"In today's volatile and fast moving ... N
things really work on the global stage ... d
practitioners from around the worl ... id
dynamics from a variety of perspect ... ...n
invaluable and interesting read for anyone who ... of
international relations."
- Marta Dyczok. Associate Professor, Departments of History and Political Science, University of Western Ontario.

"With the turbulence all around us, everyone is affected by what happens elsewhere and no one can afford not to understand international relations. This is an essential guide to learning how to navigate our interconnected world".
- Mukesh Kapila, CBE. Professor of Global Health & Humanitarian Affairs, University of Manchester.

"A thoughtful, well-written, intelligently presented and engaging narrative introduction to international relations."
- Richard Ned Lebow. Professor of International Political Theory, Department of War Studies, King's College London.

"A concise and comprehensive introduction to the study of international affairs. Adopting a student-centred approach and using strong examples, this book is essential for promoting understanding about international relations."
- Yannis Stivachtis. Associate Chair, Department of Political Science, and International Studies Program Director, Virginia Tech.

International Relations

EDITED BY

STEPHEN McGLINCHEY

E-INTERNATIONAL
RELATIONS
PUBLISHING

E-International Relations
www.E-IR.info
Bristol, England
2017

ISBN 978-1-910814-17-8 (paperback)
ISBN 978-1-910814-18-5 (e-book)

Elements of chapter seven appeared in *Globalisation, Multilateralism, Europe: Towards a Better Global Governance?* (Ashgate 2014). Used with permission.

Production: Michael Tang
Copy-editing: Gill Gairdner
Cover Image: yuliang11 via Depositphotos

A catalogue record for this book is available from the British Library

E-IR Foundations

Series Editor: Stephen McGlinchey
Editorial Assistants: Stacey Links, Max Nurnus, Kanica Rakhra & Rosie Walters.

E-IR Foundations is a series of beginner's textbooks from E-International Relations (E-IR) that are designed to introduce complicated issues in a practical and accessible way. Each book will cover a different area connected to International Relations. This is the first book in the series, with more to follow.

You can find the books, and much more, on E-IR's Student Portal:
http://www.e-ir.info/students

E-IR is developing our Foundations series as part of our mission to provide the best source of freely available scholarly materials for students of International Relations. Each book is available to buy in bookstores in paperback and, uniquely for textbooks, also freely accessible in web and PDF formats. So, readers can have each book at their fingertips and on all their devices without any restrictions or hassle.

Typically, textbook publishing is designed to appeal to professors/lecturers and, consequently, even the introductory books are intended less as an aid to the student and more to assist the instructor in the classroom. Our books are designed to meet the needs of the student, with the focus on moving readers from no prior knowledge to competency. They are intended to accompany, rather than replace, other texts, while offering the student a fresh perspective.

About E-International Relations

E-International Relations is the world's leading open access website for students and scholars of international politics, reaching over three million readers per year. E-IR's daily publications feature expert articles, blogs, reviews and interviews – as well as student learning resources. The website is run by a non-profit organisation based in Bristol, England and staffed by an all-volunteer team of students and scholars.

http://www.e-ir.info

Acknowledgements

This book would not have been possible without the assistance of E-IR's Student Review Panel. Members of the panel gave up their spare time to read drafts of each chapter and offer their thoughts on how they could be improved. The panel was chaired by Christian Scheinpflug and comprised Janja R. Avgustin, Laura Cartner, Tom Cassauwers, Caroline Cottet, Jessica Dam, Scott Edwards, Phoebe Gardner, Daniel Golebiewski, Jane Kirkpatrick, Matthew Koo, Naomi McMillen, Mohamed Osman, Robert Ralston, Bryan Roh, Daniel Rowney, Ana Carolina Sarmento, Loveleena Sharma, Ljupcho Stojkovski, Anthony Szczurek, Jan Tattenberg and Jonathan Webb.

I would also like to thank all members of the E-International Relations team, past and present, for their many acts of kindness in feeding back on ideas and providing a supportive climate for the book's development. Of special note in that respect is E-IR's co-founder Adam Groves, without whom this project would not have been possible.

Countless others have helped me through the year-long process of moving the book from concept to completion – especially Robert Oprisko, who was instrumental in getting the project off the ground during the early stages. I would also like to thank Michael Tang and Ran Xiao for their friendship and expertise.

This book has been developed in part due to conversations and experiences in and around the classroom, so I would also like to thank my colleagues, and my students, at the University of the West of England, Bristol. I am very fortunate to be part of such a vibrant and supportive scholarly environment.

Finally, and most importantly, I would like to thank the authors of each of the chapters for working so hard on this project and helping me deliver such an excellent book.

Stephen McGlinchey

Contents

Contributors

Shazelina Z. Abidin is a Foreign Service officer with the Malaysian Ministry of Foreign Affairs. After postings in Washington, DC, and to the UN in New York, she completed her PhD at the University of Sheffield on the Responsibility to Protect.

James Arvanitakis is Dean of the Graduate Research School, and Professor, at Western Sydney University. He is also a Visiting Professor at University of the Witwatersrand, South Africa.

Alex J. Bellamy is Professor of Peace and Conflict Studies and Director of the Asia Pacific Centre for the Responsibility to Protect, University of Queensland, Australia.

Katherine E. Brown is Lecturer in Islamic Studies at the University of Birmingham. She specialises in religious terrorism, radicalisation and counter-radicalisation with a focus on questions of gender.

Carmen Gebhard is Lecturer in Politics and International Relations at the University of Edinburgh. She has a particular interest in small states as well as in inter-organisational relationships in security and defence matters.

Dana Gold is a Doctoral Candidate in the Department of Political Science at the University of Western Ontario in London, Canada. Her PhD research explores how mental representations of the 'Other' are constructed and reproduced in the Israeli educational system.

Andreas Haggman is a Doctoral Candidate in the Centre for Doctoral Training in Cyber Security at Royal Holloway University of London, where he is writing his PhD thesis on wargaming cyber-attacks.

Jeffrey Haynes is Professor of Politics at London Metropolitan University and Director of the Centre for the Study of Religion, Conflict and Cooperation.

David J. Hornsby is Associate Professor in International Relations and Assistant Dean of Humanities (Teaching and Learning) at the University of the

Witwatersrand, Johannesburg. His research interests pertain to the politics of science and risk in international governance, Canadian foreign policy in Sub-Saharan Africa, middle power cooperation, and pedagogy in higher education.

Raffaele Marchetti is Senior Assistant Professor in International Relations at the Department of Political Science and the School of Government of LUISS, Rome. His research focuses on global politics and governance, hybrid diplomacy, transnational civil society, cyber-security and political risk and democracy.

Stephen McGlinchey is Senior Lecturer in International Relations at the University of the West of England, Bristol and Editor-in-Chief of E-International Relations. His main research interests are in US-Iran relations during the Cold War.

Raul Pacheco-Vega is an Assistant Professor in the Public Administration Division of the Center for Economic Teaching and Research (CIDE) in Mexico. His research focuses on North American environmental politics, primarily sanitation and water governance, solid waste management, neoinstitutional theory, transnational environmental social movements and experimental methods in public policy.

John A. Rees is Associate Professor of Politics and International Relations at The University of Notre Dame Australia. He is also Convenor of the Religion and Global Society Program at Notre Dame's Institute for Ethics and Society.

Ben Richardson is an Associate Professor in International Political Economy at the University of Warwick. His research focuses on the political economy of food and agriculture.

Erik Ringmar is Senior Lecturer in Political Science at Lund University, Sweden. He worked for 12 years at the London School of Economics and was a Professor of International Relations in China for seven years.

Harvey M. Sapolsky is Professor of Public Policy and Organization, Emeritus, at the Massachusetts Institute of Technology and former Director of the MIT Security Studies Program.

Knut Traisbach is Programme Director of the Venice Academy of Human Rights at the European Inter-University Centre for Human Rights and Democratisation, Venice.

Peter Vale is Director of the Johannesburg Institute for Advanced Study & Professor of Humanities at the University of Johannesburg. He is also Nelson Mandela Professor of Politics Emeritus, Rhodes University.

Günter Walzenbach is Senior Lecturer in European Politics at the University of the West of England. His main academic interest lies in the interaction between political and economic institutions for the purpose of social problem solving.

Getting Started

Before we go forward you should know that this book is available in e-book (PDF), web and paperback versions. While we know that many will use the digital versions of the book, we encourage you to buy a paperback copy as well if you are able. A growing body of research offers strong evidence that it is more effective to study from paper sources than from digital. Regardless of how you engage with the book, we hope it is an enjoyable read.

You can get the paperback version of this book in all good bookstores – from Amazon right down to your local bookstore – and the digital versions are always freely available on the E-International Relations Students Portal: http://www.e-ir.info/students/

Hello

This book is designed to be the very first book you will read in the area of International Relations. As a beginner's guide, it has been structured to condense the most important information into the smallest space and present that information in the most accessible way.

The book is split into two sections, each of nine chapters. Together they offer a broad sweep of the basic components of International Relations and the key contemporary issues that concern the discipline. The narrative arc forms a complete circle, taking you from no knowledge to competency. Our journey will start by examining how the international system was formed and end by reflecting that International Relations is always adapting to events and is therefore a never-ending journey of discovery.

Unlike typical textbooks, there are no boxes, charts, pictures or exercises. The philosophy underpinning this book is that these things can be a distraction. This book, like others in the E-IR Foundations series, is designed to capture attention with an engaging narrative. The chapters are short, with simple paragraphs and clear sentences.

We recommend that you read the book as it is presented and avoid cherry-picking chapters. Remember, the book is an unfolding narrative and each chapter builds on the one before it. Think of it like this: you would not skip to chapter seven of a novel and expect to understand who the characters were and what the setting was! Start at the beginning. If you find a chapter difficult, leave it for a little while then come back and give it another try. All chapters are equally important.

Key terms

Each discipline has its own unique language. This comprises a range of specific terms that have been developed by scholars to describe certain things. As a result, a lot of the time you spend learning a discipline is spent learning its jargon so that you can access and understand the literature. Instead of packing this book with jargon we have tried as far as possible to explain things in ordinary language while easing you into the more particular terminology of International Relations. This approach should keep you engaged while giving you the confidence to read the more advanced literature that you will soon encounter. We have also tried to avoid over-using acronyms.

Understanding key terms even applies to something as basic as how to express the term 'International Relations'. The academic convention is to capitalise it (International Relations, abbreviated as 'IR') when referring to the academic discipline – that is, the subject taught in university campuses all over the world. IR does not describe events; rather, it is a scholarly discipline that seeks to *understand* events. On the other hand, 'international relations' – not capitalised – is generally used by both scholars and non-scholars to *describe* relations between states, organisations and individuals at the global level. This term is interchangeable with terms such as 'global politics', 'world politics' or 'international politics'. They all mean pretty much the same thing. We have maintained this capitalisation convention in the book.

IR examines just about everything that concerns how we, as human beings, have organised our world. As a discipline it is often described as 'broad church' as it has delved into other disciplines for the tools to examine the wide range of issues within its scope. Although the chapters will progressively build up the picture, it may be helpful to skim through a few of the key terms here as an introduction.

Political power has found its ultimate form (so far) in the creation of the nation-state. Yet, 'nation-state', most commonly referred to in the shorter form of 'state', is a jargon term that you might not often hear. Instead you may hear people say 'country' or 'nation'. But, these terms are technically incorrect at describing the prime units that comprise international relations. France is a nation-state. It also happens to be a country and a nation, but then so is Wales. But, Wales is *not* a nation-state. It is part of the United Kingdom, which *is* a nation-state because, unlike Wales, it possesses something called 'sovereignty' – which is yet another key jargon term central to IR. These issues cannot be understood without IR delving into the discipline of Politics and borrowing and adapting its insights. But you need not worry, as all these terms are explained in the book as they appear.

You may not be satisfied that international relations is just politics between or among nation-states. Economics is also involved, and this has evolved to the extent that we are often said to be living in a globalised world characterised by the relatively free exchanges of goods, people and information. Understandably, this adds new elements to IR and requires it to incorporate an understanding of actors beyond nation-states, such as international organisations and corporations. And you may like to look even wider than the role of states, economics and organisations. Individuals – you and I – are of course also important. After all, international relations is essentially a system of interaction between human beings. To understand and analyse this, IR has had to borrow tools from other disciplines such as Sociology. As it has done so, it has added yet more jargon and the complexity has increased.

The paragraph above also introduces the word 'globalisation' – a buzzword of our time, even though scholars still heatedly debate what it actually means. Is globalisation the description of a shared idea of what international politics should be? Is it a description of the growing cultural connections we share globally? Is it the description of a world linked by a single global economic model – capitalism? Is it all of these things together? Is it new or has it always existed? If we try to answer these questions we quickly find new questions emerging, such as whether we think globalisation is a positive or negative thing. For example, if we settle on an idea of globalisation as the emergence of a shared global culture where we all recognise the same symbols, brands and ideals, what does that mean for local cultures and customs? Some even question whether globalisation exists at all. One of IR's foremost scholars, Kenneth Waltz, famously called it 'globaloney'.

However, this book purposefully avoids getting too bogged down in big debates over contested terms such as globalisation. We have also avoided packaging complex terms in simplified definitions. Instead, where such issues arise, we aim to give you sufficient context for you to think for yourself and read deeper and wider. We wish to open your mind, not to tell you what to think or attempt to give you pre-packed answers.

IR's dense library of key terms and jargon may appear a dizzying prospect for new students. But, it should be clear to see how unavoidable they are and why IR scholars need to use them. Even making the simplest point about something within the sphere of IR draws on specific terms that need to be understood. Some readers of this book will not be beginners. They may have started their IR journey in other places and landed here for a pit stop due to jargon overload. The book is also designed with those readers in mind.

We should also mention that as this book is published in the UK it is presented in British English. This means words like 'globalisation' and 'organisation' are spelt with an 's' rather than a 'z'.

Sources

Referencing sources is very important in academia. It is the way scholars and students attribute the work of others, whether they use their exact words or not. For that reason it is usual to see numerous references in the expert literature you will progress to after completing this book. It is an important element of scholarly writing, and one that you should master for your own studies.

In this book we have tried to summarise issues from an expert perspective so as to give you an uninterrupted narrative. When we need to point you to more specialist literature, for example to invite you to read a little deeper, we do so by inserting in-text citations that look like this: (Vale 2016b). These point you to a corresponding entry in the references section towards the back of the book where you can find the full reference and follow it up if you want to. Typically, these are books, journal articles or websites. In-text citations always include the author's surname and the year of publication. As the reference list is organised alphabetically by surname, you can quickly locate the full reference. Sometimes you will also find page numbers inside the brackets. For example, (Vale 2016b, 11–13). Page numbers are added when referring to specific arguments, or a quotation, from a source. This referencing system is known as the 'Author-Date' or 'Harvard' system. It is the most common, but not the only, referencing system used in IR.

When the time comes for you to make your own arguments and write your own assignments, think of using sources as if you were a lawyer preparing a court case. Your task there would be to convince a jury that your argument is defensible, beyond reasonable doubt. You would have to present clear, well-organised evidence based on facts and expertise. If you presented evidence that was just someone's uninformed opinion, the jury would not find it convincing and you would lose the case. Similarly, in academic writing you have to make sure that the sources you use are reputable. You can usually find this out by looking up the author and the publisher. If the author is not an expert (academic, practitioner, etc.) and/or the publisher is unknown/obscure, then the source is likely unreliable. It may have interesting information, but it is not reputable by scholarly standards.

It should be safe to assume that you know what a book is (since you are reading one!) and that you understand what the internet is. However, one type of source that you will find cited in this book and may not have encountered before is the journal article. Journal articles are typically only accessible from your university library as they are expensive and require a subscription. They are papers prepared by academics, for academics. As such, they represent the latest thinking and may contain cutting-edge insights. But, they are often complex and dense due to their audience being fellow experts, and this makes them hard for a beginner to read. In addition, journal articles are peer reviewed. This means they have gone through a process of assessment by other experts before being published. During that process many changes and improvements may be made – and articles often fail to make it through peer review and are rejected. So, journal articles are something of a gold standard in scholarly writing.

Most journal articles are now available on the internet, which leads to confusion as students can find it difficult to distinguish a journal article from an online magazine or newspaper article. Works of journalism or opinion are not peer reviewed and conform to different standards. If you follow the tip above and 'search' the publisher and author, you should be able to discern which is which. Another helpful tip is length. A journal article will typically be 10–20 pages long (7,000–11,000 words); articles of journalism or commentary will usually be shorter.

A final note on the subject of sources: the internet is something of a Wild West. There is great information there, but also a lot of rubbish. It can often be hard to tell them apart. But, again, if you follow the golden rule of looking up the author and looking up the publisher (using the internet), you can usually find your way. However, even some of the world's biggest websites can be unreliable. Wikipedia, for example, is a great resource, but it often has incorrect information because it is authored, and usually edited, by ordinary people who are typically enthusiasts rather than experts. In addition, its pages are always changing (because of user edits), making it hard to rely on as a source. So the rule of thumb with the internet is to try to corroborate anything you find on at least two good websites/from at least two reputable authors. Then you can use the internet with confidence and enjoy its benefits while avoiding its pitfalls. When preparing assignments, however, you should only use the internet to supplement the more robust information you will find in academic journals and books.

Read smart

Try to set aside time to read. You will need to put your devices on silent, close your internet browsers and find a quiet space to work. Take ten-minute mini-breaks every hour or so to do other things and make sure to eat a decent meal midway through your study session to give you a longer break. Finally, get a good night's sleep before and after you study. Your brain does not absorb or retain information very well when you are sleep deprived or hungry. There will be times in the year when panic sets in as deadlines approach, but if you have already developed a good reading strategy you will find you are in good shape for the task at hand.

Reading for scholarly purposes is not the same as reading for pleasure. You need to adopt a reading strategy. Everyone has their own way of doing this, but the basic tip is this: take notes as you read. If you find that you don't have many notes or your mind goes a little blank, then you might be reading too quickly or not paying enough attention. This is most likely if you are reading digitally on a computer or tablet, as it is very easy for the eyes to wander or for you to drift onto a social media site. If this happens, don't worry: just go back and start again. Often, reading something a second time is when it clicks.

Best practice is to make rough notes as you read through each chapter. When you get to the end of a chapter, compile your rough notes into a list of 'key points' that you would like to remember. This will be useful when you come to revise or recap an issue because you won't necessarily have to read the entire chapter again. Your notes should trigger your memory and remind you of the key information. Some textbooks do this for you and provide a list of key points at the end of each chapter. This book, being a foundational book for beginners, does *not* do so: we want readers to develop the important skills of reading and note-taking for themselves and not take short cuts.

By making notes you will form a reading strategy that will allow you to retain the most important information and compress it into a smaller set of notes integral to revision for examinations and preparation for discussions and assignments. You should adopt this approach with everything you read during your studies. It's best to use digital means (laptop/tablet) so you can create backups and not risk losing valuable handwritten paper notes. You should also note down the citation information for each set of notes at the top of the page so that you can identify the source you took the notes from if you need to reference it later in any written work.

Part One

THE BASICS

1

The Making of the Modern World

ERIK RINGMAR

International relations, as it is presented in the flow of daily news, concerns a large number of disparate events: leaders are meeting, negotiations are concluded, wars are started, acts of terror committed, and so on. In order to make sense of all this information we need to know a lot about the contemporary world and its history; we need to understand how all the disparate events hang together. At university, we study these topics, but it is a basic tenet of the academic study of international politics that this rather messy picture can be radically simplified. Instead of focusing on the flow of daily news, we focus on the basic principles underlying it. This is what we will try to do in this chapter. So, let us begin by thinking big: what is international relations, how was it made, and how did it come to be that way?

The state is a good place to start. There are a lot of states in the world – in fact, according to the latest count, there are no fewer than 195 of them. States are obviously very different from each other, but they are also similar to each other in important respects. All states are located somewhere, they have a territorial extension; they are surrounded by borders which tell us where one state ends and another begins. In fact, with the exception of Antarctica, there is virtually no piece of land anywhere on earth's surface that is not claimed by one state or another and there is no piece of land that belongs to more than one state (although, admittedly, the ownership of some pieces of land is disputed). Moreover, all states have their own capitals, armies, foreign ministries, flags and national anthems. All states call themselves 'sovereign', meaning that they claim the exclusive right to govern their respective territories in their own fashion. But states are also sovereign in relation to each other: they act in relation to other states, declaring war, concluding a peace, negotiating a treaty, and many other things. In fact, we often talk about states as though they were persons with interests to defend and plans to carry out. According to a time-honoured metaphor, we can talk about international politics as a 'world stage' on which the states are the leading actors.

Over the course of the years there have been many different kinds of states, yet this chapter is mainly concerned with the European state and with European developments. There are good reasons for this. For much of its history, Europe was of no particular relevance to the rest of the world. Europe had few connections to other continents and European states were not more powerful, and certainly no richer, than those elsewhere. But this began to change from around the year 1500. This was when the Europeans first developed extensive trading links with the rest of the world. That trade helped to spur both economic development and social change. As a result, the Europeans began to assert themselves. Eventually, in the latter part of the nineteenth century, European states occupied and colonised the bulk of the world, dramatically transforming the course of world history. Yet, as we will see, it was only when the colonised countries became independent in the twentieth century that the European state and the European way of organising international relations finally became the universal norm. Today's international system is, for good and for bad, made by Europeans and by non-Europeans copying European examples.

The rise of the sovereign state

In medieval Europe international politics consisted of a complicated pattern of overlapping jurisdictions and loyalties. Most of life was local and most political power was local too. At the local level there was an enormous diversity of political entities: feudal lords who ruled their respective estates much as they saw fit, cities made up of independent merchants, states ruled by clerics and smaller political entities such as principalities and duchies. There were even brotherhoods – such as the Knights Hospitaller, a military order – who laid claims to a political role. There were also, especially in northern Europe, many peasant communities that were more or less self-governing. There were kings too of course, such as the kings of France and England, but their power was limited and their poverty looked like wealth only in comparison with the conditions of the near-destitute members of the peasant class underneath them.

In medieval Europe there were two institutions with pretensions to power over the continent as a whole – the (Catholic) Church and the Empire. The Church was the spiritual authority, with its centre in Rome. Apart from a small Jewish minority, all Europeans were Christian and the influence of the Church spread far and penetrated deeply into people's lives. As the custodian, from Roman times, of institutions like the legal system and the Latin language, the Church occupied a crucial role in the cultural and intellectual life of the Middle Ages. The Empire – known as the *Holy Roman Empire* – was established in the tenth century in central, predominantly German-speaking, Europe. It also included parts of Italy, France and today's Netherlands and Belgium. It too derived legitimacy from the Roman Empire, but had none of its political power. The Holy Roman Empire is best compared to a loosely structured federation of many hundreds of separate political units.

The political system of medieval Europe was thus a curious combination of the local and the universal. Yet, from the fourteenth century onward this system was greatly simplified as the state emerged as a political entity located at an intermediate level between the local and the universal. The new states simultaneously set themselves in opposition to popes and emperors on the universal level, and to feudal lords, peasants and assorted other rulers on the local level. This is how the state came to make itself independent and self-governing. The process started in Italy where northern city-states such as Florence, Venice, Ravenna and Milan began playing the pope against the emperor, eventually making themselves independent of both. Meanwhile, in Germany, the pope struggled with the emperor over the issue of who of the two should have the right to appoint bishops. While the two were fighting it out, the constituent members of the Holy Roman Empire took the opportunity to assert their independence. This was also when the kings of France and England began acting more independently, defying the pope's orders. Between 1309 and 1377, the French even forced the pope to move to Avignon, in southern France. In England, meanwhile, the king repealed the pope's right to levy taxes on the people.

With the Reformation in the sixteenth century the notion of a unified Europe broke down completely as the Church began to split apart. Before long the followers of Martin Luther, 1483–1546, and John Calvin, 1509–1564, had formed their own religious denominations which did not take orders from Rome. Instead the new churches aligned themselves with the new states. Or rather, various kings, such as Henry VIII in England or Gustav Vasa in Sweden, took advantage of the religious strife in order to further their own political agendas. By supporting the Reformation, they could free themselves from the power of Rome. All over northern Europe, the new 'Protestant' churches became state-run and church lands became property of the state. Yet, the new divisions were cultural and intellectual too. With the invention of the printing press, power over the written word moved away from the monasteries and into the hands of private publishers who sought markets for their books. The biggest markets were found in books published not in Latin but in various local languages. From the early eighteenth century onwards

Latin was no longer the dominant language of learning. As a result, it was suddenly far more difficult for Europeans to understand each other.

In this climate, the increasingly self-assertive states were not only picking fights with universal institutions but also with local ones. In order to establish themselves securely in their new positions of power, the kings rejected the traditional claims of all local authorities. This led to extended wars in next to all European countries. Peasants rose up in protest against taxes and the burdens imposed by repeated wars. There were massive peasant revolts in Germany in the 1520s with hundreds of thousands of participants and almost as many victims. In the latter part of the sixteenth century, there were major peasant uprisings in Sweden, Croatia, England and Switzerland. In France, in the middle of the seventeenth century, the nobility rose up in defence of its traditional rights and in rebellion against the encroachments of the king.

Medieval kings were really quite powerless. They had no proper bureaucracies at their disposal, no standing armies and few ways of raising money. In fact, there were few good roads, ports and not many large cities. These, however, soon came to be constructed. From the sixteenth century onwards the states established the rudiments of an administrative system and raised armies, both in order to fight their own peasants and in order to defend themselves against other states. Since such state-building was expensive, the search for money became a constant concern. The early modern state was more than anything an institutional machinery designed to develop and extract resources from society. In return for their taxes, the state provided ordinary people with defense and a rudimentary system of justice. If they refused to pay up, state officials had various unpleasant ways to make them suffer.

Early modern Europe was the golden age of political economy. During this period, the economy was not thought of as a distinct sphere separated from politics but instead as a tool of statecraft which the state could manipulate to serve its own ends. Economic development meant higher revenues from taxes and gave the kings access to more resources which they could use in their wars. The state was keen to encourage trade, not least since taxes on trade were a lot easier to collect than taxes on land. It was now that a search began for natural resources – agricultural land, forests, iron and copper ore, but also manpower – which the state might make use of. Maps were drawn up which located these resources within the country's borders, and lists were made of births, marriages and deaths in order to better keep track of the population. Domestic industries were set up and given state subsidies, above all in militarily significant sectors such as metal works and in sectors that were easy for the state to tax. In addition, various 'useful sciences' were encouraged, by the newly established scientific academies, and prizes were given to innovations and discoveries. In state-sponsored universities, future members of the emerging administrative class were taught how best to regulate society and assure peace and social order.

The Westphalian system

The European states emerged in the midst of struggle and strife, and struggle and strife have continued to characterise their existence. Yet, in early modern Europe it was no longer the competing claims of local and universal authorities that had to be combated but instead the competing claims of other states. The Thirty Years' War, 1618–1648, was the bloodiest and most protracted military confrontation of the era. As a result of the war Germany's population was reduced by around a third. What the Swiss or the Scottish mercenaries did not steal, the Swedish troops destroyed. Many of the people who did not die on the battlefield died of the plague. The Thirty Years' War is often called a religious conflict since Catholic states confronted Protestants. Yet, Protestant and Catholic countries sometimes fought on the same side and religious dogma was clearly not the first thing on the minds of the combatants. Instead the war concerned which state should have hegemony (or dominance) over Europe. That is, which state, if any, would take over from the universal institutions of the Middle Ages. The main protagonists were two Catholic states, France and Austria, but Sweden – a Protestant country – intervened on France's side and in the end no dominant power emerged.

The Treaty of Westphalia, 1648, which concluded the 30 years of warfare, has come to symbolise the new way of organising international politics. From this point onwards, international politics was a matter of relations between states and no other political units. All states were sovereign, meaning that they laid claims to the exclusive right to rule their own territories and to act, in relation to other states, as they themselves saw fit. All states were formally equal and they had the same rights and obligations. Taken together, the states interacted with each other in a system in which there was no overarching power. Sovereignty and formal equality led to the problem of anarchy. Within a country 'anarchy' refers to a breakdown of law and order, but in relations between states it refers to a system where power is decentralised and there are no shared institutions with the right to enforce common rules. An anarchical world is a world where everyone looks after themselves and no one looks after the system as a whole. Instead, states had to rely on their own resources or to form alliances through which the power of one alliance of states could be balanced against the power of another alliance. Yet, as soon became clear, such power balances were precarious, easily subverted, and given the value attached to territorial acquisitions, states had an incentive to engage in aggressive wars. As a result, the new international system was characterised by constant tensions and threats of war – which often enough turned into actual cases of warfare.

At the same time various practices developed which helped regulate common affairs. The foremost example was the practice of diplomacy as exemplified by the way peace treaties were negotiated. From the seventeenth century onward, European states met after each major war in order to reach a settlement and lay down the terms of their future interaction. These diplomatic practices had their origin in relations between the city-states of northern Italy. Once these states had made themselves independent both of the pope and the emperor, they soon discovered that their relations had become vastly more complicated. In order to avoid misunderstandings and unnecessary conflicts, the different rulers began dispatching ambassadors to each other's courts. This diplomatic network provided a means of gathering information, of spying, but also a way of keeping in touch with one another, of carrying out negotiations and concluding deals. The practices of diplomacy soon expanded to include a number of mutually advantageous provisions: the embassies were given extraterritorial rights and legal immunity, diplomatic dispatches were regarded as inviolable and ambassadors had the right to worship the god of their choice. These originally north Italian practices gradually expanded to embrace more states and by the middle of the seventeenth century the system included France, Spain, Austria, England, Russia, Poland, Denmark, Sweden and the Ottoman Empire. Diplomatic practices were never powerful enough to prevent war, indeed wars continued to be common, but they did provide Europeans with a sense of a common identity. A European state was, more than anything, a state that participated in the system of shared diplomatic practices.

An inter-national system

The early modern state was a coercive machinery designed to make war and to extract resources from society. Yet at the end of the eighteenth century, this machinery came to be radically transformed. Or rather, the 'state' was combined with a 'nation' forming a compound noun – the 'nation-state' – which was organised differently and pursued different goals. A nation, in contrast to a state, constitutes a community of people joined by a shared identity and by common social practices. Communities of various kinds have always existed but they now became, for the first time, a political concern. As a new breed of nationalist leaders came to argue, the nation should take over the state and make use of its institutional structures to further the nation's ends. In one country after another the nationalists were successful in these aims. The nation added an interior life to the state, we might perhaps say; the nation was a soul added to the body of the early modern state machinery.

The revolutions that took place in Britain's North American colonies in 1776, and in France in 1789, provided models for other nationalists to follow. 'We the People of the United States' – the first words of the Preamble to the US Constitution – was a phrase which itself would have been literally unthinkable in an earlier era. In France, the king was officially the only legitimate political actor and the people as a whole were excluded from politics. In addition, the power of the aristocracy and the church remained strong, above all in the countryside where they were the largest landowners. In the revolution of 1789, the *old regime* was overthrown and with it the entire social order. The French nation was from now on to be governed by the people, the nation, and in accordance with the principles of *liberté, égalité et fraternité* – liberty, equality and brotherhood.

Already in 1792, confrontation began between the revolutionary French nation and the kings of the rest of Europe. The wars were to go on for close to 25 years, most ferociously during the Napoleonic Wars of the early nineteenth century named after the French general, Napoleon Bonaparte, who made himself emperor of France. In contrast to the kings of the old regimes, the revolutionary French government could rely on the whole people to make contributions to the war due to the power of patriotism. This allowed first the revolutionaries, and later Napoleon, to create a formidable fighting machine which set about conquering Europe. Germany was quickly overrun and its sudden and complete defeat was a source of considerable embarrassment to all Germans. The Holy Roman Empire, by now in tatters, was finally dissolved in 1806 in the wake of Napoleon's conquest. Yet, since there was no German state around which prospective nationalists could rally, the initial response was formulated in cultural rather than in military terms. Nationalist sentiment focused on the German language, German traditions and a shared sense of history. Before long a strong German nation began looking around for a unified German state. The goal was eventually achieved in 1871, after Germany – appropriately enough, perhaps – had defeated France in a war.

The Congress of Vienna of 1815, where a settlement was reached at the end of the Napoleonic Wars, was supposed to have returned Europe to its pre-revolutionary ways. Yet, nationalist sentiments were growing across the continent and they constantly threatened to undermine the settlement. All over Europe national communities demanded to be included into the politics of their respective countries. Nationalism in the first part of the nineteenth century was a liberal sentiment concerning self-determination – the right of a people to determine its own fate. This programme had far-reaching implications for the way politics was organised domestically, but it also had profound ramifications for international politics. Most obviously, the idea of self-determination undermined the political legitimacy of Europe's empires. If all the different peoples that these empires contained gained the right to determine their own fates, the map of Europe would have to be radically redrawn. In 1848 this prospect seemed to become a reality as nationalist uprisings quickly spread across the continent. Everywhere the people demanded the right to rule themselves.

Although the nationalist revolutions of 1848 were defeated by the political establishment, the sentiments themselves were impossible to control. Across Europe an increasingly prosperous middle-class demanded inclusion in the political system and their demands were increasingly expressed through the language of nationalism. The Finns wanted an independent Finland; the Bulgarians an independent Bulgaria; the Serbs an independent Serbia, and so on. In 1861 Italy too – long divided into separate city-states and dominated by the Church – became a unified country and an independent nation. Yet it was only with the conclusion of the First World War in 1918 that self-determination was acknowledged as a right. After the First World War most people in Europe formed their own nation-states.

As a result of the nationalist revolutions, the European international system became for the first time truly 'inter-national'. That is, while the Westphalian system concerned relations between states, world affairs in the nineteenth century increasingly came to concern relations between nation-states. In fact, the word 'international' itself was coined only in 1783, by the British philosopher Jeremy Bentham. In most respects, however, the inter-national system continued to operate in much the same fashion as the Westphalian inter-state system. Nation-states claimed the same right to sovereignty which meant that they were formally equal to each other. Together, they interacted in an anarchical system in which power was decentralised and wars were a constant threat. Yet, the addition of the nation changed the nature of the interaction in crucial ways. For one thing, leaders who ruled their countries without at least the tacit support of their national communities were increasingly seen as illegitimate. This also meant that newly created nation-states such as Italy and Germany were automatically regarded as legitimate members of the European community of nations. They were legitimate since the people, in theory at least, were in charge.

There were also new hopes for world peace. While kings wage war for the sake of glory or personal gain, a people is believed to be more attuned to the aspirations of another people. Inspired by such hopes, liberal philosophers devised plans for how a 'perpetual peace' could be established. For some considerable time, these assumptions seemed quite feasible. The nineteenth century – or, more accurately, the period from 1815 to 1914 – was indeed an uncharacteristically peaceful period in European history. At the time, great hopes were associated with the increase in trade. As Adam Smith pointed out in *The Wealth of Nations* (1776), a nation is rich not because it has a lot of natural resources but because it has the capacity to manufacture things that others want. In order to capitalise on this capacity, you need to trade and the more you trade the wealthier you are likely to become. Once the quest for profits and market shares has become more important than the quest for a neighbouring state's territory, world peace would naturally follow. In a world in which everyone is busy trading with each other, no one can afford to go to war.

By the twentieth century most of these liberal hopes were dashed. As the First World War demonstrated, nation-states could be as violent as the early-modern states. In fact, nation-states were far more lethal, not least since they were able to involve their entire population in the war effort together with the entirety of its shared resources. The peaceful quest for profits and market shares had not replaced the anxious quest for security or the aggressive quest for pre-eminence. In the Second World War, the industrial might of the world's most developed nations was employed for military ends with aerial bombardments of civilian populations, including the dropping of two atomic bombs on Japan. Between 1939 and 1945 over 60 million people were killed – around 2.5 per cent of the world's population. This figure included the six million Jews exterminated by Germany in the Holocaust, which was one of the worst genocides in recorded history. After the Second World War, the military competition continued between the United States and the Soviet Union. This was known as a 'cold war' since the two superpowers never engaged each other in direct warfare, but they fought several wars by proxy such as those in Korea and Vietnam.

The Europeans and the rest of the world

Most of what happened in Europe before the nineteenth century was of great concern to the Europeans but of only marginal relevance to people elsewhere. Europe certainly had a significant impact on the Americas, North and South. However, it had far less impact on Asia and relations with Africa were largely restricted to a few trading ports. The large, rich and powerful empires of East Asia were organised quite differently than the European states, and international politics followed different principles. The same can be said for other parts of the world such as the Indian subcontinent, Central Asia, sub-Saharan Africa and the Arab world. And yet, it was the European model of statehood and the European way of organising international relations that eventually came to organise all of world politics.

As previously mentioned, trade was an important source of revenue for states in early modern Europe, and no trade was more lucrative than the trade with East Asia. Europeans had developed a taste for East Asian goods already in the Middle Ages – for spices above all, but also for silk and other exotic commodities. During the Mongol Empire, 1206–1368, much of the vast stretch of the Eurasian landmass was unified under one set of rulers and it was easy to obtain goods via the great caravan routes which criss-crossed Asia. When the Mongol Empire fell, overland trade became more insecure and the Europeans began looking for ways to get to East Asia by sea. It was when Vasco da Gama rounded the Cape of Good Hope, at the southernmost tip of Africa, in 1497 that the Europeans for the first time discovered a direct way to travel by sea to East Asia. The Portuguese took the lead in this trade, but they were soon replaced by the Dutch, and above all, by the Dutch East India Company, founded in 1602. All over Europe similar trading companies were soon established and they were all granted monopolies on the highly profitable East Asian trade. These monopolies were sold to the highest bidder, and for European kings this was an easy and quick way to raise revenue.

The Europeans who came back from travels in East Asia were amazed at the wondrous things they had seen. East Asian kings, they reported, were far richer and more powerful than European rulers. Europe seemed a provincial backwater compared to the centres of civilisation they had stumbled upon. From an East Asian point of view, however, the Europeans were nothing but a small contingent of traders who docked at a few ports, conducted their trade, and then left. Yet, the increase in trade which the opening of new trade routes produced was nevertheless important to the countries of East Asia. The Europeans paid for their goods in silver – often mined at Potosí, an enormous mine in today's Bolivia – and this inflow of precious metal helped spur inter-Asian trade. In order to facilitate commerce, various European trading companies were given the right to establish small trading posts. The Portuguese established outposts in Goa in India, Macau in China, East Timor and Malacca in today's Malaysia; while the Dutch founded Batavia, a trading post on the island of Java in today's Indonesia.

In the Americas, the Europeans were far more ruthless. The Spanish conquered the Aztecs in Mexico and the Incas in Peru and gradually took over the bulk of the continent. In North America the English established themselves, together with the Dutch and the French. The European invasion was associated with widespread genocide. In South America many natives died as a result of being overworked in mines and plantations and in North America the European settlers made outright war on the natives. Yet in both North and South America the largest number of natives died through exposure to European diseases such as the measles. Africa, meanwhile, remained largely unknown to the Europeans.

It was only in the nineteenth century that relations between Europe and the rest of the world were irrevocably transformed. The reason is above all to be found in economic changes taking place in Europe itself. At the end of the eighteenth century, new ways of manufacturing goods were invented which made use of machines powered by steam, and later by electricity, which made it possible to engage in large-scale factory production. As a result of this so called 'industrial revolution', the Europeans could produce many more things and do it far more efficiently. As cheap, mass-produced goods flooded European markets, the Europeans began looking for new markets overseas. They also needed raw material for their factories, which in many cases only could be found outside of Europe. These economic imperatives meant that the Europeans took a renewed interest in world trade. This time it was the British who took the lead. It was in Britain that the industrial revolution had started and the British, an island nation with a long history of international commerce, had a navy second to none. Before long they had established commercial outposts from Canada to South Africa and Australia, but it was India that became the most important colony. The commercial outposts and colonial settlements soon grew in size as the British sought to protect their economic investments by means of military force.

Towards the end of the nineteenth century, other European countries joined in this scramble for colonies, not least in Africa. Colonial possessions became a symbol of 'great power' status, and the new European nation-states often proved themselves to be very aggressive colonisers. France added West Africa and Indochina to its growing empire, and the Germans and Italians also joined the race once their respective countries were unified. This explains how, by the time of the First World War in 1914, most parts of the world were in European hands. There were some exceptions to this rule – China, Japan, Siam, Persia, Ethiopia and Nepal, among others – but even in these ostensibly independent countries the Europeans had a strong presence.

But this was not how the European state and the European way of organising international relations came to spread to the rest of the world, at least not directly. After all, a colonised country is the very opposite of a sovereign state; the colonised peoples had no nation-states and enjoyed no self-determination. It was instead through the process of liberating themselves from the colonisers that the European models were copied. Since the Europeans only would grant sovereignty to states that were similar to their own, the only way to become independent was to become independent on European terms. To create such Europe-like states was thus the project in which all non-European political leaders engaged. Once they finally made themselves independent in the decades after the Second World War, as an international climate of decolonisation took hold, all new states had a familiar form. They had their respective territories and fortified borders; their own capitals, armies, foreign ministries, flags, national anthems and all the other paraphernalia of European statehood. Whether there were alternative, non-European, ways of organising a state and its foreign relations was never discussed. Whether it made sense for the newly independent states to try to live up to European ideals was never discussed either. This, briefly, is how the modern world was made.

Conclusion

In this chapter we focused on Europe since contemporary international politics, for good and for bad, was shaped by Europeans and by non-Europeans copying European examples. This is a story of how the state emerged as a sovereign actor in the late Middle Ages by simultaneously rejecting the traditional claims made by universal and local institutions. It is a story of how the state went on to strengthen its power by means of bureaucracies and armies. European states were always competing with each other, and while the military competition had disastrous effects in terms of human suffering, the economic competition that took place was a spur to development and social change. In the course of the nineteenth century, the state was transformed into a nation-state in which, in theory at least, the people as a whole were in charge. There were great hopes that nation-states would be more peaceful in their relations with one another, but these hopes were soon dashed. Nation-states were ferocious colonisers and in the twentieth century the world as a whole suffered through two devastating world wars and came to the brink of nuclear Armageddon during the Cold War. In the twenty-first century there are once again hopes for a better future, but as long as the European state-system (now the international system) lasts a more enduring peace is unlikely.

2

Diplomacy

STEPHEN McGLINCHEY

As the previous chapter showed, war compels and focuses public attention, leaves a clear mark on human life, and is responsible for shaping our world. On the other hand, despite its importance, diplomacy rarely gains much attention. When military theorist Carl von Clausewitz remarked in the early 1800s that war was the continuation of policy by other means, he sought to normalise the idea of war in modern politics. But, his words also indicated that actions short of war are available to help states achieve their objectives. These are typically the actions of diplomats. And, their work is often far less expensive, far more effective and much more predictable a strategy than war. In fact, unlike in centuries gone by when war was common, diplomacy is what we understand today as the normal state of affairs governing international relations. And, in the modern era, diplomacy is conducted not only between nation-states, but also by a range of non-state actors such as the European Union and the United Nations.

What is diplomacy?

Diplomacy has probably existed for as long as civilisation has. The easiest way to understand it is to start by seeing it as a system of structured communication between two or more parties. Records of regular contact via envoys travelling between neighbouring civilisations date back at least 2500 years. They lacked many of the characteristics and commonalities of modern diplomacy such as embassies, international law and professional diplomatic services. Yet, it should be underlined that political communities, however they may have been organised, have usually found ways to communicate during peacetime, and have established a wide range of practices for doing so. The benefits are clear when you consider that diplomacy can promote exchanges that enhance trade, culture, wealth and knowledge.

For those looking for a quick definition, diplomacy can be defined as a process between actors (diplomats, usually representing a state) who exist within a system (international relations) and engage in private and public dialogue (diplomacy) to pursue their objectives in a peaceful manner.

Diplomacy is not foreign policy and must be distinguished from it. It may be helpful to perceive diplomacy as part of foreign policy. When a nation-state makes foreign policy it does so for its own national interests. And, these interests are shaped by a wide range of factors. In basic terms, a state's foreign policy has two key ingredients; its actions and its strategies for achieving its goals. The interaction one state has with another is considered the act of its foreign policy. This act typically takes place via interactions between government personnel through diplomacy. To interact without diplomacy would typically limit a state's foreign policy actions to conflict (usually war, but also via economic sanctions) or espionage. In that sense, diplomacy is an essential tool required to operate successfully in today's international system.

In the modern context then, a system dominated by states, we can reasonably regard diplomacy as something being conducted for the most part between states. In fact, the applicable international law that governs diplomacy – the Vienna Convention on Diplomatic Relations (1961) – only references states as diplomatic actors. Yet, the modern international system also involves powerful actors that are not states. These tend to be international non-governmental organisations (INGOs) and international governmental organisations (IGOs). These actors regularly partake in areas of diplomacy and often materially shape outcomes. For example, the United Nations and the European Union (two IGOs) materially shaped diplomacy in the case studies highlighted later in this chapter. And, a range of INGOs – such as Greenpeace – have meaningfully advanced progress toward treaties and agreements in important areas tied to the health and progress of humankind such as international environmental negotiations.

While readers of this book will be familiar with the concept of war to some extent due to its ubiquity in modern life, diplomacy may present itself as something alien or distant. On the one hand this is a consequence of what diplomacy is and how it is carried out. Diplomacy is most often an act carried out by representatives of a state, or a non-state actor, usually behind closed doors. In these instances, diplomacy is a silent process working along in its routine (and often highly complex) form, carried out by rank-and-file diplomats and representatives. This is perhaps not the best place to shine a light on diplomacy for beginners. On the other hand, sometimes the public are presented with briefings, statements, or – more rarely – full disclosures of a diplomatic matter. These usually drift into the public consciousness when they involve critical international issues and draw in high-ranking officials. Because they do get headlines and work their way into the history books, examples drawn from this type of diplomacy are used in this chapter to offer a more palatable access point.

To enable the reader to get a sense of what diplomacy is and why it is important, this chapter will use two interrelated case studies. The first case study involves the quest to manage the spread of nuclear weapons. The second half of the twentieth century came to be dominated by conflict between two nuclear-armed superpowers, the United States of America (US) and the Union of Soviet Socialist Republics (USSR) – often called the Soviet Union. In this tense climate, diplomacy ensured that few other nation-states developed nuclear weapons. Hence, the diplomatic success in curbing the proliferation of nuclear weapons is a major one, and one that involved non-state as well as nation-state actors. US-Iran relations form the second case study. This case spans several important decades from the end of the Second World War, to the present day. As times changed, the structure of international relations also changed, often causing material shifts in the patterns of diplomacy between both nations. By visiting that relationship, it is possible to not just show the importance of high-level diplomacy between two pivotal states but also to consider the importance of an international governmental organisation – the European Union. The case studies were chosen as they offer a glimpse of diplomacy between states that were sworn enemies and had had little in common due to incompatible economic, political, or even religious, systems. Yet, through diplomacy, they were able to avoid war and find ways to achieve progress in the most critical of areas.

Regulating nuclear weapons

After the first use of an atomic bomb by the US on Japan in August 1945, the world was transformed. Reports and pictures of the total devastation caused by the two bombs that the US dropped on Nagasaki and Hiroshima confirmed that the nature of warfare had changed forever. As one reporter described the scene:

> There is no way of comparing the Atom Bomb damage with anything we've ever seen before. Whereas bombs leave gutted buildings and framework standing, the Atom bomb leaves nothing.

> (Hoffman 1945)

Although the US was the first state to successfully detonate a nuclear bomb, other nations were also researching the technology. The second state to successfully detonate a bomb was the Soviet Union (1949). The United Kingdom (1952), France (1960) and China (1964) followed. As the number of nations possessing nuclear weapons increased from one to five, there were genuine fears that these dangerous weapons would proliferate uncontrollably to many other nations.

Proliferation was not only a numbers issue. As the weapons developed in sophistication from those dropped in Japan they became many orders of magnitude more destructive, representing a grave threat to humankind as a whole. By the early 1960s, nuclear weapons had been built that could cause devastation for hundreds of kilometres beyond the impact zone. The United States and the Soviet Union, who were locked into a system of rivalry known as the Cold War, seemed to be in a race to outdo each other in terms of the quantity and quality of bombs each possessed. The Cold War was known as such because the presence of nuclear weapons on both sides made a traditional war between the two almost unfathomable. If somehow they were to end up engaged in a direct conflict they each had the power to destroy the other entirely and in doing so jeopardise human civilisation as a whole.

It may seem strange but, despite their offensive power, nuclear weapons are primarily held as defensive tools – unlikely to be ever used. This is due to a concept known as deterrence. By holding a weapon that can wipe out an opponent, such an opponent is unlikely to attack you. Especially if your weapons can survive that attack and allow you to retaliate. In an environment as insecure as the Cold War, gaining a nuclear arsenal was a way to achieve deterrence and a measure of security that was not otherwise attainable. This was obviously an attractive option for states. For this reason, any hope of creating an international regime of moderation over nuclear weapons seemed doomed during the Cold War.

To the brink and back

The United Nations (UN), which was created in 1945 in part to give international diplomacy a focal point and create a more secure world, attempted in vain to outlaw nuclear weapons in the late 1940s. Following that failure, a series of less absolute goals were advanced, most notably to regulate the testing of nuclear weapons. Weapons that were being developed required test detonations, and each test released large amounts of radiation into the atmosphere, endangering ecosystems and human health.

By the late 1950s, high-level diplomacy under a United Nations framework had managed to establish a moratorium (or suspension) on nuclear testing by the United States and the Soviet Union. However, by 1961 a climate of mistrust and heightened tensions between the two nations caused testing to resume. One year later, in 1962, the world came to the brink of nuclear war in what is now known as the Cuban Missile Crisis when the Soviet Union sought to place nuclear warheads in Cuba, a small island nation in the Caribbean less than 150 kilometres off the southern coast of the United States. Cuban leader Fidel Castro had requested the weapons to deter the United States from meddling in Cuban politics following a failed US-sponsored invasion by anti-Castro forces in 1961. As Soviet premier Nikita Khrushchev (1962) put it, 'the two most powerful nations had been squared off against each other, each with its finger on the button.' After pushing each other to the brink, US president John F. Kennedy and Khrushchev found that via diplomacy, they could agree to a compromise that satisfied the basic security needs of the other. Over a series of negotiations Soviet missiles were removed from Cuba in return for the United States removing missiles they had deployed in Turkey and Italy. As the two sides could not fully trust each other due to their rivalry, the diplomacy was based (and succeeded) on the principle of verification by the United Nations, which independently checked for compliance.

Once the immediate crisis over Cuba was resolved, high-level diplomacy continued. Neither nation desired such a dramatic break down in communications to occur again, so a direct hot line was established linking the Kremlin in Moscow and the Pentagon in Washington. Building further on the momentum, in July 1963 the Partial Test Ban Treaty was agreed, confining nuclear testing to underground sites only. It was not a perfect solution, but it was progress. And, in this case it was driven by the leaders of two superpowers who wanted to de-escalate a tense state of affairs.

Although early moves to regulate nuclear weapons were a mixed affair, the faith that Kennedy and Khrushchev put in building diplomacy was pivotal in the course of the Cold War and facilitated further progress in finding areas of agreement. In the years that followed the Cuban Missile Crisis, Cold War diplomacy entered a high watermark phase in what became known as a period of 'détente' between the superpowers as they sought to engage diplomatically with each other on a variety of issues, including a major arms limitation treaty. In that climate, progress was also made on nuclear proliferation.

The Non-Proliferation Treaty

Building on earlier progress, the 1970s opened with the entering into force of the Treaty on the Non-Proliferation of Nuclear Weapons (1970) – often known as the Non-Proliferation Treaty (NPT). The Treaty sought to channel nuclear technology into civilian uses and to recognise the destabilising effect of further nuclear weapons proliferation on the international community. It was a triumph of diplomacy. The genius of the treaty was that it was aware of the realities of the international politics of the time. It was not a disarmament treaty as great powers would simply not give up their nuclear weapons, fearful their security would be diminished. So, instead of pursuing an impossible goal of eliminating nuclear weapons, the Non-Proliferation Treaty sought to freeze the number of nations that had nuclear weapons at the five nations which already possessed them: the United States, the Soviet Union, the United Kingdom, France and China. Simultaneously, those five nations were encouraged to share non-military nuclear technology with other nations – such as civilian nuclear energy – so that those nations would not feel tempted to pursue nuclear weapons. In short, those who had nuclear weapons could keep them. Those who didn't have them would be allowed to benefit from the non-military research and innovation of the existing nuclear powers.

Due to the well-considered design of the treaty and its enforcement, it has been deemed highly successful. Following the end of the Cold War, the Non-Proliferation Treaty was permanently extended in 1995. Granted, it has not kept the number of nuclear nations to five, but there are still fewer than ten – which is far from the twenty or more projected by diplomats on both sides of the Atlantic before the treaty entered into force in 1970. States with nascent nuclear weapons programmes, such as Brazil and South Africa, gave them up due to international pressure to join the treaty. Today, only a small number of states are outside its bounds. India, Pakistan and Israel never joined as they (controversially in each case) had nuclear ambitions that they were not prepared to give up due to national security priorities. Underlining the weight of the Non-Proliferation Treaty, in 2003, when North Korea decided to rekindle earlier plans to develop nuclear weapons, they withdrew from the treaty rather than violate it. To date, North Korea remains the only nation to withdraw from the Non-Proliferation Treaty.

The non-proliferation regime is not perfect of course – a situation best underlined by North Korea's quest to proliferate despite international will. It is also a system with an inherent bias, since a number of nations are allowed to have nuclear weapons simply because they were first to develop them – and this continues to be the case regardless of their behaviour. Yet, while humankind has developed the ultimate weapon in the nuclear bomb, diplomacy has managed to prevail in moderating its spread. When a nation is rumoured to be developing a nuclear bomb, as in the case of Iran, the reaction of the international community is always one of common alarm. In IR we call ideas that have become commonplace 'norms'. Due to skilful diplomacy in decades gone by, non-proliferation is one of the central norms underpinning our international system.

The US and Iran

Following the end of the Second World War, Iran found itself placed in a geostrategic hotspot. It shared a long border to its north with the Soviet Union and as a result acted as a geographical buffer to any Soviet moves into the Middle East. Iran's wider location, known as the Persian Gulf, was a region that contained the world's largest-known pool of oil – the steady supply of which was vital for the fuelling of Western-orientated economies. So, a coincidence of time, place, politics and economics judged Iran – in most ways a weak and underdeveloped state – important. When Iran's king, known as the Shah, found himself side-lined by a powerful left-leaning government, the United States, in league with the British, conspired to restore him to power via a covert coup in 1953. During the Cold War the United States feared that leftward political developments in nations would result in a domestic communist revolution and/or an alliance with the communist Soviet Union. In certain cases, therefore, the United States took interventionist action to contain communism from spreading. The coup was a watermark in US-Iranian history. It set up a pattern of close relations that would last 25 years, as the Shah became a loyal ally of the United States in a volatile region. This volatility was not just due to Cold War geostrategic rivalry between the United States and Soviet Union. The wider region was embroiled in a series of crises caused by decolonisation and the resulting phenomenon of Arab nationalism, regional opposition to the creation of Israel, and a major ongoing conflict between India and Pakistan. Then, as now, this was a highly unstable area of the world to live in.

Iran has always been a nation that, despite different manifestations of its internal shape and character, has aspired to greater stature internationally, or at the very least regional predominance. For example, the Shah, whose autocratic rule was brought to an end by the 1979 revolution that erased his regime and created the Islamic Republic of Iran, harboured grand designs for Iran as the premier nation of the Middle East. This vision was shared by the United States, which armed Iran with advanced weaponry, of the non-nuclear kind, during the Shah's rule. The United States hoped its support of the Shah would allow him to widen and deepen Iranian power in order to help stabilise the region. Iran today is not much different to the Shah's Iran in the sense that it exists within the same borders and is a nation of the same peoples. However, a significant caveat is that the regional and global role Iran was to play under the Shah was largely in line with American desires, while the role envisioned by the Islamic Republic of Iran is deeply antagonistic to just about every facet of American politics. Hence, US-Iran relations are packed with insight and intrigue due to the history and divergent paths both nations have experienced.

The Iran hostage crisis

To connect our US-Iran case study to the issue of diplomacy, we do not need to look far beyond the birth of the Islamic Republic of Iran to an episode known as *the Iran hostage crisis*. In November 1979 a gang of Iranian students invaded the US Embassy in Tehran, Iran's capital city, and captured the personnel they found there. This occurred after the Shah, who was in exile, had taken residence in New York for cancer treatment. The protesters demanded his return to stand trial for various crimes committed by his regime, such as torturing political dissidents. So the prisoners, most of them US diplomatic personnel, were taken hostage as a bargaining chip, their freedom offered in exchange for the return of the Shah. The United States and Iran found themselves in uncharted waters when Iran's new government, led by the once-exiled anti-Shah cleric Ruhollah Khomeini, officially sanctioned the hostage-taking.

Due to established diplomatic customs, an embassy – although hosted on foreign soil – is forbidden from being entered by the host state unless permission is given. So, when the Iranian protesters invaded the US Embassy in Tehran they violated a key feature of diplomacy developed over centuries to allow diplomats the freedom to do their work. This is why, to use a more contemporary example, WikiLeaks founder Julian Assange was able to avoid arrest by British police by taking up residence in an innocuous-looking terraced house in London – the house is the Embassy of Ecuador and police were refused entry. Strange as it may sound, police officers were then stationed outside the door waiting to arrest Assange should he decide to leave – an operation that has cost the British taxpayer millions of pounds. It is evident from the Assange example how highly such diplomatic customs are regarded by nations and how little this changes over time – even when those nations are in conflict.

In Iran's case, its disregard for established diplomatic principles was both shocking and extreme. Not only did it violate established diplomatic principles, but hostage-taking by a state is defined as a war crime under the Geneva Conventions. Predictably, the United States rejected Iran's demands and the hostage crisis became a tense diplomatic stand-off lasting 444 days. It turned Iran into an international pariah: there was worldwide outrage at its disregard not only for the rules of the international system but also for human decency as it paraded the hostages – bound and gagged – in front of news cameras. It also marked a new anti-Western political path for Iran, one in stark opposition to its pro-US stance during the time of the Shah. Despite the eventual freeing of the hostages in January 1981, the once-friendly nations had become foes. Following the crisis, all direct diplomatic links between the United States and Iran were severed until an issue of nuclear proliferation brought them to the same table over thirty years later.

Nuclear Iran

The idea of Iran possessing nuclear weapons is understandably controversial. Iran's known disregard for international laws and customs, as evidenced by the hostage crisis and reinforced by the regular accusation that it supports terrorist and radical groups, creates an atmosphere of mistrust in the international community. News of Iran's nuclear ambitions has been a point of major international diplomatic focus since 2002, when news leaked out that Iran had begun the development of a modern nuclear programme that showed signs of weaponisation (see Sinha and Beachy 2015 and Patrikarakos 2012). This was in spite of the fact that Iran is a signatory of the Non-Proliferation Treaty and therefore bound to neither receive nor develop nuclear arms. Iran protested that its programme was for civilian and peaceful purposes only. However, due to Iran's international profile, few believed this. Given that the United States had just declared its 'Global War on Terrorism' following the 9/11 terrorist attacks, it was a tense period.

In 2002 the United States had no appetite for diplomacy with Iran over the nuclear issue. The US had already invaded Afghanistan in late 2001 and was preparing to invade Iraq in early 2003 as part of its campaign to rid the Middle East of regimes which might provide safe harbour to transnational terrorist groups such as Al Qaeda – the perpetrators of the 9/11 attacks. The United States also had a larger goal: to secure regime change in Iran, which it considered the world's leading state-sponsor of terrorism. Seen through that logic, a war on terror was meaningless if it did not target the world's chief terrorist. This would be done by demonstrating the might of the United States through its invasion of Iran's neighbours – note that Afghanistan borders Iran to the east and Iraq borders Iran to the west. This would then create internal pressure on Iran's leadership to reform of its own accord; it might even incite another revolution. If that failed, the United States was prepared to engage with Iran in some fashion in order to destroy its nuclear research facilities and possibly engineer regime change via military means, as it did in Iraq and Afghanistan. This is best encapsulated by president George W. Bush's oft-repeated phrase that 'all options are on the table' regarding dealing with Iran – outlined in more complete terms by the following passage from an official government document:

The Iranian regime sponsors terrorism; threatens Israel; seeks to thwart Middle East peace; disrupts democracy in Iraq; and denies the aspirations of its people for freedom. The nuclear issue and our other concerns can ultimately be resolved only if the Iranian regime makes the strategic decision to change these policies, open up its political system, and afford freedom to its people. This is the ultimate goal of U.S. policy. In the interim, we will continue to take all necessary measures to protect our national and economic security against the adverse effects of their bad conduct.

(The National Security Strategy of the United States of
America 2006, 20)

In that climate, diplomacy seemed a non-starter. However, an unlikely candidate entered the fray – the European Union (EU). In 2003, three EU nations, the UK, Germany and France, initiated high-level diplomacy with Iran in an attempt to prevent a war and introduce mediation to the situation. The talks were rejected by the United States, which refused to take part, given its above-mentioned objectives. For the European nations, diplomacy was worth pursuing. Despite the UK, France and Germany being traditional allies of the United States, there was no appetite in Europe for more war in the Middle East. The war in Iraq was controversial, as many – including the United Nations, which refused to mandate the war – did not accept its rationale. The 2003 invasion of Iraq also divided Europe politically and caused mass popular protests. In this context, engaging Iran was a bold move of diplomacy – effectively stepping in the way of the world's sole superpower when it was at its most belligerent. The talks were initially inconclusive, but they at least succeeded in engaging Iran in diplomacy, stalling its nuclear programme and offering a path to resolution other than confrontation.

In the years that followed invasion, military operations in Iraq and Afghanistan became deeply troubled as both nations (for different reasons) descended into instability. This required a longer-term, and more substantial, military presence by the United States than had been planned. As a result, the US became bogged down and was not in a position to realistically pursue a military strategy against Iran. Thus, it joined the EU-Iran talks, albeit reluctantly, in 2006. China and Russia also joined, making it a truly international diplomatic affair. It took almost a decade, but the parties finally reached agreement in July 2015. That agreement is a marvel of diplomacy. What were once mutually opposing positions characterised by decades of mistrust between the United States and Iran were painstakingly worked on by diplomats at all levels over many rounds of diplomacy until compromises acceptable to both sides were found.

Personal relationships between the diplomats were also built during the years of the negotiations, and these helped transcend state rivalries. Wendy Sherman, the US lead negotiator, recalled how she and her Iranian counterpart, Abbas Araghchi, both became grandparents during their negotiations and shared videos of their grandchildren with each other. Personal relationships like this do not dissolve or change pre-set national interests on either side, but they were instrumental in both sides developing the resolve to work tirelessly and not give up until they were able to agree on key parameters. Similar personal relations were developed between officials at the highest level when they spent 17 days locked in intense discussions in Vienna during the concluding phase of the negotiations. Sherman later described the scene on the final day, with all the diplomatic personnel gathered together, as US Secretary of State John Kerry addressed the parties:

> Secretary Kerry was the last person to speak. He recounted that when he was 21 he went off to war in Vietnam. He made a commitment that he would do whatever he could in his life to make sure that there was never war, ever again. The room was absolutely still. There was quiet. And then everyone, including the Iranians, applauded. Because, I think for all of us we understood that what we had done was to try to ensure peace, not war.

> (Sherman 2016)

Much like the resolution of the Cuban Missile Crisis, the key to the success of the diplomatic strategy underlining the agreement was to focus on verification rather than the seemingly impossible goal of establishing trust. The diplomats laboured in the one area where a resolution was possible and found a way to make it acceptable for both sides. For Iran this overtly involved the phased removal of punitive economic sanctions that had been sponsored by the United States and also the tacit removal of any direct military threat. For the Americans, the deal placed Iran under a strict regime of verification to ensure that it cannot easily develop nuclear weapons, and if they appeared to be doing so there would be time for the international community to react before those weapons became useable. This is known as a 'breakout' period (see Broad and Peçanha 2015). Such a thing is only possible via an unprecedented system of strict international inspection of Iran's facilities, which Iran agreed to.

The resolution of the US-Iran nuclear standoff would not have been possible without the bold move of three European Union nations to start a diplomatic process during the tense year of 2003. Not only was a serious confrontation between Iran and the United States avoided, but the important non-proliferation principle that has become central to international relations was upheld by securing Iran's commitment to the Non-Proliferation Treaty. The Iran nuclear deal, although a clear example of a diplomatic success in the face of tall odds, is contentious and fragile. It will need to weather multiple political shifts in the United States and Iran that might unseat it in years to come – and it does not remove the enmity between the states, which continue to mistrust each other. However, it may be seen in retrospect as the opening act on a path of rapprochement between the two nations that may gradually replace the toxic pattern of relations begun in 1979 with the hostage crisis. Even if the United States and Iran resume a path of confrontation, it does not take away from the triumph of diplomacy in this case, with nuclear weapons in the Middle East prevented from proliferating during a critical period and an alternative offered to what might have been a major war.

Conclusion

Diplomacy in the modern era, an era sometimes called the 'long peace' (Gaddis 1989) due to the absence of major war since 1945, has deepened and widened in complexity. Nowadays, it would be ill advised to base a description of diplomacy on actions short of, or in response to, war between states. Diplomacy today is integral to ensuring that our period of long peace gets longer and that the world we live in is as conducive as possible to the progress of the individual, as well as the state. As today's world is more linked and interdependent than ever before, effective and skilful diplomacy is vital to ensure that humankind can navigate an ever-growing list of shared challenges such as climate change, pandemics, transnational terrorism and nuclear proliferation that may be our undoing if left unresolved. So, while you may not know the names of many of those engaged in diplomatic endeavours, nor see much of their hard work credited in the media, their work is more important than ever to all of us.

3

One World, Many Actors

CARMEN GEBHARD

The previous two chapters have set the foundations for understanding our world as one determined by centuries of warfare. At the same time, we have developed mechanisms for 'getting along' via diplomacy. With that context in mind, we must turn to unpacking how International Relations as an academic discipline analyses our world. International Relations (IR) traditionally focused on interactions between states. However, this conventional view has been broadened over the years to include relationships between all sorts of political entities ('polities'), including international organisations, multinational corporations, societies and citizens. IR captures a vast array of themes ranging from the growing interconnectedness of people to old and new forms of security, dialogue and conflict between visions, beliefs and ideologies, the environment, space, the global economy, poverty and climate change. The sheer number of actors and issues that are relevant to IR can be overwhelming. This can make it seem like a daunting task to not just study various aspects of IR but to try to grasp the bigger picture.

All the more important are the analytical tools that scholars have developed in an attempt to make the field more manageable – not just for newcomers to the discipline but also for themselves. Social scientists in general spend quite a lot of time thinking about effective ways of structuring their thinking and of processing the complexity of the reality they endeavour to study, analyse and understand. A lot of this kind of analytical sense-making in IR happens in the form of theories. Scholars use theories to explain and capture the meaning of real-life events in the form of abstract interpretations and generalised assumptions. On the one hand, theories can be 'empirical' – based on measurable experiences, usually through observation or experimentation. Empirical theories generally seek to try to explain the world *as it is*. On the other hand, theories can be 'normative' – meaning that they build on principles and assumptions about how social interactions should occur. In other words, normative theories generally seek to present a version of world that *ought to be*.

Before scholars develop or adopt any specific theories, however, they take what is often a subconscious decision in selecting the focus of their analysis. Following this, they normally stick with their choice without reflecting very much on alternative approaches to the issue. As students of IR it can be helpful to equip ourselves with a basic overview of the perspectives one can adopt when analysing just about any topic. This chapter will do this by looking at different 'levels of analysis' as one of the most common ways of structuring scholarly debates in IR.

Levels of analysis

Thinking of different levels of analysis in IR means that the observer and analyst may choose to focus on the international system as a whole, parts of the system in interaction with each other, or some of its parts in particular. What forms the parts or components of this system is again a matter of perspective. The international system can be conceived of as made up of states, groups of states, organisations, societies or individuals within and across those societies. IR generally distinguishes between three levels of analysis: the system, the state, and the individual – but the group level is also important to consider as a fourth. To be able to use the level of analysis as an analytical device, we need to be clear about what we are most interested in. We have to clarify for ourselves what it is exactly that we want to look at when discussing a particular theme or issue concerning the 'international' sphere. If we were to study and understand the 2008 global financial crisis and its consequences, for example, there would be various ways of approaching, discussing and presenting the issue. To determine the level of analysis we would need to determine what those levels are and ask ourselves some questions, which we can explore below.

The individual level

Would we look at the actions of individuals responding to the financial crisis according to their own position or responsibilities? For example, a prime minister encountering the leader of another state to negotiate an important financial agreement, the head of a large corporation adopting a policy to rescue their business or even the situation of individual citizens and their attitude towards austerity measures?

The group level

Would we be more interested in the actions of groups of individuals, such as all voters of a country and the way they express their views in the general election, political parties picking up on the issue in their campaigns or social movements forming to counter the effects of the crisis on society?

Would we be interested in activist/pressure groups like 'Anonymous' that seek to influence the global debate about the winners and losers of globalisation and capitalism?

The state level

Would we look at states as actors in their own right as if they were clearly defined entities that have certain preferences, and accordingly, look at their actions and decisions to find an answer to our analytical questions?

Would we then be looking at how states interact with each other to deal with the crisis – in other words, their foreign policy? How they build off each other's suggestions and react to international developments and trends? How they cooperate, say, in the framework of international organisations?

Or would we be looking at them as competitors and antagonists, each of them pushing for a stronger position in what makes up the world economy?

The system level

Finally, might we try to look at the global level, the big picture, and try to grasp wider ranging dynamics that emerge from the global economic 'system' to affect its various components, states, national economies, societies, individuals?

A much-debated example of this kind of system perspective has been presented by Daniel W. Drezner (2014), who argued controversially that the international system of financial governance did well at coping with the 2008 global financial crisis. He looked at how various parts of the system worked together to mitigate wider repercussions. After all, while we call it the global financial crisis, the world has really not changed much since then and you might argue it has been business as usual for the system.

How the level of analysis determines our findings

Being aware of various possible perspectives helps us to develop an understanding of where we stand as analysts and observers. It also guides us through the process of investigation and analysis. First of all, the particular perspective we assume determines the kind of information we would need to gather and look at in order to be able to answer our questions and draw meaningful conclusions.

A system-level ('systemic') study would need to consider global linkages that go beyond single interactions between states. It would need to look at such things as the balance of power between states and how that determines what happens in global politics. This could include developments that are even outside the immediate control of any particular state or group of states, such as the global economy, transnational terrorism or the internet.

A state-level study would require careful consideration of what kinds of states we are looking at (how they are ordered politically), their geographical position, their historical ties and experiences and their economic standing. It would likely also look at the foreign policy of states, meaning their approach to and practice of interacting with other states. Key indicators of the foreign policy of states would be the policies proposed and decided by governments, statements of top-level politicians but also the role and behaviour of diplomats and their adjoining bureaucratic structures.

A group level analysis would again need to try and break the analysis down into certain kinds of groups, how they relate to the state level and where they position themselves with respect to the global dimension of the issues they are dealing with. An example of this can be seen in the work of Engelen et al. (2012), who discuss the global financial crisis as the 'misrule of experts', pointing at the politicised role of technocratic circles and the relative lack of democratic control over the boards of large banks and corporations. A group-level analysis focusing on foreign policy would look, for example, at the role of lobbying groups and the way they influence national decision-making on an issue.

If looking at the actions of individuals, we would likely also need to engage with the implications of human nature. This can be seen in the psychology and emotions behind people's actions and decisions, their fears and their visions as well as their access to information and capacity to make a difference. Psychological factors do not only matter at the level of individual members of society or of a group. They are also an important factor in the analysis of foreign policy, whenever particular mindsets and perceptions of political leaders and key actors might influence their decisions and behaviour.

Which one of these specific perspectives we choose would greatly influence our findings. In other words, the focus or level of analysis determines the outcome of our scholarly investigations. Meanwhile, the real-life events we are analysing remain the same, of course. That is a particularly important consideration if we aim at developing generalised conclusions from our observations. Strictly speaking, our conclusions would only be valid within the scope of the level of analysis we chose to focus on. Insights provided by other perspectives would remain outside the remit of our analysis. To illustrate this, let's stick with the above example of the global financial crisis as it is one of the more debated issues in contemporary politics.

From the system level

If we studied the global financial crisis from a system-level perspective, for instance, we would expect to gain an insight into the global dynamics that make up the international financial system. Focusing on the big picture would enable us to develop a comprehensive model of explanation that could potentially capture the states and national economies within that global system. The explanations we derive from this systemic model, however, might exaggerate the system-level factors that have conditioned the global financial crisis. As a consequence, we might overlook a lot of psychological and sociological issues that would be the subject of a group-level or individual-level analysis.

From the state level

If we studied the same theme from a state perspective, we would develop a greater level of detail about specific circumstances in particular states as well as in their interaction with each other. The distinction here, as will be discussed further below, is not quite this rigid in practice as the state level is rarely looked at in isolation but more in its wider systemic context. For our example this would mean that the world financial system is taken as the framework in which state actors operate, so state action is often conditioned by factors beyond the state's control.

From the group level

If we studied the issue from a group-level perspective, we would yet again reach a different result in our findings. We would potentially emphasise aspects of the global financial crisis that would escape a more comprehensive global level analysis. This includes analysing the impact of the crisis on society and the livelihoods of individuals as exemplified in the UN Report 'The Global Social Crisis' (2011).

From the individual level

Finally, focusing on the individual level and, say, particular actions of specific personalities in the public realm – be they politicians, diplomats or bankers – would lead to us drawing different conclusions again about the causes and consequences of the financial crisis.

The bigger picture

In short, being aware and acknowledging the potential gaps in our observation – that is to say, all of what is not directly captured by our perspective or level of analysis – is important. Applying rigour in our analysis is also important. These guidelines for scholarly investigation are applied in many academic disciplines, including the natural sciences. What German theoretical physicist Werner K. Heisenberg (1962, 58) said in respect to research in his field very much also applies to IR; 'we have to remember that what we observe is not nature in itself, but nature exposed to our method of questioning.' Scholarly writings are nevertheless not always explicit about their particular perspective or level of analysis. So, as a reader, it is important to stay critical and to look closely and enquire whenever an argument presented to us appears to straddle potentially conflicting analytical lenses.

As you start to read deeper on particular IR issues, always remind yourself of the importance of analytical clarity. Do not hesitate to expect and demand it even from renowned authors and established publications outlets. Note that clarity concerning one's level of analysis does not necessarily mean that different perspectives could not be used in conjunction with each other – on the contrary. As will be argued further below, many of today's political challenges are so complex that they require our analyses to span across various levels.

Foreign policy

A crucial area where the need to broaden our levels of analysis is particularly important is the analysis of the foreign policy of states. Hopefully, we can see this immediately due to the fact that any state activity that crosses their national borders, such as a foreign policy, will have implications for other states. We can look at foreign policy at the state level by analysing government policies and diplomatic decisions in isolation. However, governments are also actors on the world stage and their foreign policies contribute to what we call international relations. As highlighted above, foreign policy can also be explained by looking at the individual level, for example, the psychological and political factors that guide leaders and their advisers in their foreign policy decisions. Those decisions in turn then feed into national decisions that matter at the state level and in relation to other states.

It can be helpful to think of foreign policy behaviour as something that is influenced by a range of factors. Some of them can be found within a state, in its political traditions, its socio-economic profile, its political party system or in the minds of leading politicians. Others come from outside, from the global system that builds the context within which states operate. This does not mean that every meaningful discussion of foreign policy needs to look at all these aspects: investigations at one particular level should be used very carefully to draw conclusions about a different level. Where the levels overlap, we need to be aware that each one will require us to look at different kinds of evidence.

To help lock in the foreign policy example, we can draw on the case of British prime minister Tony Blair. Blair is often remembered for his decision to take the UK to war with Iraq in 2003, in coalition with the United States. To examine this important foreign policy decision from the individual level, we might draw on Blair's personal convictions as a committed anti-terrorist with a strong moral sense based on his Christianity, something that helped him forge a common personal bond with the US president, George W. Bush. If we move our focus to the state level, we can judge equally as fairly that Blair might have been acting to preserve the Anglo-American 'special relationship' that was vital to British national security. The Iraq war period was a contentious one in Europe, with many European nations rejecting American plans for war. If Blair had followed some of his European colleagues and not supported the war, then he may have put a vital bilateral relationship in danger. Finally, we move to the international, or systemic, level. Here, we are not so much focused on Blair himself since the systemic level often supposes that it is forces operating at the international level that shape behaviour. By this reading, Blair may have felt compelled to participate in what he saw as a shift in world order that was defined by the existence of dangerous transnational terrorism on one hand, and a coalition led by the United States on the other hand who were waging a war on terrorism. Of course, as has been noted already, you would also be able to argue that Blair's motives might have been drawn from more than one of these levels – perhaps even all of them.

Levels of analysis and the changing ambitions of a discipline

Apart from making us more critical and discerning readers, being aware of the issue of different levels of analysis can also help us understand the way in which the academic discipline of IR has developed over time. To begin with, in the early days of IR – say, from 1919 until the after the Second World War – a lot of what could be called traditional or conventional IR was not concerned with any potential distinctions between different levels of analysis or theoretical perspectives. J. David Singer (1961, 78) lamented that scholars would simply

> roam up and down the ladder of organizational complexity with remarkable abandon, focusing upon the total system, international organizations, regions, coalitions, extra-national associations, nations, domestic pressure groups, social classes, elites, and individuals as the needs of the moment required.

Singer's criticism of this 'general sluggishness' (Singer 1961, 78) highlights another value in thinking of IR as something that can be studied from different and distinctive perspectives. Being clear about our level of analysis can prevent us from indulging in analytical 'cherry-picking', that is to say, from randomly gathering evidence across different levels in pursuit of an answer to our research questions. This 'vertical drift', as Singer calls it, can compromise the accuracy of our observations and undermine the validity of our findings. That in turn can obscure some of the detail that might have otherwise turned out to be the key to a conclusive explanation. This does not mean that any one piece of scholarly work must not consider aspects from different levels of analysis. However, when moving between different levels of analysis, we need to do so openly and explicitly. We also need to acknowledge the analytical consequences of drifting between levels: that our search for evidence will need to be comprehensive and that we might have to look at a different set of data or material for each additional aspect. For example, if you were to explain Germany's decision to open its borders to hundreds of thousands of refugees in 2015 you might want to look at the external pressures as much as the personal motivations of German chancellor Angela Merkel. You would investigate factors at the system level (such as economic indicators, refugee flows, the attitude of key partners) and at the individual level (such as Merkel's ideological background, her interests and perceptions of the problem as it emerges from statements and key decisions throughout her career). Each would contribute to an overall explanation, but you would need to be prepared to look at different sets of information.

From the 1950s onwards, more and more IR scholars endeavoured to specify the focus of their analysis more clearly. The most prominent example was Kenneth Waltz's *Man, the State and War: A Theoretical Analysis* (1959) which introduced an analytical framework for the study of IR that distinguished between what he referred to as different 'images' of an issue: the individual, the state and the international system. Waltz's contributions to the discipline generated interest in analysing the international system as a place of interactions between states. From this perspective, the global system is conceived of as the structure or context within which states cooperate, compete and confront each other over issues of national interest. You might visualise it as a level above the state. Particularly important in that context is the distribution of power amongst states, meaning, whether there is one main concentration of power ('unipolarity'), two ('bipolarity') or several ('multipolarity'). Global circumstances are seen to condition the ability and opportunity of individual states and groups of states to pursue their interests in cooperative or competitive ways. The view of states being embedded in a global context traditionally comes with the assumption that our international system is 'anarchic'. An anarchic system is one that lacks a central government (or international sovereign) that regulates and controls what happens to states in their dealings with each other.

Although this idea of the global or system level as a context of anarchy features in many contributions to the IR literature, the main focus remains on the state as the dominant unit of analysis. This enduring focus on the state, and therefore, on the state level of analysis, is referred to as the relative 'state-centrism' of the discipline. This means that IR scholars would generally not only regard states as the central unit of analysis as such, they also conceive of the state as a point of reference for other types of actors. From this perspective, the state acts as the arena in which state officials, politicians and decision-makers operate. The state is seen as the framework that encapsulates society and as the main point of reference for the individual. This predominant focus on the state is strongly related to an assumption IR scholars have made about the state also being the main location of power within the international sphere. This idea that the state is where power is primarily concentrated and located has to be seen against the historical context within which some of the most prominent IR scholars operated – the Cold War. It was an era in which much of international affairs appeared to be run via state channels and in line with particular state interests. Other actors that we would consider important from today's perspective, such as those explored in later chapters in this book, seem to have had little leverage during the Cold War. This was because the period was dominated by great power confrontation and overwhelming military might on each side of the systemic conflict.

Although the Cold War has long since passed, a lot of today's political life remains managed in the state framework, based on issues like national security, domestic cohesion or internal stability. States form the primary kind of actor in major international organisations such as the United Nations, they feature prominently in the global discourse on most of the major challenges of our time, and states still hold what famous German sociologist Max Weber called the monopoly on violence – the exclusive right to the legitimate use of physical force. States continue to matter and thus have to be part of our considerations about what happens in the world and why. The state as a unit of analysis and frame of reference will certainly not go away any time soon, nor will the interactions of states as a key level of analysis in IR.

IR as arena or process?

It is important to highlight that thinking from the point of view of different – and to a degree, separate – levels of analysis as discussed up to this point has been contested by some. Leftwich (2004), for instance, has argued that thinking of international politics as something that takes place in a certain site or location is just one possible way of looking at things. He calls this the 'arena' approach given the way in which it focuses on the location, or 'locus' of interactions, on different platforms that provide the stage to particular events and instances of international relations. He distinguishes this 'arena' approach from what he calls the 'processual' approach, which assumes that international relations should not primarily be looked at as something that happens in a particular location or at a particular level of analysis but that it can instead be thought of as a complex web of processes that takes place between people.

Some theoretical approaches have what is often an implicit preference for a conception of IR as a process rather than an arena with various distinctive levels. This is because they aim to highlight the meaning of interactions as opposed to the meaning of physical structures and locations, such as the state or particular institutions within states. An example of such a perspective can be found in environmentalism or so-called 'Green Politics', which traditionally refuses to think of the practice of international relations as something that can be studied at different 'levels' of analysis. This is mainly because analysts pertaining to this approach perceive any proposed division of political reality into arenas or any attempts at physically locating a problem in a particular context as arbitrary and misleading. They would also argue that thinking in those divisions conveys a false sense of structure, when all aspects of any societal challenge are fundamentally interconnected and should thus be studied in a 'holistic' way – meaning, in conjunction with each other.

Another example of such a theoretical approach is feminism, which would argue that politics does not exclusively occur in public places such as state institutions and international organisations. Feminists would instead argue that 'the personal is the political', meaning that all human interactions carry and reproduce political meaning, and are therefore part of the intricate process of global affairs. Other thinkers would even go as far as to suggest that politics as a process is not even confined to the human species. Frans de Waal (1982) argues that even the interactions between animals, such as chimpanzees, can carry political meaning and should thus not be excluded from any intellectual accounts of politics including its international and global dimensions.

We will not develop these kinds of perspectives further at this point, but it is nevertheless useful to note how such contentions challenge any assumption of there being any kind of clear cut structure or specific levels of analysis that we can rely on as students and analysts of IR. Regardless of perspective, it is important to be aware of the multiplicity of actors and processes that make up the global system. Reminding ourselves of the complexity of international relations equips us with the ability to recognise any overgeneralisations as they are being presented to us by the media, by political leaders, activists, pressure groups and through our social networks, making us more informed, nuanced and rounded in our thinking.

Beyond the state

While the legacy of conventional Cold War-style thinking still looms large in contemporary analyses, researchers have been interested in developing non-state-centric and more fluid perspectives. We already mentioned environmentalism and feminism as examples of analytical perspectives that acknowledge the importance of actors other than the state, and the role of individuals in particular. Some analysts have not completely abandoned the state perspective but suggest looking into what exactly it is inside states that might be contributing to what happens in the global sphere. This could be related to their internal characteristics, such as their form of government, their economic profile, their cultural and ideological composition or their demography. This perspective includes a distinctive focus on the societies that make up a specific state as much as particular groups and individuals within those societies. Many analysts invite their readers to open the 'black box' that way. In other words, to break up the conventional IR habit of treating states as secluded units and containers of power, politics and societies. They also openly challenge the assumption that there is such a thing as 'unitary' state action. They would dispute, for instance, that 'Germany' – as a nation-state – would push for austerity measures in Greece. Rather, they would insist that related policies are initiated by specific German politicians that advocate such measures out of a particular sentiment, out of an individual interpretation of current developments, or for reasons that might be linked to their own political future or specific preferences of their electorate.

Apart from a focus on the individual and group level of official decision-making, this 'sub-state' (meaning, 'below the state') level of analysis also attempts to expand the scope of scholarly investigation beyond formal interactions of the state, its official representatives and of its constituent parts to include informal relationships and non-official exchanges, such as flows and transfers of goods, information, communications, services and people – above and below the purview of the state.

Contemporary IR is interested in looking at actors that operate across state borders instead of being specifically confined by them – for instance, citizens of a particular state or proponents of a particular ethnic or cultural minority within that state. The study of IR has gradually widened to include all kinds of interactions between a variety of actors, including the general public and individual members of it, people like you and me.

Such an analytical move seems welcome if we think of how potent the influence of individual actors can be that do not officially represent or act on behalf of states or any of their constituent parts. An example of this is the activist Julian Assange, who spearheaded a widely publicised whistleblowing campaign leaking government secrets via the website WikiLeaks. Another example is Osama Bin Laden, who built a global terrorist network (Al Qaeda) based on his own religious and political visions. Both Assange and Bin Laden, although very different in nature, have had lasting impact on top-level global politics from the position of a private persona with no official political status or role.

What is significant in this context is that the traditional conception of the state as the main framework of political interaction and the main point of reference for both society and the individuals within it has lost a lot of its meaning and importance. If we look at the world around us, state borders do not seem to accurately delimitate global affairs. The majority of global interactions – be they related to global finance, production, education, personal and professional travel, labour migration or terrorism – no longer occur via state channels the way they once did. We could say that the increased focus on non-state actors and cross-border issues has marked a close-to-revolutionary turn in IR; something that could be interpreted as a shift away from the inter-national ('between-states') to the 'trans-national' ('across/beyond-states' and their borders). Robert Keohane, one of the leading scholars in the field, recently stated that 'International Relations' is no longer a suitable label and that we should instead refer to the discipline as 'Global Studies' or 'World Politics' (Keohane 2016). In today's world, few societal and political issues, challenges and problems are neatly confined by the borders of individual states or even groups of states. Thinking about world affairs in 'trans-national' rather than in purely 'inter-national' terms therefore seems more of an analytical necessity than just a choice.

Individuals and groups interact across borders and thus relativise the meaning of space and territory as conventional IR knew it. International commercial aviation and the rapid spread of information technologies has further increased people's mobility and the rate at which interactions occur across and beyond state borders. The ability for common people to store, transfer and distribute large amounts of information, the possibility for data to travel across the world in virtually no time, and the increasing availability of high-speed internet have not only changed lives at personal and community levels but also dramatically altered the general dynamics in politics and global affairs.

Social media provide accessible platforms of communication that allow for the projection and promotion of ideas across borders at virtually no cost to the individual or group generating and advocating them. Various political agendas – be they progressive, revolutionary or outright dangerous – can unfold in a relatively uncontrolled and unregulated way, posing real challenges to governmental agencies and the political leaders that try to improve and direct them. Random individuals can potentially start a revolution from their homes, bypassing any conventional conceptions of power and transcending spatial and material boundaries to the point where political activity and even confrontation become weightless and immaterial altogether. A powerful illustration of this can be found in Thomas Neuwirth, an Austrian singer, who is most commonly known by the stage persona 'Conchita Wurst'. The political messages displayed during a show at the Sydney Opera House in March 2016 multiplied and spread through social media. This eventually urged various representatives of the Australian government to take a stance on gay, lesbian, bisexual and transgender (LGBT) issues and also gave momentum to the global LGBT movement. A national politician from, say, Austria, would likely not have been able to influence the domestic debate in Australia to that extent, let alone spark a worldwide debate that way.

IR and you

This chapter has introduced you to the idea of levels of analysis as an analytical device that makes the variety of issues in IR more manageable and structured. More specifically, we distinguished between the system level, the state level, the group and the individual level, highlighting differences as well as connections between them. We have shown that the academic discipline of IR has gradually moved away from a dominant focus on the state and the system to deal more with the role and perspective of groups and individuals. As you are reading this book it should be an inspirational thought that never in the history of humanity has it been easier for individuals like you to become directly involved in the practice of international relations, or should we say transnational relations. As an individual you are not just a passive subject of international relations as directed by political elites and official state actors; you have the means of being an actor in your own right – or at the very least being counted as more scholars focus beyond the narrow confines of the state level of analysis.

4

International Relations Theory

DANA GOLD & STEPHEN McGLINCHEY

Theories of International Relations allow us to understand and try to make sense of the world around us through various lenses, each of which represents a different theoretical perspective. In order to consider the field as a whole for beginners it is necessary to simplify IR theory. This chapter does so by situating IR theory on a three-part spectrum of traditional theories, middle-ground theories and critical theories. Examples are used throughout to help bring meaning and perspective to these positions. Readers are also encouraged to consult this book's companion text, *International Relations Theory* (2017), which expands greatly on the subject matter of this chapter.

Before we get started, one very important note. You may notice that some of the theories you are introduced to here are referred to by names that also occur in other disciplines. Sometimes this can be confusing as, for example, realism in IR is not the same as realism in art. Similarly, you may hear the word 'liberal' being used to describe someone's personal views, but in IR liberalism means something quite distinct. To avoid any confusion, this note will serve as a caveat that in this chapter we only refer to the theories concerned as they have been developed within the discipline of International Relations.

Traditional theories

Theories are constantly emerging and competing with one another. For that reason it can be disorientating to learn about theoretical approaches. As soon as you think you have found your feet with one approach, you realise there are many others. Thomas Kuhn's *The Structure of Scientific Revolutions* (1962) set the stage for understanding how and why certain theories are legitimised and widely accepted. He also identified the process that takes place when theories are no longer relevant and new theories emerge. For example, human beings were once convinced the earth was flat and accepted this as fact. With the advancement of science and technology, humans discarded this previously accepted belief. Once such a discovery takes place, a 'paradigm shift' results and the former way of thinking is replaced with a new one. Although changes in IR theory are not as dramatic as the example above, there have been significant evolutions in the discipline. This is important to keep in mind when we consider how theories of IR play a role in explaining the world and how, based upon different time periods and our personal contexts, one approach may speak to us more than another. Traditionally there have been two central theories of IR: liberalism and realism. Although they have come under great challenge from other theories, they remain central to the discipline.

At its height, liberalism in IR was referred to as a 'utopian' theory and is still recognised as such to some degree today. Its proponents view human beings as innately good and believe peace and harmony between nations is not only achievable, but desirable. Immanuel Kant developed the idea in the late eighteenth century that states that shared liberal values should have no reason for going to war against one another. In Kant's eyes, the more liberal states there were in the world, the more peaceful it would become, since liberal states are ruled by their citizens and citizens are rarely disposed to desire war. This is in contrast to the rule of kings and other non-elected rulers who frequently have selfish desires out of step with citizens. His ideas have resonated and continue to be developed by modern liberals, most notably in the democratic peace theory, which posits that democracies do not go to war with each other, for the very reasons Kant outlined.

Further, liberals have faith in the idea that the permanent cessation of war is an attainable goal. Taking liberal ideas into practice, US President Woodrow Wilson addressed his famous 'Fourteen Points' to the US Congress in January 1918 during the final year of the First World War. As he presented his ideas for a rebuilt world beyond the war, the last of his points was to create a general association of nations, which became the League of Nations. Dating back to 1920, the League of Nations was created largely for the purpose of overseeing affairs between states and implementing, as well as maintaining, international peace. However, when the League collapsed due to the outbreak of the Second World War in 1939, its failure became difficult for liberals to comprehend, as events seemed to contradict their theories. Therefore, despite the efforts of prominent liberal scholars and politicians such as Kant and Wilson, liberalism failed to retain a strong hold and a new theory emerged to explain the continuing presence of war. That theory became known as realism.

Realism gained momentum during the Second World War when it appeared to offer a convincing account for how and why the worst conflict in known history originated after a period of supposed peace and optimism. Although it originated in named form in the twentieth century, many realists have traced its origins in earlier writings. Indeed, realists have looked as far back as to the ancient world where they detected similar patterns of human behaviour as those evident in our modern world. As its name suggests, advocates of realism purport it reflects the 'reality' of the world and more effectively accounts for change in international politics. Thomas Hobbes is often mentioned in discussions of realism due to his description of the brutality of life during the English Civil War of 1642–1651. Hobbes described human beings as living in an orderless 'state of nature' that he perceived as a war of all against all. To remedy this, he proposed that a 'social contract' was required between a ruler and the people of a state to maintain relative order. Today, we take such ideas for granted as it is usually clear who rules our states. Each leader, or 'sovereign' (a monarch, or a parliament for example) sets the rules and establishes a system of punishments for those who break them. We accept this in our respective states so that our lives can function with a sense of security and order. It may not be ideal, but it is better than a state of nature. As no such contract exists internationally and there is no sovereign in charge of the world, disorder and fear rules international relations. That is why war seems more common than peace to realists, indeed they see war as inevitable. When they examine history they see a world that may change in shape, but is always characterised by a system of what they call 'international anarchy' as the world has no sovereign to give it order.

One central area that sets realism and liberalism apart is how they view human nature. Realists do not typically believe that human beings are inherently good, or have the potential for good, as liberals do. Instead, they claim individuals act in their own self-interests. For realists, people are selfish and behave according to their own needs without necessarily taking into account the needs of others. Realists believe conflict is unavoidable and perpetual and so war is common and inherent to humankind. Hans Morgenthau, a prominent realist, is known for his famous statement 'all politics is a struggle for power' (Morgenthau 1948). This demonstrates the typical realist view that politics is primarily about domination as opposed to cooperation between states. Here, it is useful to briefly recall the idea of theories being lenses. Realists and liberals look at the very same world. But when viewing that world through the realist lens, the world appears to be one of domination. The realist lens magnifies instances of war and conflict and then uses those to paint a certain picture of the world. Liberals, when looking at the same world, adjust their lenses to blur out areas of domination and instead bring areas of cooperation into focus. Then, they can paint a slightly different picture of the same world.

It is important to understand that there is no single liberal or realist theory. Scholars in the two groups rarely fully agree with each other, even those who share the same approach. Each scholar has a particular interpretation of the world, which includes ideas of peace, war and the role of the state in relation to individuals. And, both realism and liberalism have been updated to more modern versions (neoliberalism and neorealism) that represent a shift in emphasis from their traditional roots. Nevertheless, these perspectives can still be grouped into theory 'families' (or traditions). In your studies, you will need to unpack the various differences but, for now, understanding the core assumptions of each approach is the best way to get your bearings.

For example, if we think of the simple contrast of optimism and pessimism we can see a familial relationship in all branches of realism and liberalism. Liberals share an optimistic view of IR, believing that world order can be improved, with peace and progress gradually replacing war. They may not agree on the details, but this optimistic view generally unites them. Conversely, realists tend to dismiss optimism as a form of misplaced idealism and instead they arrive at a more pessimistic view. This is due to their focus on the centrality of the state and its need for security and survival in an anarchical system where it can only truly rely on itself. As a result, realists reach an array of accounts that describe IR as a system where war and conflict is common and periods of peace are merely times when states are preparing for future conflict.

Another point to keep in mind is that each of the overarching approaches in IR possesses a different perspective on the nature of the state. Both liberalism and realism consider the state to be the dominant actor in IR, although liberalism does add a role for non-state actors such as international organisations. Nevertheless, within both theories states themselves are typically regarded as possessing ultimate power. This includes the capacity to enforce decisions, such as declaring war on another nation, or conversely treaties that may bind states to certain agreements. In terms of liberalism, its proponents argue that organisations are valuable in assisting states in formulating decisions and helping to formalise cooperation that leads to peaceful outcomes. Realists on the other hand believe states partake in international organisations only when it is in their self-interest to do so. Many scholars have begun to reject these traditional theories over the past several decades because of their obsession with the state and the status quo.

The middle ground

The thinking of the English school is often viewed as a middle ground between liberal and realist theories. Its theory involves the idea of a society of states existing at the international level. Hedley Bull, one of the core figures of the English school, agreed with the traditional theories that the international system was anarchic. However, he insisted that this does not imply there are no norms (expected behaviours), thus claiming there is a societal aspect to international politics. In this sense, states form an 'Anarchical Society' (Bull 1977) where a type of order does exist, based on shared norms and behaviours. Due to its central premise, the English school is often characterised as having an international society approach to IR. This describes a world that is not quite realist and not quite liberal – but rather a world that has elements of both.

Constructivism is another theory commonly viewed as a middle ground, but this time between mainstream theories and the critical theories that we will explore later. It also has some familial links with the English school. Unlike scholars from other perspectives, constructivists highlight the importance of values and shared interests between individuals who interact on the global stage. Alexander Wendt, a prominent constructivist, described the relationship between agents (individuals) and structures (such as the state) as one in which structures not only constrain agents but also construct their identities and interests. His famous phrase 'anarchy is what states make of it' (Wendt 1992) sums this up well. Another way to explain this, and to explain the core of constructivism, is that the essence of international relations exists in the interactions between people. After all, states do not interact; it is agents of those states, such as politicians and diplomats, who interact. As those interacting on the world stage have accepted international anarchy as the defining principle, it has become part of our reality. However, if anarchy is what we make of it, then different states can perceive anarchy differently and the qualities of anarchy can even change over time. International anarchy could even be replaced with a different system if a critical mass of other individuals (and by proxy the states they represent) accepted the idea. To understand constructivism is to understand that ideas, or 'norms' as they are often called, have power. IR is, then, a never-ending journey of change chronicling the accumulation of the accepted norms of the past and the emerging norms of the future. As such, constructivists seek to study this process.

Critical theories

Critical approaches refer to a wide spectrum of theories that have been established in response to mainstream approaches in the field, mainly liberalism and realism. In a nutshell, critical theorists share one particular trait – they oppose commonly held assumptions in the field of IR that have been central since its establishment. Thus, altered circumstances call for new approaches that are better suited to understand, as well as question, the world we find ourselves in. Critical theories are valuable because they identify positions that have typically been ignored or overlooked within IR. They also provide a voice to individuals who have frequently been marginalised, particularly women and those from the Global South.

Marxism is a good place to start with critical theories. This approach is based upon the ideas of Karl Marx, who lived in the nineteenth century at the height of the industrial revolution. The term 'Marxist' refers to individuals who have adopted Marx's views and believe that society is divided into two classes – the business class (the bourgeoisie) and the working class (the proletariat). The proletariat are at the mercy of the bourgeoisie who control their wages and therefore their standard of living. Marx hoped for an eventual end to the class society and overthrow of the bourgeoisie by the proletariat. Critical theorists who take a Marxist angle often argue that the internationalisation of the state as the standard operating principle of international relations has led to ordinary people around the globe becoming divided and alienated, instead of recognising what they all have in common as a global proletariat. For this to change, the legitimacy of the state must be questioned and ultimately dissolved. In that sense, emancipation from the state in some form is often part of the wider critical agenda.

Postcolonialism differs from Marxism by focusing on the inequality between nations or regions, as opposed to classes. The effects of colonialism are still felt in many regions of the world today as local populations continue to deal with the challenges created and left behind by the former colonial powers. Postcolonialism's origins can be traced to the Cold War period when much activity in international relations centred around decolonisation and the ambition to undo the legacies of European imperialism. This approach acknowledges that politics is not limited to one area or region and that it is vital to include the voices of individuals from other parts of the world. Edward Said (1978) developed the prominent 'Orientalist' critique, describing how the Middle East and Asia were inaccurately depicted in the West. As a result, more focus within the discipline was placed on including the viewpoints of those from the Global South to ensure that Western scholars no longer spoke on their behalf. This created a deeper understanding of the political and social challenges faced by people living within these regions as well as an acknowledgement of how their issues could be better addressed. Postcolonial scholars are, therefore, important contributors to the field as they widen the focus of enquiry beyond IR's traditionally 'Western' mindset.

Another theory that exposes the inequality inherent in international relations is feminism. Feminism entered the field in the 1980s as part of the emerging critical movement. It focused on explaining why so few women seemed to be in positions of power and examining the implications of this on how global politics was structured. You only need look at a visual of any meeting of world leaders to see how it appears to be a man's world. Recognising this introduces a 'gendered' reading of IR, where we place an issue such as gender as the prime object in focus. If it is a man's world, what does that mean? What exactly is masculinity as a gender and how has it imposed itself on international relations? As V. Spike Peterson (1992) argues, as long as gender remains 'invisible' it may be unclear what 'taking gender seriously' means. Once it is recognised that gender is essentially a social construction permeating all aspects of society, the challenges it presents can be better confronted in a way that benefits all individuals. Here, you might be beginning to see some overlaps – with constructivism for example. We are doing our best to present each approach separately so that you have a clearer starting point, but it is wise to caution you that IR theory is a dense and complex web and not always clearly defined. Keep this in mind as you read on, and as your studies develop.

The most controversial of the critical theories is poststructuralism. It is an approach that questions the very beliefs we have all come to know and feel as being 'real'. Poststructuralism questions the dominant narratives that have been widely accepted by mainstream theories. For instance, liberals and realists both accept the idea of the state and for the most part take it for granted. Such assumptions are foundational 'truths' on which those traditional theories rest – becoming 'structures' that they build their account of reality around. So, although these two theoretical perspectives may differ in some respect in regards to their overall worldviews, they share a general understanding of the world. Neither theory seeks to challenge the existence of the state. They simply count it as part of their reality. Poststructuralism seeks to question these commonly held assumptions of reality that are taken for granted, such as the state – but also more widely the nature of power. Jacques Derrida's contribution in this area was in how he showed that you could deconstruct language to identify deeper, or alternative, meanings behind texts. If you can deconstruct language (expose its hidden meanings and the power it has), then you can do the same with fundamental ideas that shape international relations – such as the state. By introducing doubt over why the state exists – and who it exists for – poststructuralists can ask questions about central components of our political world that traditional theories would rather avoid. If you can shake the foundations of a structure, be that a word or an idea, you can move beyond it in your thinking and become free of the power it has over you. This approach introduces doubt to the reality we assume to share and exposes the often thin foundations that some commonly held 'truths' stand upon.

Theory in practice: examining the United Nations

The United Nations (UN) is a highly respected international organisation created at the conclusion of the Second World War from the ashes of the League of Nations. Although it continues to exist, many doubt its claims to success. The United Nations General Assembly is an organ that provides every country with a seat at the table. However, the United Nations Security Council is where power ultimately resides. The Security Council has ten elected non-permanent members, each with their own vote. More importantly, the Security Council also contains five permanent members – the United States, Russia, China, France and the United Kingdom – reflecting the victors of the Second World War who stood dominant in 1945 as the United Nations was created. Any of those five permanent members can, through the use of a veto, stop any major resolution.

The United Nations does not possess complete power over states. In other words, it has limited authority to interfere in domestic concerns since one of its main purposes has generally been to mediate diplomatically when issues between countries arise. To better understand this last point, one can point to the challenges faced by the UN's peacekeepers, who comprise civilian, police and military personnel positioned in areas of conflict to create conditions for lasting peace. Irrespective of any actual desire to maintain peace in a certain area, peacekeepers are typically only permitted to apply force in matters of self-defence. This draws on the common (though not always accurate) description of the United Nations as 'peace*keeper*' rather than 'peace*maker*'. For these reasons, among others, it is possible to argue that the United Nations as an organisation is merely symbolic. At the same time, despite its limited ability to influence heads of state or prevent violence, it is also possible to argue that many nations have benefitted from its work. Aside from its mission to maintain peace and security, the United Nations is also committed to promoting sustainable development, protecting human rights, upholding international law, and delivering humanitarian aid around the world.

From a theoretical point of view, the effectiveness and utility of the United Nations differs depending on which perspective we choose to adopt. Liberals tend to have faith in the capacity of international organisations, primarily the United Nations, along with others organisations such as the International Monetary Fund, the World Health Organization and the World Bank, to uphold the framework of global governance. International organisations may not be perfect, but they help the world find alternatives to war through trade and diplomacy (among other things), which are staples of the liberal account of

IR. On the other hand, middle-ground theories such as constructivism focus on ideas and interests. As constructivists focus often on the interactions of elite individuals, they see large organisations like the United Nations as places where they can study the emergence of new norms and examine the activities of those who are spreading new ideas.

Realists, although they do not reject the United Nations completely, argue that the world is anarchic and states will eventually resort to war despite the efforts of international organisations, which have little real authority. Generally, realists believe that international organisations appear to be successful when they are working in the interests of powerful states. But, if that condition is reversed and an organisation becomes an obstacle to national interests, then the equation may change. This line of enquiry is often used by realists to help explain why the League of Nations was unsuccessful – failing to allow for Germany and Japan's expansionist desires in the 1930s. A contemporary example would be the United States invading Iraq in 2003 despite the Security Council declining to authorise it. The United States simply ignored the United Nations and went ahead, despite opposition. On the other hand, liberals would argue that without the United Nations, international relations would likely be even more chaotic – devoid of a respectable institution to oversee relations between states and hold bad behaviour to account. A constructivist would look at the very same example and say that while it is true that the United States ignored the United Nations and invaded Iraq, by doing so it violated the standard practices of international relations. The United States disregarded a 'norm' and even though there was no direct punishment, its behaviour was irregular and so would not be without consequence. Examining the difficulties the United States faced in its international relations following 2003 gives considerable weight to the constructivist and liberal viewpoints.

In contrast to liberals and constructivists, who value the United Nations to an extent, critical theories offer different perspectives. Marxists would argue that any international body, including the United Nations, works to promote the interests of the business class. After all, the United Nations is composed of (and was built by) states who are the chief protagonists in global capitalism – the very thing that Marxism is opposed to. Likewise, the United Nations can be said to be dominated by imperial (or neo-imperial) powers. Imperialism, according to Marxist doctrine, is the highest stage of capitalism. The United Nations, then, is not an organisation that offers any hope of real emancipation for citizens. Even though it may appear humanitarian, these actions are merely band-aids over a system of perpetual state-led exploitation that the United Nations legitimises.

Poststructuralists would seek to question the meanings behind the role of the United Nations and the arbitrary power structure of the Security Council. They would also look at how key terms are used by the United Nations and what they mean. For example, examining the wording of concepts like 'peacekeepers' and 'peacekeeping' as opposed to 'peace-making' and 'peace-enforcing'. Or similarly, 'collective security' versus 'international security': poststructuralists would be sceptical as to whether these terms really differ in meaning and would point to the power of language in advancing the agenda of the United Nations – or perhaps that of the powerful states controlling it. Even the name of the dominant organ of the United Nations – the 'Security' Council – begs the question, security for whom? A critique here would point out that at its core, the United Nations is primarily concerned with facilitating the *national* security of powerful states rather than *human* security. In instances like these, the tools that poststructuralism provides to deconstruct and analyse wording have real value.

Feminists would look to how those in positions of power, whether politicians or those working for the United Nations such as officials and delegates, perpetuate a discourse of masculinity. Alternative feminine perspectives are still not adequately recognised and those in decision-making positions of power continue to be disproportionately male. Many countries that make up the United Nations marginalise the feminine voice domestically and thus perpetuate this at the international level. This is especially true of states where women hold more traditional roles in society and are therefore less likely to be considered suitable for what may be traditionally viewed as masculine roles, such as a delegate or ambassador.

Finally, postcolonialists would argue that the discourse perpetuated by the United Nations is one based on cultural, national or religious privilege. They would suggest, for instance, that, as it has no African or Latin American permanent members, the Security Council fails to represent the current state of the world. Postcolonialists would also point to the presence of former colonial powers on the Security Council and how their ability to veto proposals put forward by other countries perpetuates a form of continued indirect colonial exploitation of the Global South.

Hopefully, this brief reading of the United Nations from these varied perspectives has opened your eyes to the potential of IR theory as an analytical tool. We have barely scratched the surface, but it should be clear why so many divergent views are needed in IR and how, in a basic sense, they may be applied.

Conclusion

This chapter has surveyed the main approaches in IR theory, each of which possesses a legitimate, yet different, view of the world. It is important to note that the theories listed in this chapter are not exhaustive and there are many more that could be examined. However, this is a good starting point for achieving an overall understanding of the field and where the most common approaches are situated. Hopefully this has helped you consider your own theoretical inclination – or at least piqued your interest in determining where you might stand. It is not necessary to adopt one theory as your own. But it is important to understand the various theories as tools of analysis that you can apply in your studies. Using a theory to critique an issue, as this chapter did with the United Nations, is to understand the reason why these theories exist. Simply, they offer a means by which to attempt to understand a complex world. As international relations has grown in complexity, the family of theories that IR offers has grown in number. Due to its complexity and diversity, it is common for newcomers to have some difficulty in grasping IR theory, but this chapter should give you the confidence to get started.

5

International Law

KNUT TRAISBACH

International law is an important area to understand and much of it is theoretical or historical in nature – building on themes explored in the previous chapters. You have seen in the preceding chapter that some of the discussed theories regard 'norms' as a regulatory force in international relations, although the theories differ in their understanding of the relevance and function of these norms. This chapter takes up this notion and introduces you to the role of international legal norms as a particular means for the social regulation of international affairs.

Imagine a small settlement with a number of properties on each of which stands one house in which lives one family. This settlement has no common government, parliament, court system or police force. The internal affairs of each family as much as the borders of each property are respected as inviolable. The families have predominantly bilateral relations with each other and engage in commercial exchanges of goods and services. It is commonly accepted that if the head of a family dies, the established promises to other families and agreed exchanges are respected by the heirs. When children decide to delineate a new property or when a new family from elsewhere wants to settle in, the other families must agree first and recognise this new property. When disputes between families arise, they may result in violence, especially if someone challenges an established border or intervenes with a family's interests. It is commonly accepted that one may have recourse to force to defend one's interest in family and property. Other families do not intervene in these disputes as long as their interests are not affected or they have formed a special alliance with another family.

Ask yourself now whether you would call this settlement a 'legal system'? Would you even speak of 'laws'? Perhaps intuitively you would say no. Yet, consider for a moment which kind of rules and principles must exist even in such a setting. How does any form of regulation work? Why does it work? If you delve a little on these questions, you will encounter some of the foundational legal institutions that exist in most legal systems. The concept of property, title, territory and border are there; a principle of autonomy and supreme authority seems to apply to the families; and the institution of contract certainly exists. You will also detect rules of some sort in the form of established customs and you might even identify a principle that says that 'agreements need to be kept'. Lawyers make use of the Latin phrase 'pacta sunt servanda' to express this basic principle. Thus, even in such a rudimentary setting, some customary rules and principles exist even if they are not called 'law' or written down in any form.

You will also note that some characteristics of what you may intuitively regard as essential to a legal order are missing: There is no authority 'above' the families which makes laws for all, adjudicates conflicts or enforces laws and judgements. There is no government, parliament, court or police system. The rules and principles seem to stem from established practices motivated by the functional needs of cohabitation, pragmatism or mere common sense. Whatever rules exist in this settlement, their validity and effectiveness are routed exclusively in the will of the families and their members.

This settlement resembles many peculiarities of the international legal order. In fact, the settlement resembles a certain depiction of the international legal order that most international lawyers today would call outdated, even though it is precisely this depiction of a primitive legal order that haunts international law even today. If you translate the situation of the settlement to the international plane and substitute the families with states, you will get a picture of international law characterised by states as the principal actors. In this depiction, states hold the supreme and exclusive authority over their polities and follow predominantly customary and contractual rules in the relations between them but have no world government above them.

The principle of sovereignty expressed this supreme and exclusive authority of states over their territory, and it confirmed the equal status of all states. It developed its current meaning through the writings of legal and political philosophers between the sixteenth and eighteenth century. Sovereignty continues to be the foundational pillar of the international legal order. For many decades this foundational pillar of international law read: sovereign states are the masters of international law with no world government above them. This meant that the validity of any legal rule depended on the will of states or, conversely, that states are only bound by authoritative legal precepts (norms) that they have consented to. In a famous judgement in the *Lotus case,* the Permanent Court of International Justice in The Hague – the principal judicial organ of the League of Nations, the predecessors to the

International Court of Justice (ICJ) of the United Nations (UN) – stated in 1927 (The Case of the S.S. 'Lotus', judgement of the Permanent Court of International Justice, 7 September 1927, 18):

> International law governs relations between independent States. The rules of law binding upon States therefore emanate from their own free will as expressed in conventions or by usages generally accepted as expressing principles of law and established in order to regulate the relations between these co-existing independent communities or with a view to the achievement of common aims. Restrictions upon the independence of States cannot therefore be presumed.

What law is international law?

It is this depiction of international law that often culminated in the question of whether international law was really law. How could international legal norms be effective if their validity depended on the will of states, the very subjects international law should govern? This doubt in the validity and effectiveness of international law ultimately led to a rupture between the two disciplines of international law and international relations theory after the Second World War. Two scholars, Edward Hallett Carr and Hans Morgenthau, suggested around this time that international law was particularly inept for understanding the behaviour of nations. They were disappointed by what they identified as an idealistic belief in international law which, after all, had not prevented – for the second time – a world war. They proposed instead a more 'realistic' assessment of international relations based on power and interest. The founding realist school of international relations theory thus questioned the effectiveness and relevance of international law as a decisive influencing factor for the behaviour of states and for the assurance of international peace and security.

Much has changed since then. The international legal order has diversified in every possible way. There are countless bilateral and multilateral contracts between states (called treaties or conventions in international law), and more than 5,000 intergovernmental organisations and their different organs engage in the regulation and administration of nearly all aspects of international life.

International legal norms pervade global affairs. Every time you travel internationally, send an email, or update your social media profiles, there are not only domestic but supranational legal norms at play, including regional norms as in the European Union. Be it border control, diplomatic and consular relations between countries, the determination of flight and navigation routes, internet regulation, privacy, the use of postal and telecommunication services, industrial standards or cross-border environmental hazards – international law permeates these areas as much as the better-known fields of the protection of human rights, humanitarian interventions and the fight against transnational terrorism.

It is important to understand, then, that the question of whether and how international law matters depends not least on one's conceptual outlook on international life. This chapter introduces you foremost to the (traditional 'occidental' or 'Western') normative understanding of international law in order to show you how international lawyers think and how they use international law. This implies a focus on valid legal rules that authoritatively regulate international life. Yet the understanding of international law as a system of legal norms is not the only possible approach, nor is it the solely valid one. In fact, there are numerous other approaches that complement the normative outlook on global law (Walker 2014). It is also important that the occidental depiction of international law is not the only one existing in the world. Scholars from outside the West have shown, for example, how the dominant view of international law neglects important and often earlier contributions to international law by other cultures. Asian, African and Latin American countries should form part of our understanding of international law. For example, international treaties existed already in Africa and Asia over three thousand years ago. Islamic legal thought, present in Persia, India, South Asia and Europe, also had legal regulations of how to conduct hostilities at least since the seventh century. There is not one single conception of international law or international politics.

By focusing on the normative understanding of international law, the chapter takes a modest approach and steers a middle ground. There are also conceptualisations that portray international law as a cosmopolitan order securing solidarity and peace in a 'post-Westphalian' world in which states have largely lost their status as sole sovereigns. On the other hand, there are theories that continue to question the social effectiveness and relevance of international legal norms to shape the behaviour of international actors. In addition, one can also analyse international law through empirical research that uses collected data about the social behaviour of actors as it is done, for example, to scrutinise the effectiveness of human rights norms. Yet, a purely empirical analysis has difficulty in conveying the idiosyncrasy of normative thinking and argumentation in international law. Even if collected data shows instances of non-compliance with human rights norms, it would be wrong to draw conclusions from this about the binding character or range of social effects of these norms.

International lawyers as a particular group of professionals learn techniques to determine which legal norms exist and which are applicable to the relevant actors in a certain situation. Lawyers speak of the sources and subjects of law. They learn how to apply these norms using specific techniques, such as interpretation or the balancing of conflicting rights. These professional techniques are not value-neutral or objective but involve subjective choices and politics. An approximation to objectivity and ideals of justice is achieved only through specific procedures that need to be followed, recognised modes of argumentation and particular processes of decision-making. In a nutshell, international law consists of certain conventions on argumentation and modes of conflict resolution that some regard as a craft, others as an art. Most likely it is both.

The contents of international law

One distinguishes broadly between domestic, regional and (public and private) international law. Domestic law stems from domestic lawmakers and regulates the life of the citizens of a particular state. Regional law, such as European Union law or the law of regional human rights mechanisms, stems from regional intergovernmental institutions and addresses the governments and individuals of a particular geographical region or legal regime. Public international law is the subject of this chapter and addresses – in most general terms – relations involving states, intergovernmental organisations and non-state actors, which include today individuals, non-governmental organisations (NGOs) and private corporations. Private international law concerns conflicts of laws that may arise in cases where the domestic laws of different states could apply, for example in cases of cross-border e-commerce, marriages or liabilities.

Within public international law, a distinction is traditionally drawn between the law of peace and the law of war (humanitarian law). The law of peace regulates peaceful relations and includes such subject matters as international treaty law, the law of diplomatic and consular relations, international organisation law, the law of state responsibility, the law of the sea, the environment and outer space or international economic law.

International humanitarian law (IHL) is the law of armed conflicts (*jus in bellum* – the law applicable in war) and regulates the conduct of international and non-international hostilities. In times of war, the use of force, including the killing of human beings, is not prohibited. The legal regulation of armed conflicts goes back to the mid-nineteenth century and comprises a large body of customary rules and a series of important conventions and additional protocols to these conventions adopted primarily in The Hague and Geneva.

International humanitarian law regulates, among other things, the methods and means of warfare and the protection of certain categories of persons – for example, the sick and wounded, prisoners of war and civilians. More specific treaties prohibit the use of certain types of weapons (such as chemical or biological weapons, mines or cluster munitions) or the protection of cultural property during armed conflict. Much of the development and codification of this body of law is the merit of the International Committee of the Red Cross, founded in 1863 by Henry Dunant, which is a private humanitarian institution based in Geneva and forms part of the International Red Cross and Red Crescent Movement.

At the transitional points between the law of peace and the law of armed conflict lies the legal regulation of the resort to force (*jus ad bellum* – the law to engage in war) which concerns the conditions that need to be met to use force legally as, for example, in instances of self-defence (Article 51, UN Charter). More recently, scholars also speak of the regulation of the transition to peace after the end of armed conflicts (*jus post-bellum* – the law after war) which includes questions over how to end armed conflicts, transitional justice and post-war reconstruction.

The strict distinction between the law of peace and the law of armed conflict has been somewhat blurred with the rise of international human rights law and international criminal law. Human rights law builds on and develops fundamental principles of humanitarian law for the protection of individuals. On the other hand, human rights have considerably influenced the refinement of humanitarian rules for the protection of combatants and civilians. International criminal law has seen a rapid development after the end of the Cold War first with the establishment of the international criminal tribunals for the former Yugoslavia and Rwanda and then with the establishment of the International Criminal Court in 2002.

From 'no world government' to global governance

Consider now what it meant to establish, for example, an international legal prohibition of torture. Torture was a common and legal method of interrogation before the seventeenth century. A legal prohibition of torture would mean that governments are obliged by international law not to allow their officials to use torture. How did an international legal norm prohibiting torture develop? What were its effects?

Subjects: Who makes international law and to whom does it apply?

You have seen already that traditionally only states (for historical reasons also the Holy See/Vatican and the Maltese Order) were subjects of international law and bearers of privileges and obligations. Privileges included sovereign status, immunities, jurisdiction or membership in international organisations, for example. Obligations towards other states arose from voluntary contracts, from the principle of non-intervention or from responsibilities for wrongful acts.

The status of a sovereign state implied full membership in the international society of states. It is a contentious issue in international law whether a territorial entity gains the legal status of a sovereign state depending only on a number of factual criteria (such as the existence of a population, territory, effective government and capacity to enter into international relations) or whether this requires also a formal recognition by other states. Already the criteria of statehood are contentious, and in practice it is not always easy to determine whether all conditions are met. In addition, for political reasons states have sometimes recognised other states that did not fulfil one or more criteria of statehood, or they have not recognised states despite them fulfilling all criteria. After the break-up of the former state of Yugoslavia, for example, Kosovo declared its independence from Serbia in 2008. Serbia has not formally recognised Kosovo as an independent sovereign state. Neither have a number of other states such as Russia, China and Spain, which all try to control movements for regional independence or autonomy in their own territory.

Coming back now to the example of the prohibition of torture, which options did individuals have under international law to seek redress for acts of torture? If a foreigner was tortured by officials of another state, the home state could complain to the latter. The individuals themselves, however, could do very little under international law, for individuals were not subjects of this body of law. Even worse, if a state tortured its own citizens, this was an internal matter in which other states could not intervene.

Sources: How is international law made?

The most important and most concrete sources of international law are bilateral and multilateral treaties. Multilateral treaties are usually prepared during long negotiations at diplomatic state conferences where a final treaty text is adopted and then opened for signature and ratification by states. When an agreed number of states have ratified the treaty, it enters into force and becomes binding on the member states.

Article 38 of the Statute of the International Court of Justice lists as sources of international law on which the court may rely in its decisions: treaties, customary international law, general principles of law that exist in most domestic legal systems (such as behaving in 'good faith') and, as a subsidiary means, also judicial decisions and scholarly writings.

Customary practices are even today still a common and highly contentious source of law. Customary law refers to the established practices of states that are supported by a subjective belief to be required by law. If a customary rule exists, it is binding on all states except where a state has persistently objected to this rule. You can imagine already that the deduction of legal rules from social practices and subjective beliefs poses many difficulties and bears many insecurities regarding proof and actual content. Also during diplomatic conferences that prepare a treaty text, many difficult compromises are brokered. To paraphrase a saying that is often attributed to Otto von Bismarck, laws are like sausages. It is better not to see them being made.

In the context of our example of the prohibition of torture, imagine the following scenario: state A has signed and ratified the International Covenant on Civil and Political Rights, which contains a prohibition of torture in Article 7, and is also party to the Convention against Torture and Other Cruel, Inhuman or Degrading Treatment or Punishment. This country fights terrorism and brings suspected terrorists to secret prisons in countries which are not party to any of the above conventions. In these prisons, the suspects endure intense interrogations which include sleep deprivation, waterboarding (causing the sensation of drowning) and other measures.

As an international lawyer faced with this case your starting point would be the aforementioned international treaties that contain a prohibition of torture. You would need to determine whether the interrogation measures amount to torture. Here, the codified definition in international treaties and the interpretation of this definition in previous cases can give you important guidance. You would also need to determine whether the particular state in question has ratified the pertinent treaty or treaties. In our example, the situation is complicated by the fact that both treaties limit the territorial applicability of the treaty to all individuals within a state's territory and subject to its jurisdiction. Hence one could argue that instances of torture on the territory of non-state parties do not fall within the ambit of the treaties. Also a counterargument is possible. One could make a case for the extraterritorial application of the treaty if the acts of torture on foreign soil were effectively controlled by a state that is a member to the treaty.

You would then proceed to see whether a customary rule exists that prohibits the use of torture. Even if the treaties prohibiting torture have not been ratified by a state, you could argue that the treaty has codified an already existing customary rule or, if a large majority of states has ratified the treaties, that this is evidence that a customary rule has been formed. In light of horrendous historical experiences, you may also argue that the prohibition of torture is of such fundamental importance that today no derogation from this rule is permitted. In other words, you would argue that the prohibition of torture is a peremptory rule of international law (*ius cogens* – peremptory law) that does not permit any exception.

You can see now how the early idea of state consent as a necessary requirement for an international rule still permeates these argumentations. The main difficulty often consists in establishing state consent or, at times, in constructing alternatives for it.

Global organisation: The United Nations era

The end of the Second World War and the end of the Cold War are probably the most significant historical watersheds in the development of recent public international law. The end of the Second World War in 1945 led to the establishment of the United Nations and the rapid development of several areas of international law, including human rights law, international criminal law and international economic law.

The United Nations is the most important global intergovernmental organisation with major offices in New York, Geneva, Nairobi and Vienna. It was established with the principal aim to ensure peace and security through international co-operation and collective measures. As of 2017, it has 193 member states. Article 2 of the UN Charter, the founding treaty of the United Nations, confirms as guiding principles the sovereign equality of the member states, the peaceful settlement of disputes, the prohibition of the use of force and the principle of non-intervention.

Delegates of all member states meet once a year during the General Assembly to discuss pertinent issues of world politics and vote on non-binding resolutions. The Security Council is the highest executive organ of the United Nations in which the representatives of ten selected member states and five states with permanent seats decide on issues of peace and security through binding resolutions, which may result in economic sanctions or even military actions. The 'permanent five' (the People's Republic of China, France, Russia, the United Kingdom and the United States) hold the privilege of a veto right allowing them to prevent the adoption of resolutions of the Security Council on any substantial (as opposed to procedural) issues. Major reform initiatives of the composition or voting procedures of the Security Council have been unsuccessful so far. This taints the effectiveness and the democratic legitimacy of the Security Council and, especially during the Cold War, it severely constrained the Security Council as two of its key members (the United States and the Soviet Union) were engaged in an ideological conflict. Politically, however, the right to veto was a necessary concession to ensure the participation of the most powerful nations in a world organisation.

Numerous principal and subsidiary UN organs and specialised agencies engage in the application, enforcement and development of international law. This work comprises, for example, classical legal work in the International Law Commission and special committees of the General Assembly, practical work in the field and diplomatic efforts by Offices of High Commissioners and their staff, or actions taken by the Security Council. All of these bodies, and many more, promote and shape international law in various ways. In the International Law Commission, for example, a group of experts create reports and drafts on specific topics that are then submitted to a committee of the General Assembly and can provide an important basis for later treaty negotiations. The Offices of the High Commissioners for Human Rights and Refugees do important work in the field where their staff endeavour to uphold international law often in crisis situations. Their experiences influence also subsequent interpretations of international law, for example, regarding who qualifies as a refugee. The United Nations Educational, Scientific and Cultural Organization (UNESCO) fulfils a crucial function in disseminating knowledge about international law by promoting education and research on human rights, justice and the rule of law.

Community and governance: The changing structure of international law

The existence of a world organisation, the legal prohibition of the use of force, the establishment of a system of collective security and the protection of human rights have caused fundamental changes in the international legal order. International lawyers and politicians speak frequently of the 'international community' that co-operates to pursue community interests which cannot be achieved by single states alone. These community interests may range from environmental challenges and cultural heritage to issues of human security.

How much the meaning of sovereignty has changed, one can see, for example, in the principle of a shared 'responsibility to protect' (R2P). According to this principle, states have an obligation to prevent gross human rights violations not only at home but also abroad, if necessary through forceful United Nations measures. The protection of the individual from severe atrocities has thus become a matter of national, regional and international concern. This means that states can no longer claim that gross human rights violations are internal matters and that they are protected by their sovereignty.

Today there are countless actors that engage in the making, interpretation, use and enforcement of international norms. States still are the major international actors and the principal makers and addressees of international norms. Yet the bureaucracies of intergovernmental organisations and their organs, numerous international, regional and domestic courts and tribunals, non-governmental organisations and even groups or single persons (so-called 'norm entrepreneurs') engage in the pronunciation, interpretation and dissemination of international legal norms, standards and other types of 'soft law'. And, they often do this without, or even against, the will of states. For example, a NATO-led intervention in Kosovo in 1999 was executed without the authorisation of the UN Security Council. NATO (the North Atlantic Treaty Organization) is a collective security organisation, effectively a military alliance, of Western states. It was originally created to help contain the spread of communism in Europe during the Cold War but has endured in the years since. Its actions in Kosovo contributed to the establishment of the International Commission on Intervention and State Sovereignty which was a private expert group under the auspices of the Canadian Government to respond to UN Secretary-General Kofi Annan's challenge on how to respond to large-scale violations of human rights and humanitarian law. The commission produced a report on 'The Responsibility to Protect' to which both the UN Security Council and the General Assembly have repeatedly referred to and which is used as an argumentative tool by civil society actors, including many non-governmental organisations. You can thus see how a private initiative has transformed into public normative authority.

This multitude of norms, legal regimes, actors and normative processes is reflected in more recent approaches to international law that focus more on pluralistic governance processes than on a unified legal system, and more on informal law-making than on formal sources.

The functioning of international law

In order to understand how different actors make normative claims and how they use international law, the aforementioned broader perspectives offer valuable insights. The emergence of a norm like the prohibition of torture and its influence start long before such a norm is codified in an international treaty. Political scientists and legal scholars have described a normative 'life cycle' that relies on a (transnational) social process which is characterised by an initial norm emergence, followed by early adoption of this new norm, spreading of this acceptance and ultimately by widespread internalisation of the norm and compliance with it.

For the first stage of norm emergence, the influence of so-called 'norm-entrepreneurs' (such as private individuals, lobbying groups, non-governmental organisations) is essential. Through a combination of means (e.g. framing of issues, campaigning, empathy appeal, persuasion, shaming, claiming, declaring, etc.) and on different organisational platforms, the norm-entrepreneurs try to enunciate norms and persuade governments to embrace them. In the case of torture, this meant that even literary novels and political pamphlets contributed to a change in social perception and an increase of empathy with victims which in turn led to the social unacceptability of torture.

Once a 'critical mass' of actors have adopted a new norm prohibiting torture or of a responsibility to protect, a threshold or tipping point is reached. At this second stage, the norm starts to spread through international society. Here an active process of transnational – domestic, regional and international – socialisation takes place which, primarily, states, international organisations and networks of norm entrepreneurs carry forward. Those state and non-state actors that have endorsed the norm engage in a process of redefining what qualifies as appropriate behaviour within international society. Social movement theory, which studies mobilisations in society to make collective claims about social changes, provides valuable insights on the conditions and effects of this process.

A third phase of internalisation or obedience is reached when norms 'achieve a "taken-for-granted" quality that makes conformance with the norm almost automatic' (Finnemore and Sikkink 1998, 904). If this process succeeds, norms such as the prohibition of torture become truly transnational in the course of this process. They exert normative force domestically through constitutional guarantees and through the work of civil society groups. In addition, the norms are invoked in regional and in international human rights fora such as regional and international courts or human rights bodies. Thus, these norms acquire a transnational character through interactions between a variety of actors – both state and non-state – across issues areas and across historic public/private and domestic/international dichotomies (Koh 1997, 2612).

This, however, does not mean that international law is a guarantor for a just global order. Much rests on the will and interests of the actors involved. International law itself cannot solve injustices and cannot manufacture solutions. Ultimately, many of the politically charged issues simply reflect in the language of international law. For example, we have seen already that international law prohibits the use of force by states in peace times except when the forceful measures have been authorised by the UN Security Council or when a state acts in self-defence (Article 51, UN Charter). In this scenario, not only politicians but also international lawyers will argue in legal terms whether the use of force against an (allegedly) imminent terrorist attack that has not *yet* occurred can be justified as a form of 'pre-emptive' self-defence. Similarly, since it is not illegal to kill enemy combatants during an armed conflict, international lawyers will exchange legal arguments about whether terrorists qualify as combatants and whether the killing of terrorist suspects in a foreign country is permissible under international law because of a continuing global war on terror that amounts to a state of armed conflict. Finally, also in the ambit of our example on the prohibition of torture, lawyers will argue about whether the situation of a hidden ticking bomb might exceptionally permit torturing the apprehended attacker if this could save innocent lives.

This is not to say, however, that international law is inherently indeterminate or arbitrary. The normative force of international law lies in the creation of new argumentative needs, in the possibility to challenge established positions, in the specific required modes of argumentation, in the institutionalised fora for conflict resolution and in the justificatory potential that rests in law.

Conclusion

Although questions about the relevance and effectiveness of international law persist, especially when powerful nations use their political power to 'bend' international law, today hardly anyone declares international law as irrelevant. Accordingly, the discussion has shifted from 'whether international law is really law' to 'how do international norms matter'. Also the divide between international law and IR theory has been closing for some time now. Liberal approaches to IR acknowledge that norms have an important role to play for the shaping of state preferences and in international co-operation to attain common aims by setting common normative frameworks. The English school argues for an international society in which states through interaction naturally create rules and institutions, as exemplified in the example of the families at the beginning of this chapter. The constructivist school focuses on social processes, including legal norms that shape the self-understanding, role, identity and behaviour of actors. Social movement theory analyses the creation and effects of group organisation in civil society and how campaigning, for example for human rights, gains social force and translates into political results.

International lawyers, on the other hand, have been opening up towards empirical, sociological and political approaches to understand how norms develop and how actors exert normative authority. This goes beyond understanding international law exclusively as a coherent legal system with recognised sources of law and specific techniques of legal practice. International lawyers increasingly adopt a more pluralistic and holistic outlook and an understanding of international law as a social process. This social process results in normative regulations that function as standards of conduct to guide and evaluate the behaviour of international actors. That the individual has acquired such a prominent role in international law as a central subject beyond state confines is truly remarkable. Today, each individual has rights that permeate the international and that are fundamentally embedded in an – albeit imperfect – global law which in turn permeates each of our lives. This law is not static but in a constant process of development. It requires to be made effective, challenged, defended and reformulated in order to fulfil its emancipatory potential.

6

International Organisations

SHAZELINA Z. ABIDIN

As you may have picked up in the previous chapter, we live in a world of laws. While sovereign states are the principal legal actors, international organisations are increasingly important in helping us govern our world. Today's international system is made up of a cacophony of different voices and interests. In addition to states there are also non-governmental organisations, multinational corporations and hybrid organisations which are a mix of all the different categories.

Imagine stepping off a plane into a foreign country. As you disembark you switch on your phone to check the messages that may have come through while you were in transit. You follow the sign that directs you to the airport's exit, clear immigration, and then pick up your luggage at the designated carousel. You then head straight for the 'nothing to declare' green lane to exit the airport. Those routine actions would have already brought you into contact with the work of at least four different international organisations. The aircraft that you arrived in would have been one of the many planes under the International Air Transport Association (IATA) and regulated by standards set by the International Civil Aviation Organization (ICAO); that you were able to use your phone to check messages would have been courtesy of the work of the International Telecommunication Union (ITU); and your customs clearance would have been facilitated by the Kyoto Convention set by the World Customs Organization (WCO) to simplify the customs process.

These are just some of the ways in which international organisations form an integral part of our everyday lives. Whether these organisations are working to build houses for the impoverished like UN-Habitat does, or working to ensure a standard of health for everyone like the World Health Organization (WHO) does, there is no running away from international organisations. Today, it is increasingly difficult to imagine an international system in which the only voices that matter are those of states.

International governmental organisations

An international governmental organisation (IGO), also referred to as an intergovernmental organisation, is an organisation with a membership of only states. The organisation is usually founded upon a treaty, or a multilateral agreement, and consists of more than two states. Member states determine the way in which the organisation is run, vote within the organisation and provide its funding.

Established in 1945 following the end of the Second World War, the United Nations (UN) is a prime example of an international governmental organisation with almost universal membership. Only states can be members of the United Nations and membership is valued because it confers upon the member state international recognition of its sovereignty. As of 2017 there are 193 UN member states – but it is important to note that a small number of states are not members. Taiwan, for example, has repeatedly requested membership but has had its request blocked by China. This is because China regards Taiwan as a part of its sovereign territory and does not recognise it as an independent nation. Taiwan, of course, wants United Nations membership because this will mean that the international community fully accepts its sovereignty. The Taiwan example has gone unresolved for decades due to the major role that China plays within the United Nations as one of its most powerful members.

There are six main organs of the United Nations. Once a state is a member, it is automatically a member of the General Assembly. This is the most democratic organ where each state gets one vote, no matter how big or small, rich or poor the country. It is also the place where, every September, world leaders give their address to the international community from behind a dark green podium with the UN crest clearly visible. The other organs are the Security Council, the Economic and Social Council (ECOSOC), the Trusteeship Council, the Secretariat and the International Court of Justice. By far the most powerful organ is the Security Council, which has 15 members. Five states – China, France, Russia, the United Kingdom, and the United States – are permanent members of the Security Council. The other ten are voted in by the General Assembly for two-year tenures. The Security Council is the only organ that can impose sanctions on states or deploy military forces on behalf of the international community to keep the peace in a certain area, region or country. The United Nations itself does not have its own military force, but it can muster military and police personnel through contributions by its members. These UN peacekeepers are distinguished by their trademark blue helmets, giving rise to the nickname 'Blue Berets'.

In order to be inclusive the United Nations has welcomed the participation (note participation, not membership) of civil society groups during some of its meetings, but never at the sessions of the all-important Security Council. Organisations may speak as observers to the General Assembly, or as organisations with 'consultative status' with the UN Economic and Social Council for example. There are civil society organisations on all issues, ranging from disarmament to oceanic noise pollution, and from mental health to refugees. There are also private individuals who are invited to speak at special United Nations meetings. It is therefore common to witness heart wrenching first-hand accounts of sexual abuses, torture, or discrimination. Such testimonies have the power to galvanise the international community. Yet, no matter how powerful these testimonies are, it is ultimately up to the member states to determine the course of action. The Secretariat, including the Secretary-General who leads the United Nations, cannot take action on its own and can only appeal to member states to 'do something'. Because of this, the United Nations remains undeniably and irrevocably an international governmental organisation and not a level of authority above the states.

Here, the other designation sometimes used to describe IGOs – 'intergovernmental organisation' – is helpful in appreciating the difference in 'global governance' (which IGOs bring to our international system) and 'global government' (which does not currently exist). Virtually all IGOs are intergovernmental. This means that their power rests with governments (the member states) not with the organisation. States are free to leave the organisations, or even in some cases to ignore them. There are usually consequences for both actions, but the fact remains that even in extreme cases – when an organisation like the United Nations imposes sanctions, or authorises war, on a state – international governmental organisations do not rule over states. Such punitive measures are only possible when the members of the UN Security Council are in accord, agree with such proposals, and a coalition of states agrees to finance and partake in the operation. Therefore, the power rests with the states themselves, especially the more powerful states, and there are regular examples of states rejecting a certain course of action because it was not in their national interest. Here, the failures of the United Nations to establish a coordinated response to the Syrian war comes to mind, despite hundreds of thousands killed and millions displaced since 2011.

If an IGO was not intergovernmental, as explained above, it would be in the rare category of 'supranational'. To have supranational powers means that an organisation is actually able to govern its members and have a degree of independence from its member states. The only clear example of a major organisation such as this is the European Union (EU). For that reason, it is often described as *sui generis*, or 'unique' in its own right. The European

Union is unique because, unlike the United Nations and other international governmental organisations, it can actually be said to exercise a degree of sovereignty over its members via law-making powers in certain areas that its members agreed to relocate to the supranational level. It also has its own currency which, together with other capabilities, gives it some of the powers otherwise only seen in states. This is not without controversy in Europe and there is a rising tide of discontent with the growing power of the European Union and a desire in some political circles to weaken, or even dissolve, the organisation so that more of the power returns to the states. The 'Brexit' debate, when the British public voted in a 2016 referendum to leave the European Union, raised many of these issues and is an interesting instance of the idea of supranationalism being challenged.

Leaving aside bigger organisations like the European Union and the United Nations, international governmental organisations are typically more specific in nature – often dealing with just one particular issue or a specific geographical area. The work that they do is often clear from their names – for example, the International Whaling Commission (IWC) or the International Criminal Police Organization (INTERPOL). These are issue-based organisations and their members are worldwide. Then there are organisations of states in specific regions, such as the Association of Southeast Asian Nations (ASEAN) and the African Union (AU). These often emulate elements of the European Union, but none (as yet) feature supranational powers. Other organisations are neither geographically limited nor limited to a single issue. The Commonwealth of Nations, for example, is an organisation whose membership is restricted to former colonies of the United Kingdom. Having been around since 1949, the Commonwealth also has its own permanent secretariat. An international governmental organisation that does not have its own fixed secretariat is the BRICS – an intergovernmental organisation of only five countries (Brazil, Russia, India, China and South Africa) focusing on economic and financial issues of interest to its members. The point to remember is that as long as an organisation is composed exclusively of states, or governments (including government agencies), it is an international governmental organisation operating according to international norms.

These international governmental organisations are outside the United Nations but are almost always tied to the UN in some way or another. For some, these ties are explicitly spelled out in the document that establishes them. For others, the simple goal of ensuring that their work is relevant ties them to the United Nations at least tangentially. Take the International Atomic Energy Agency (IAEA), for example. The founding statute of the Agency dictates that its reports should go to the United Nations so that the Security Council may take action against any countries that fail to meet their obligations. This works out well for the international community – as the

International Atomic Energy Agency monitors the use of nuclear technology while the UN Security Council enforces measures to ensure state compliance over nuclear safety and security.

International non-governmental organisations and hybrid international organisations

International non-governmental organisations (INGOs) are non-governmental organisations that either work at the international level or have international members. International non-governmental organisations are a mixed bag, best described as those organisations that are not intergovernmental, business entities or terrorist organisations (Davies 2014, 3). There is no exact figure for the number of international non-governmental organisations that are currently active. The United Nations lists over 4,000 with consultative status – which may only be a fraction of their true number.

Some spectacular and headline-grabbing protests are organised by certain international non-governmental organisations. Images of Greenpeace protestors chaining themselves to ships, or of anti-globalisation protestors blocking streets, are usually well covered in the media. These are the organisations whose mission is to raise awareness among the general public on issues of concern. No less effective are those that carry out their missions away from the limelight. Mercy Corps, for example, helps disaster survivors in countries around the globe, Médecins Sans Frontières (Doctors Without Borders) is often the first highly skilled responder to a crisis and Oxfam is at the forefront of various poverty eradication programmes around the world. Former UN Secretary-General Kofi Annan termed groups like these the 'unsung heroes' of the international community.

Hybrid organisations are those international organisations whose membership comprises both states and civil society members. The states may be represented by government departments or agencies; while civil society, as we have seen earlier, can be just about anyone or any organisation. One such hybrid international organisation is the International Union for the Conservation of Nature (IUCN), which deals primarily with the preservation of the environment and whose members include government agencies from countries such as Fiji and Spain and non-governmental organisations from all corners of the globe. Individual members are often experts and affiliated to one of the IUCN's six commissions. The number of hybrid organisations has increased as more and more partnerships are forged between states and civil society. There is now an understanding that hybrid organisations, where governments, non-governmental organisations and multinational corporations all have a say, can be highly effective because of the reach, expertise and funding that such groupings can command.

How international organisations shape our world

One of the more visible international non-governmental organisations in the world is the International Red Cross and Red Crescent Movement. Today, the Red Cross is synonymous with work with victims of humanitarian crises, but before its founding there was no organisation to carry out such work and no guidelines for humanitarian concerns arising out of war and conflict. In 1862, Swiss businessman Henry Dunant published a book describing the aftermath of the 1859 Battle of Solferino, which he had experienced first-hand. He wrote how the soldiers were left wounded on the field with no medical care even after the battle had ended. Dunant managed to organise the local population into providing assistance to the sick and wounded. Many were moved by his account and in 1863 Dunant founded the International Committee of the Red Cross. Dunant's efforts prompted a push to provide for the care of wounded soldiers and civilians caught in places of conflict. This was the start of the Geneva Conventions, which all UN members have since ratified. The Geneva Conventions form part of the international law that governs humanitarian concerns arising out of war and conflict and stand as testimony of how an international non-governmental organisation (in this case the Red Cross) can start a movement that later develops into international norms and standards.

States were once the judge, jury and executioner of all matters related to the conduct of international affairs. Under the guise of state sovereignty, the state could act with impunity as far as its citizens and lands were concerned. Those days are effectively over as the pressure of outside interests, amplified through international non-governmental organisations, have eroded state impunity. In no other area has there been such a major leap forward than in the development of norms involving international human rights. It also used to be the case that monarchs, presidents, prime ministers and other state leaders held immunity from any kind of criminal prosecution while they were in power. That too, has now changed. The International Criminal Court, which sits in The Hague, now has the jurisdiction to hold individuals responsible for a range of crimes. The United Nations briefly discussed the idea of an international criminal court in the 1950s, but it took the efforts of a coalition of international non-governmental organisations, calling themselves the Coalition for the International Criminal Court, to realise the vision of a world court for heinous crimes. In 1997, the Coalition eventually managed to garner the political will, and within a few short years the Court had been established. Today, approximately two thirds of the world's states are members and dozens of individuals have been prosecuted for war crimes, genocide and other crimes against humanity.

There are many success stories of how international organisations, once thought to be the tools of states, have come into their own and set the agenda for the international community. Nowhere is this more evident than in the area of environmental preservation. It took the combined efforts of vocal non-governmental organisations and might of the United Nations to bring states together for a watershed conference on the environment in Rio de Janeiro in 1992. Often called the Earth Summit, the UN Conference on Environment and Development was revolutionary because it emphasised the collective responsibility of states towards the wellbeing of the earth. Due to the Earth Summit, states signed the UN Framework Convention on Climate Change, the Convention on Biological Diversity, and the Convention to Combat Desertification – treaties that became important milestones in the fight to save the environment from the harmful practices of mankind. The momentum the Earth Summit generated still has an impact today as nations continue to work together, albeit often acrimoniously, to combat climate change.

For the average citizen, the most important international organisations might be those whose work can be felt on the ground. The UN Development Programme has been a lifeline for many impoverished nations, helping to raise populations out of absolute poverty, developing programmes to allow the people to be economically sustainable and closing the gender equality gap that exists in many developing nations. In these cases, instead of states contributing to the organisation and keeping it financially afloat, it is sometimes international governmental organisations such as the World Bank that provide the means for the states to pursue development policies that would otherwise not be possible. However, the results of these assistance programmes have been mixed and they are often contentious, as they have sometimes left countries in significant debt or failed to improve their economies.

Conclusion

Like most other things, international organisations are only as good as the results they yield, but there is no denying that they play a central role in international affairs. Their growth, particularly in the twentieth century when the concept of global governance came of age, means that nearly every aspect of life is regulated in some way at the global level. International organisations, in their vast array of forms, complement and sometimes positively challenge the role of the state. Going back to the airport analogy used at the start of this chapter, we may not always be aware of how international organisations affect even the most mundane things in our lives. But, our lives would be materially different without them.

7

Global Civil Society

RAFFAELE MARCHETTI

Patterns of globalisation have challenged the exclusivity of states as actors in international affairs. Globalisation links distant communities and opens up spaces for new social actors. Among the non-state actors benefiting from this change are public-interest-orientated non-governmental actors, often known as civil society groups. Alongside the state, profit-orientated corporate actors (which we will explore in the next chapter) and international governmental organisations (which we explored in the previous chapter), these civil society groups complete the mosaic of actors on the international stage.

The standard definition of civil society identifies it as the space outside of government, family and market. A place in which individuals and collective organisations advance allegedly common interests. Civil society organisations can include community groups, non-governmental organisations, social movements, labour unions, indigenous groups, charitable organisations, faith-based organisations, media operators, academia, diaspora groups, lobby and consultancy groups, think tanks and research centres, professional associations, and foundations. Political parties and private companies can also be counted as borderline cases. The presence of civil society organisations in international affairs has become increasingly relevant. They have played a role in agenda setting, international law-making and diplomacy. Further, they have been involved in the implementation and monitoring of a number of crucial global issues. These range from trade to development and poverty reduction, from democratic governance to human rights, from peace to the environment, and from security to the information society. Because of these reasons, international relations cannot be fully captured without taking into account the actions of civil society organisations.

Different theoretical perspectives can be used to interpret global civil society. Liberals may understand it as the actor that provides a bottom-up contribution to the effectiveness and legitimacy of the international system as a whole. In essence, it is democracy in action as power is being held to account by the populace. Realists, however, may interpret global civil society as a tool used by the most powerful states to advance their ultimate interests abroad, often promoting and popularising ideas that are key to the national interest. Marxists may see global civil society as political vanguards that can spread a different world view that challenges the dominant order. Finally, some even argue that the concept of civil society as a sphere distinct from the family, state and market remains a Western concept that does not apply easily to societies where the boundaries between these spheres are more blurred. It is useful to keep these various perspectives in mind as you read through the chapter.

Conditions for transnational activism

The activism of global civil society groups has been facilitated by a number of specific conditions. First, a number of international organisations have supported the inclusion of civil society actors within international decision-making. For example, the 1992 UN Earth Summit in Rio de Janeiro provided a means for previously scattered groups to meet and create common platforms and networks. The European Union has followed a similar approach by integrating different types of civil society organisations within its governance mechanisms. Second, the state's priorities for the allocation of resources changed in the 1980s and 1990s due to a trend towards the privatisation of industries. In that climate, it was common to see state-owned enterprises (such as utilities) being sold off to private companies. For that reason, in many Western nations, the state's overall role in public affairs was reduced. In this context, civil society organisations were able to subcontract many functions from the state and take up new roles as service providers. Third, the globalisation process has generated a sense of common purpose among civil society actors. This has been a trigger for internal unification – increasing the sense of solidarity among civil society organisations. It has also united the groups that want to highlight the negative sides of globalisation. Finally, through the internet, groups from different parts of the world have been able to familiarise themselves with other political realities, like-minded organisations, and alternative forms of action. In this way, they have been able to increase their political know-how and their ability to join forces in addressing common targets.

The wider international system itself has offered an environment conducive to the development of these kinds of activities. By forming transnational networks, civil society organisations have used their leverage at the international level to achieve notable results. A transnational network can be defined as a permanent co-ordination between different civil society organisations (and sometimes individuals), located in several countries, collectively focused on a specific global issue. Major past examples are the Jubilee 2000 campaign, which worked through the 1990s to induce creditor governments and the International Monetary Fund to take steps toward debt relief for highly indebted poor countries. Another is the campaign to ban landmines, which led to the intergovernmental conference in Ottawa where the Mine Ban Treaty was signed in 1997. Ongoing campaigns, to mention a few, include mobilisation on environmental justice, gender recognition, LGBT rights and food security.

Global civil society as a response to transnational exclusion

In today's complex world, traditional institutions have struggled to provide effective and legitimate responses to global issues such as climate change, financial instability, disease epidemics, intercultural violence and global inequalities. As a response to these shortcomings, forms of so-called multi-level, stakeholder governance have been established that involve a combination of public and private actors. Civil society action at the international level is predominantly focused on building political frameworks with embedded democratic accountability. At present, most global governance bodies suffer from accountability deficits – that is, they lack the traditional formal mechanisms of democratic accountability that are found in states, such as popularly elected leaders, parliamentary oversight, and non-partisan courts. Instead, the executive councils of global regulatory bodies are mainly composed of bureaucrats who are far removed from the situations that are directly affected by the decisions they take. People in peripheral geographical areas and in marginalised sections of society are especially deprived of recognition, voice and influence in most contexts of global governance as it is currently practised. An apt depiction of such an international system is to describe it as characterised by 'transnational exclusion'.

In recent decades most global regulatory bodies have begun to develop closer relations with civil society organisations precisely in order to fill this legitimacy gap. For example, the Committee on World Food Security within the UN Food and Agriculture Organisation has reserved seats for different types of organisations, including non-governmental organisations and social movements, research centres, financial institutions, private sector associations and private philanthropic foundations. While the role of civil society organisations in these contexts is predominantly based on a consultative status, they allow the civil society organisations to have a seat at the table.

Given their need to balance a deeper impact on society with greater legitimacy, global governance institutions have been under pressure to be more inclusive and attentive to the political demands coming from below. Thanks to such dynamics, civil society actors have managed to increase their access to international agenda-setting, decision-making, monitoring and implementation in relation to global issues. At the same time, the challenge to the inclusion of civil society actors in global governance mechanisms remains significant. New institutional structures are continually emerging and the challenge in terms of integration is therefore endlessly renewed. New institutional filters are created and civil society actors have to constantly re-focus and adapt to new circumstances. An example is provided by the announcement in 2009 that the main economic council of wealthy nations would shift from the G-8 to the G-20 format. The G-20 meets annually and is composed of 19 states plus the European Union. Together its members account for roughly 80 per cent of the world's trade. In this instance, civil society activists have been lagging behind: activism around the G-8 was intense, but the meetings of the G-20 have only recently attracted a similar level of attention.

Values promotion and creating change

At the core of the dynamics leading to the emergence of transnational activism is the perception of the possibility of change in the area of one specific global issue. This might arise due to a new issue becoming significant or the re-interpretation of a long-standing issue. Ultimately, the key feature of transnational activism in global governance is precisely its stubborn attempt to influence the normative battle on the right and legitimate interpretation of crucial global issues. In this perspective, civil society organisations should be seen not only as traditional problem solvers (providing solutions that governments are less suited to delivering) but also as problem generators (placing new problematic issues on the international agenda). While the perception of an unjust situation necessarily constitutes a precondition for action, it is only when the actor recognises the possibility of having a positive impact on such a situation that mobilisation may start. Two elements are necessary for such mobilisation: conceptualisation and political commitment.

Transnational mobilisation on global issues should be interpreted as the result of several steps. A crucial challenge for any transnational network is to present the issue at stake in such a way that it is perceived as problematic, urgent and also soluble. Think, for instance, of the case of feminism. Through the action of a number of feminist movements, beginning with the suffragettes in the late nineteenth century, the traditional role of women was challenged and eventually replaced by a new egalitarian position entitling women to have equal standing in society. The first step in cross-border mobilisations is therefore the production of knowledge and the creation of 'frames' through which the issue at stake can be correctly interpreted.

A second step consists of the external dissemination and strategic use of such knowledge. This is a crucial stage as it is the point at which information acquires a fully public dimension – and therefore political significance. Global public opinion needs to be attracted and its imagination captured for framing the terms of the conflict in such a way that the issue at stake becomes the focus of a general interest requiring public engagement. Dissemination often passes through scientific channels. When networks become active players in the communities of experts on global issues, they tend to be perceived by public opinion as credible sources of information and this increases their influence on policymaking. However, dissemination can also be executed though other forms, including public action such as mass protests.

In order to successfully promote change a third step is necessary. The task here consists in gaining a recognised role in the public sphere as a rightful advocate of general interests. To the question 'In whose name do you speak?', transnational networks need to offer a response that enables them to claim representation of interests that are wider than just those of a small group. Once transnational networks succeed in shaping a challenge associated to a particular global issue, the political opportunity for mobilising and network building arises.

Although success necessarily depends on international circumstances, national conditions often play an important role in the rise of global social movements. In national contexts, civil society organisations are rooted in a web of social relations and common identities. They have access to important resources (such as people and money) but operate in highly formalised political systems that shape and constrain their mobilisation and impact through a number of political filters. For instance, while democratic countries tend to leave space for activism, the room for manoeuvre in countries ruled by other kinds of regime may be more limited. At the global level, however, there are few such restrictions. This factor widens the options for political action. In fact, transnational networks may help increase the political opportunities that are present in national contexts; they often perform a facilitating role, providing space for actors who are usually voiceless and excluded. Transnational networks can also amplify local voices by setting them in the context of global issues and policies, thus strengthening local or national activism.

Transnational networks can therefore be understood as organisational responses to the new global socio-political environment in which political opportunities on the one hand and scarce resources (finance, knowledge, etc.) on the other create conditions in which a network structure can perform better than other organisational forms. As this combination is inherently contingent, transnational networks tend to have a limited political life. On the one hand, networks are created in response to a specific issue; it is difficult to adapt them to a different issue and in many cases easier to simply create a new network. On the other hand, social movements and especially networks are cyclical phenomena. The interaction between the set of values shared by social movements and global political opportunities leads to the emergence of different projects of political change, reflecting also the heterogeneity of actors – for instance, balancing reformist with more radical attitudes. Individual networks, therefore, fit a specific set of conditions – internal and external to global movements – but when some of them change, the factors that led to their rise may dissolve, mobilisation may decline rapidly and networks are unlikely to maintain their significance unless they adapt their strategy and at times their own identity to the new political contexts.

Contested legitimacy

While it is clear that civil society organisations cannot aim at replacing the traditional channels of political representation, it is recognised that they often play a key role in 'broadcasting' viewpoints that struggle to be included in the political agenda. From the activist perspective the issue of political representation should not be interpreted as a matter of who they represent but, rather, what they aim to represent. It is the issues they tackle and the values they seek to uphold that are crucial – possibly more than their constituencies. Civil society organisations usually claim to advance the public interest. While it may not be clear what the public interest is with regard to many global issues, the ambition of civil society is, as argued above, to contribute within the normative battlefield of global public opinion. To explore the issue of legitimacy we can look at the two extremes of the civil society spectrum – the divide between mainstream politics and radical groups. At one extreme there are the civil society organisations established by governments and international organisations. At the other we find civil society organisations that are considered criminal, such as terrorist groups and mafia organisations. These represent the two extremes of co-optation and ostracisation. In other words, they are examples of full integration into and full exclusion from the political system.

For groups closer to the mainstream of politics, or those groups seeking to enter the mainstream, there is always the risk of co-optation by the institutional system. Civil society organisations need financial resources, public recognition and political support – all of which can be provided or facilitated by the political system. At the same time, the political system may take advantage of the fragmentation and proliferation of civil society organisations by picking and choosing, on the basis of political convenience, the groups most inclined to cooperate with the current political agenda. In this way, there is a danger that some civil society organisations may find themselves used instrumentally to facilitate top-down representation of specific interests. On the other hand, issues of violence and resistance to political systems are always controversial, depending as they do on political interpretation. To borrow an old phrase, one man's terrorist is another man's freedom fighter. Those who take an oppositional stand to the status quo and agitate for material changes have often been criminalised and/or politically marginalised. We should always remember that the term 'civil' is normatively loaded and tends to be interpreted in line with the predominant ideology. For this reason, history is at times ironic: prominent political leaders such as South African president Nelson Mandela and Palestinian leader Yasser Arafat were long considered to be leaders of criminal groups, perhaps even terrorists, and yet in due course they were both awarded the Nobel Peace Prize.

The case of the moratorium on the death penalty

The goal of abolishing the death penalty is a key aspiration of human rights activism. It is a contemporary example of how initiatives backed by civil society organisations can have lasting impact. While the topic of the death penalty has been debated for centuries, it is only in recent decades that significant institutional changes have occurred, with a number of countries removing capital punishment from their legal systems. The anti-death penalty stance only managed to gain importance at the United Nations level due to the specific transnational mobilisation of civil society organisations. While earlier activism contributed to creating the right political context at the national level, it was the campaign for a moratorium on the death penalty that specifically targeted the United Nations. This ultimately led to a significant UN General Assembly resolution in 2007 that was reconfirmed several times in subsequent years. In themselves, the resolutions and the changed attitude of a number of states are remarkable achievements in terms of human rights promotion, even if the death penalty still remains in some states.

The campaign developed through a multi-stage process of normative promotion. It began in a specific place – Italy. It then became stronger by 'going transnational' via civil society organisations networking together and sharing resources and ideas. The campaign then returned to the national domains so that key target states could be persuaded to back it. Finally, the campaign targeted the United Nations, where it successfully achieved the backing of the General Assembly. The dynamics of the process cannot be fully captured without making clear the part played by tactics of persuasion. Humanitarian diplomacy developed by civil society organisations through persuasion activities remains key. In this case the undertaking featured two main components. First, the idea of the right to life was communicated persuasively as a desirable outcome – something that attached well to several already popular international agendas. Second, an empathic process was generated by using powerful narratives drawn from individual cases. These were mainly stories told by people previously sentenced to death and now pardoned, or moving accounts by their relatives. In both cases, civil society organisations played a central role as either reason-based frame creators or emotion-based narrative disseminators. They played an important role as an alternative and/or adjunct to diplomatic politics and achieved a clear and lasting impact at the international level.

Conclusion

Over recent decades, civil society activities have been responsible for a number of important contributions. While this is still far from a decisive move towards a comprehensive democratisation of world politics, the incremental steps should not be underestimated. At least two kinds of impact can be identified. In the first instance, civil society organisations have managed to influence political decision-makers by giving voice to the voiceless and framing new issues. At the same time they have managed to pressurise global governance institutions so that today the overall level of transparency, consultation, outside evaluation and efficiency is measurably higher than it was in the past. Such results cannot be attributed solely to civil society, but they have been achieved in part by civil mobilisations.

Nevertheless, we need to acknowledge that in absolute terms the impact has been modest and uneven (see Scholte 2011). Most transnational activism has come from Western organisations, with significant exceptions in Latin America and Southeast Asia. Other parts of the world are still socially disconnected. Russia, China, most of Africa and the Arab world constitute islands which remain relatively isolated from the general growth of transnational civil society. And just as civil society organisations are unevenly concentrated in the Global North, the political results they have achieved also exhibit geopolitical imbalance. The gains realised by political activism have mostly been in line with agendas framed in northern states and benefitting northern constituencies. However, this is unlikely to continue as agendas arise from the developing world and international Western power and influence gradually declines. In such a climate, Western civil society organisations will have to share the stage with civil society organisations coming from the developing world. This will not always be easy, but it will hopefully make the future global civil society more genuinely 'global'.

8

Global Political Economy

GÜNTER WALZENBACH

Global political economy is a field of study that deals with the interaction between political and economic forces. At its centre have always been questions of human welfare and how these might be related to state behaviour and corporate interests in different parts of the world. Despite this, major approaches in the field have often focused more on the international system perspective. A side effect of this has been the relative neglect of non-elites and an all-too-often missing recognition of ordinary individuals. While states remain central to international politics, they have gradually intensified their relations with multinational corporations and strengthened their engagement with international organisations. Naturally, these changes in the world around us have led to a certain rethinking of the way we understand and position individuals as actors in the global economy. To account for this, many scholars now prefer to use the term 'global political economy' (GPE) over the more traditional term 'international political economy' (IPE). Although both terms are often used interchangeably, using the word 'global' is important as it indicates a wider scope in political economy that reaches beyond relations between states.

There are various approaches to global political economy that span the political spectrum and often overlap with the perspectives covered in chapters three and four – though they are often formulated differently to incorporate economic factors. These range from state-centred approaches to Marxist approaches that argue that international capitalism will lead to the end of the state due to capitalism's inherent flaws. Arguably, it has been the liberal approach that has given individual actors (rather than states or social groups) the centre stage for analysis. As such, liberal approaches to global political economy form the bedrock of this chapter as they offer a more tangible way to present complex issues of global economics to a beginner in a way that is relatable.

Liberal approaches

The writings of liberal political economists have become so broad a church that they can include advocates of uncontrolled markets as well as supporters of strong state intervention in the market. This is a reflection of some of the practical contradictions that Karl Polanyi (1957) first discovered in different historical manifestations of liberal ideas in the aftermath of the industrial revolution in the nineteenth century. Consider, in this respect, whether government policy takes freedom of choice away from individuals, or if the state should establish a legal order that enables individuals to make choices and function as participants in a market system. Polanyi's reasoning offers an insight into the globalising economy of the twenty-first century. In this account, markets are not just abstract constructs that settle demand and supply for goods through a specific price, as economists would make us believe. Markets are, and always have been, much more. They are social phenomena embedded in broader communities and directly connected with deliberate forms of state action. As a consequence, economic, social and political life is always interconnected. In particular, the widely held belief in the advantage of a self-regulating market process carries with it a basic contradiction in so far as it leads inevitably to a severe disruption of the social fabric in different countries. This disruption can occur because of rising levels of income inequality (why some are paid more than others), foreign takeovers of companies, or fundamental disagreement on what needs to be done during economic recessions to prevent social decay.

Essentially, Polanyi observed two interrelated processes that explain change in the international system. At first, free market principles dominate and the winners from liberal economic policies exert their influence for further political change. Over time, however, the political pressures created will inevitably generate a counter-movement that is opposed to the direction of reform. Other social groups within society will articulate their interests, slow down the speed of modernisation and demand a different form of economic management and policy making. Seen from this angle, the global political economy of the twenty-first century is an attempt to embed globalising markets in transnational social relations – quite similar to what we observed historically in terms of social and economic development at the level of the nation-state.

The early heroes of the liberal approach were Adam Smith and David Ricardo. Smith argued in favour of government non-interference and the superiority of market exchanges guided by the 'invisible hand' of the price mechanism. This is a process whereby consumers seek the best quality for the lowest price and this, in turn, compels successful producers to find the lowest-cost method of production. Ricardo explicitly added the gains deriving from a system of free trade built around the principle of comparative advantage. Accordingly, 'under a system of perfectly free commerce, each country naturally devotes its capital and labour to such employments as are most beneficial to each'. And, 'this pursuit of individual advantage is admirably connected with the universal good of the whole' (Ricardo 1817). From this point, international trade liberalisation has been seen as a useful mechanism allocating labour to its most productive uses allowing in turn a much greater consumption of goods than what would be possible in the absence of such a system.

For Smith, the specialisation in working patterns and the division of labour also created new opportunities for employees to achieve personal growth and professional careers. In the classic example, ten people working to produce pins could produce more in total if they worked together, dividing up tasks and performing each one better than if they all worked separately. Where Karl Marx identified repetitive work patterns and exploitation, early liberal political economy found skills, self-love and natural propensity (O'Brien and Williams 2010, 259). Taking these arguments into the modern era, if governments across the world de-regulated economic activity, cut taxes for the wealthy, privatised and contracted out traditional state services, then unprecedented levels of economic growth would follow. By allowing the free movement of capital, many more people can benefit from high levels of direct investment even if employees are less mobile and more tied to a particular workplace. Thus, in the modern liberal world view, often called neoliberalism, governments are expected to be active promoters and supporters of globalisation. Only left-leaning liberals, by contrast, recognise the increasingly global division of labour as responsible for rising levels of inequality.

What unifies liberal thinking in terms of global economics is an analytical inclusion of a variety of state and non-state actors that form relationships of mutual dependence. Therefore, the historical focus of one country being dependent on another due to a surplus in a vital commodity, like oil or gas, has gradually given way to a much more complex understanding. This does not mean that the classic interaction between states has become obsolete, rather that it is enriched by including and explicitly recognising an ever-increasing number of other international actors such as those explored in chapters five, six and seven. Hence, the policies of one international or regional organisation may rely on the policies of another. This has been the case with the European Union and the International Monetary Fund in the management of the 2008 global financial crisis as they adopted joint programmes to assist states such as Ireland. Another example is the successful implementation of a global environmental policy by the United Nations that benefitted significantly from collaboration with Greenpeace, an international non-governmental organisation. In the literature, however, it has been the multinational corporation (a private business operation with facilities and assets in at least two countries) that has received the most attention in the search for interdependent relationships across borders. Here, as elsewhere, the liberal account does show its broad remit, leaving room for positive evaluation as well as critical reflection. Some liberals praise the overall benefit from competition for international investments played out on the back of the rivalry between states and multinational corporations. Others, by contrast, stress the comparative disadvantage and limited success of less well-funded civil society actors when trying to change corporate behaviour on a global scale.

Individual actors

A convenient way to accommodate individual actors in the global economy has been to see them as economically dependent workers rather than as citizens capable of bringing about social change. The economic globalisation process has modified this perspective to some extent, with greater recognition of the integration of a diverse, but nationally based, workforce into production patterns that can span several sovereign jurisdictions and world regions. This is in contrast to what was mentioned above in classical approaches that envisioned goods and services produced from start to finish within a nation-state rather than anticipating the system of today where production spans across borders. Technological changes have made it possible to control transnational production processes and bring together people from different parts of the world to add value to a specific good or service. By engaging in this practice enterprises can transform their business into a global operation thriving on different wage levels and a diverse set of skills in the workforce. This naturally raises the question of how such changes in the organisation of capitalism influence the lives of everyday people. For example, if people produce only part of a good, such as a microchip for a computer, how are their wages determined?

More recently, the 2008 global financial crisis has shed light on non-elite actors at the receiving end of failures in the banking system and the reckless behaviour of financial elites. Not just blue and white-collar workers, but mortgage holders, house buyers, owners of small and medium-sized businesses, small-scale investors, shareholders, farmers, civil servants, self-employed people and students had to struggle with the implications of rescue efforts taking place simultaneously in several of the major industrialised countries. In the aftermath of government intervention and bail-out measures, many businesses had to restructure and streamline their operations for the sake of cutting costs and maintaining competitiveness. At the same time, individuals in their capacity as voters were asked to support far-reaching reform packages, austerity policies and new government strategies for job creation and employability. Non-elites have also been able to promote new alliances among a range of individual actors with more charitable goals such as income redistribution and equality in mind. Many left-leaning political economists have therefore placed their hope in transnational solidarity and broader social movements unified under the banner of alter-globalisation – which styles itself as an alternative to neoliberal forms of globalisation.

A fundamental requirement for any such processes to work is an increasing number of people-to-people contacts developing various types of cross-border relationships. International migration offers an example where Polanyi's key argument is relevant. Although governments have closely cooperated for the sake of liberalising the flow of goods, services, and capital, the same cannot be said about the flow of people. Restrictions to migration movements have become the rule rather than the exception. In a market economy, key decisions about investment, production and distribution are driven by supply and demand. This has led, as a side effect, to diverging approaches to migration control within liberal political systems. Canada, for example, was the first nation to implement a points-based system by which entry visas are granted on the basis of specialist skills or aptitude tests. Moreover, relative population density and regional distribution is also taken into consideration when residency permits are linked to particular jobs or states within the federal system. Such restrictions on personal freedom are accepted precisely to achieve a better goodness of fit with the demand side for immigration and the requirements of regional economies. Only gradually, and over time, are individual restrictions reduced, thus slowing down the pressures for adaptation that is expected from new arrivals as well as society as a whole.

Another example of the Polanyi-type adjustment process can be found in the area of philanthrocapitalism. These accounts show personal characteristics and entrepreneurial spirit through the activities of billionaires such as Warren Buffett, Bill Gates, George Soros and Mark Zuckerberg. This elitist circle is not just known for its wealth, but also for individual ambitions to transcend the business world and influence political leaders in their decision-making process. Through the funding of global campaigns, each of these entrepreneurs has tried to make a difference in terms of poverty reduction, public health, educational reform and democratisation. In other words, corporate elites are actively translating individual success into altruistic behaviour on a global level. Broadly speaking, the institutional arrangements surrounding philanthrocapitalism help to safeguard core business activities while branching out into new sectors with genuine global reach and potential. The individual actors of this emerging system use their personal wealth to construct new global policy networks that specifically include individuals from governmental and non-governmental organisations susceptible to a particular vision of the future (Cooper 2010, 229). Therefore, personal gain, shareholder benefits or compensation for aggressive business tactics may not be at the forefront of their considerations. Instead, corporate social responsibility in this interpretation can be seen as a form of enlightened self-interest, recognising the danger of a potential backlash from society at large to excessive market power and business influence.

The Chan-Zuckerberg Initiative is a useful example of philanthrocapitalism. Its aims are to administer the donation of 99 per cent of the married couple's Facebook shares to a range of global projects, which amounts to tens of billions of US dollars. Its founders chose the institutional form of a limited liability company (LLC) rather than extending the model of a charitable trust or social fund to the global level. This ensures that as an organisational form it can continue to generate profit and donate money to specific political causes. More traditional non-profit organisations have stricter requirements for the disclosure of information to qualify for tax exemptions, whereas LLCs have fewer rules in this respect and still allow for investment in profit-driven projects in addition to philanthropic activities. Thus, this type of business structure offers new degrees of flexibility to move shares between separate business operations and to extract profits for the owners, if so required. In this way, the core of the Facebook business model that generates the wealth held by Chan and Zuckerberg remains unchanged. The ambition to do good at a global level is clearly counterbalanced by the need to generate revenue and income through a lucrative commercial service.

Whether financially successful entrepreneurs with celebrity status can have a truly transformative capacity when it comes to the finding of solutions for international policy problems is open to debate. Their activities, as observed at the annual meeting of the World Economic Forum in Davos, Switzerland, at least suggest that they are increasingly recognised as important contributors to global public policy. Fame and fortune, however, is not always the main criterion to be part of an international gathering. The independently organised World Social Forum is deliberately non-elitist in that it welcomes a broad range of civil society organisations and social movements to its annual convention. The 2016 meeting in Montreal, Canada, carried the slogan 'another world is needed – together it is possible' and aimed to 'gather tens of thousands of people ... who want to build a sustainable and inclusive world, where every person and every people has its place and can make its voice heard'. What both events have in common is the continuing effort to build transnational alliances that gradually dissolve any neat distinction between the public and the private sphere and make the global count in the study of political economy.

The state and the multinational corporation

The industrialised state of the twenty-first century is going through significant stages of adaptation and transformation in response to economic globalisation and losing its privileged position in the international system. Not only the rising powers of Brazil, Russia, India and China but also multinational corporations represent a serious challenge to its once dominant role. There is now little expectation that major economies will adopt a light regulation economic policy style along the lines of the once dominant US model. Instead, the notion of the competition state captures best how since the 1990s government actors have created more business-friendly regulatory frameworks actively supporting internationally operating firms in their efforts to generate more growth and employment opportunities. A well-trained domestic workforce becomes, in this context, an important asset to promote a particular territory for the allocation of foreign direct investment.

Despite similar pressures to reduce government expenditure, states have also continued to diverge in the way they provide welfare for different social groups within their societies. It has become popular to privatise public services and leave the task of their delivery to companies rather than the state. As a consequence, the role of the civil servant is now similar to that of a business manager overseeing the spread of markets into new areas such as education, health and security. Yet, in line with the Polanyi-type adjustment process, government agencies and state organisations cannot entirely shed their responsibility for some of the negative effects of radical policies associated with market liberalisation, especially in trade and finance. Economic globalisation creates 'winners' and 'losers', which leads to the issue of inequality in societies. To win the support of the 'losers', governments typically have to offer compensatory measures through income redistribution, retraining programmes or further educational opportunities. The budgetary resources necessary for the funding of such activities brings into perspective taxation as a main attribute of modern forms of government as well as an indicator of state power relative to other actors in the international system. As the international controversy around the tax bills of large multinational corporations like Amazon has shown, there is a general public expectation that multinational corporations should make a fair contribution to the states in which they generate their profit. After all, for their business models to succeed they have to be able to draw on a well-developed infrastructure, an educated workforce and general health care.

Furthermore, through direct tax evasion, or the use of regulatory loopholes, large corporations may gain a decisive advantage over local suppliers operating in the same market sector and offering comparable services. For example, due to different tax laws within member states of the European Union, the video streaming service Netflix International was exempt from UK corporation tax despite having around 4.5 million paying customers in the UK. In line with the letter of the law, it only paid 5 per cent income tax in Luxembourg. Although this is a regional example, multinational companies with global operations can also shift profits to countries where lower taxes apply by transferring royalties between different branches of their business. What emerges is a picture of waning state power with global business actors playing off different tax regimes to their own advantage. Seen from their angle, multinational corporations are merely following the rules of the game as implemented by governments in their national systems. If the rules change, their behaviour will change as well. Indeed, due to public pressures there seems to be evidence of a step change in this issue, at least in Europe where corporations like Google and Starbucks have been reprimanded.

Multinational corporations in their interaction with civil society have sometimes been the target of non-governmental pressure groups and trade unions, which call for boycotts due to breaches of international environmental or labour standards. More frequently, however, liberal approaches have singled out their exceptional capacity to create wealth at a national, as well as international, level. Their cross-border investment activities in home or host states are often assessed positively as they ensure technology and capital transfer, develop managerial skills in diverse country contexts and ensure market access while simultaneously creating new jobs, thus providing a 'social' service in lieu of those typically seen as justifying the state and, therefore, excusing them from taxes. In the case of Apple this has taken the form of a global supply chain by which the bulk of its products are designed in the United States, but manufactured elsewhere – predominantly in China – due to lower costs. This is also an indication of the impact technological change in the production process has on the multinational corporation–state relationship. Seen from the Polanyi angle it is no surprise that when Apple's chief executive officer Steve Jobs was asked by US president Barack Obama why manufacturing could not return to the US, he simply replied, 'Those jobs aren't coming back' (Duhigg and Bradsher 2012). Even the most powerful national politicians find it hard to deal with the social consequences of these technological innovations in the global market.

Towards global economic governance?

One popular way to react to the fundamental changes in the production sphere described above has been the signing of regional and global trade agreements. At times this is combined with further steps towards market integration and intensified political cooperation among nation-states. The exponential growth of such deals has generated a major controversy in the field about whether regional and global organisations constitute a new ideal for the international economic system, making it possible to align the multitude of potential actors for the purpose of creating effective global policies.

The widespread appeal of regional governance is shown by the prominent examples of regional groupings loosely modelled on the example of the European Union. This can be seen primarily in the North American Free Trade Agreement (NAFTA), the Southern Common Market (MERCOSUR), the Association of South East Asian Nations (ASEAN) and the Economic Community of West African States (ECOWAS). The evidence available so far is inconclusive as to whether regional organisations can act as the final stepping-stone or, perhaps, present a major stumbling block for the emergence of a genuine form of governance in the global system. In the case of the European Union a prime purpose has been to build a single market, but in many areas this has necessitated a range of measures to deal with some of the undesirable consequences of market liberalisation. For the sake of economic prosperity all European Union member states agreed to remove trade barriers and reform some of their domestic regulations, while at the same time devising measures through which particular groups within society are entitled to direct financial compensation. Through its own legislative process, the European Union has also been actively trying to cushion some of the effects of an open market by enforcing environmental targets, health and safety standards and guarantees for equal opportunities.

The scope of the European Union has also revealed some of the difficulties of regional projects, with member states sometimes wishing to 'opt out' of certain areas when they are not in agreement with regional plans – such as adopting the euro currency. An extreme instance of this can be seen in the British vote to leave the European Union in the 2016 'Brexit' referendum. In a wider sense, negotiation rounds for global trade deals, as opposed to regional ones, have stalled and protectionist behaviour for whole industrial sectors has been on the rise. Although tariffs are at unprecedented low levels globally, it has proved much harder to further harmonise national business regulations and guarantee mutual market access. If the aim is to achieve higher growth rates, enhance consumer choice and create more jobs, then hidden trade barriers have to be tackled much more effectively at the global negotiation table. The liberal ambition to take transnational civil society more seriously also comes at a price. Keenly aware of the historical record and detrimental effects of free trade deals, critics are deeply concerned about the repercussions that new large-scale, inter-regional agreements might have. In different parts of the world voters and interest groups have become increasingly sensitive to the impact of trade liberalisation on labour standards, worker rights, income distribution and environmental sustainability.

More generally, there is a problem with the very institutions of global governance in how they settle a trade-off between their democratic accountability and effective economic policymaking. In the case of the World Trade Organization (WTO), with 164 member states, the implementation of trade rules is not easily reconciled with the demands articulated by international non-governmental organisations such as Greenpeace. These frequently hold the view that the management of international organisations has been captured by a few powerful countries, undermining their role as honest brokers, mediators and enforcers of joint policies (Stiglitz 2002). At the same time, not everyone agrees that giving non-state groups advisory status and better access to the organisation's internal decision-making would solve the dilemma. Due to the intergovernmental character of the World Trade Organization, its democratic legitimacy is set in a 'one country, one vote' system where the governing body consists of trade ministers delegated by the member states.

From the angle of democratic accountability things look even more problematic in other global economic institutions. Most notably, the International Monetary Fund (IMF), which is charged with the task of ensuring economic stability around the world. The International Monetary Fund allocates voting rights proportional to the size of financial contributions made by its 189 member states. At grassroots level critical voices view this as fundamentally contradicting the organisation's goal of global policy change and economic reform. They see a desperate need for new social mass movements to address the failings of deregulated capitalism, build working arrangements for global governance and arrive eventually at a fairer world. Despite pessimistic assessments of the viability of such a system of global governance, an element of optimism can be gained from historical experience of bottom-up community building and the transformative power of human agency (Hale et al. 2013). Although there is always the risk that the political adjustment process at transnational level may offer too little too late, the historical work of Polanyi suggests with a degree of certainty that, under exceptional circumstances, previously passive individual actors – the 'silent majority' in conservative terminology – can proactively instigate large-scale institutional change.

Conclusion

The examples presented in this chapter highlight the diverse social and political adjustment processes that a largely unregulated global market system necessarily entails. While we certainly live in a global economy, for the time being we lack a common response to the challenges this brings. The analytical turn from the international to the global, as mentioned in the introduction to this chapter, alerts us to the fact that change has occurred – though measuring its trajectory is difficult due to the fragmented array of actors and agendas evident at the global level. Liberal approaches stress the inevitability of economic globalisation but place some hope in the responsiveness of particular global actors as long as their activities are made accountable. Accordingly, praise of market mechanisms as a force for good across the globe has been matched by ever-growing demand for reforms enabling ordinary people to share more the spoils of the system rather than being exploited by it. As long as democratic processes such as elections are strongly tied to domestic political communities, a still-evolving global market system built around liberal principles continues to present a serious challenge. If for our own individual benefit we believe there should be an element of control over this process, then regional and international organisations with the power to devise and implement global rules are the natural place to look. Without denying the impact of other factors such as philanthropic acts, or states acting alone, these are a second-best solution in the absence of an effectively coordinated global economic policy.

9

Religion and Culture

JOHN A. REES

Religion and culture seem like complex ideas to study from the perspective of International Relations. After all, scholars and philosophers have long debated the meaning of these terms and the impact they have had on our comprehension of the social world around us. So is it an impossibly complicated task to study religion and culture at the global level? Fortunately, the answer is 'no', for we can recognise and respect complexity without being confused about what we mean by each term. In this chapter, which completes the first section of the book, we will explore why thinking about religious and cultural factors in global affairs is as integral as the other issues we have covered thus far.

What do we mean by the terms 'religion' and 'culture'? Where can we see examples of religion and culture at work in the domains of world politics? How do religious and cultural factors impact on our ability to live together? Our investigation will begin to address these questions. As we do so, we shall keep in mind the encouragement of rabbi and political philosopher Jonathan Sacks, who wrote that 'sometimes it is helpful to simplify, to draw a diagram rather than a map in order to understand what may be at stake in a social transition' (1997, 55). There has indeed been a transition in IR thinking about the value of religion and culture.

How can we define religion and culture in a way that is useful to the study of world politics? It is important to sketch each term separately before bringing them back together to form a composite picture. We begin with religion, a category that scholars and policymakers once considered irrelevant to the study of IR because it was not believed to be important for the economic and security interests of modern states and their citizens. Yet, many scholars now hold that religion cannot be ignored. While the idea of culture has equally been underplayed in IR, its inclusion in analyses of world affairs predates that of religion and is considered less controversial. We shall consider four elements of each category and then make important linkages between them so that religion and culture make sense as whole, rather than fragmented, ideas.

Elements of religion

Following the Al Qaeda attacks on the US on 11 September 2001 (often called 9/11), studies of religion in world politics increased sixfold. In the words of Robert Keohane, the events of 9/11 provoked the realisation that 'world-shaking political movements have so often been fuelled by religious fervour' (2002, 29). Indeed, whether it is the disruptions of religion-led revolution, the work of religious development agencies responding to natural disasters, peace-making efforts of religious diplomats or a myriad of other examples, even a glance at global affairs over recent decades seems to support the comment of sociologist Peter Berger that 'the world today ... is as furiously religious as it ever was, and in some places more so than ever' (1999, 2).

Such a view also seems supported by the numbers as 'worldwide, more than eight-in-ten people identify with a religious group' (Pew 2012, 9). Are you numbered among the 20 or 80 per cent? Do you think religious influence on global affairs is a welcome inclusion or a significant problem? Regardless of where we stand, it appears a closer look at the 'religion question' is in order if we are to establish a fuller picture of IR. The following four elements of religion may provide a useful introduction.

1. God(s) and forces in the public square

The first element of religion is the belief that divine beings and/or forces hold relevance to the meaning and practice of politics today and throughout history. These beings are sometimes understood as a knowable God or gods, sometimes as mythical and symbolic figures from our ancient past and sometimes as impersonal forces beyond the physical realm.

Different religious traditions understand the influence of religion upon politics in different ways. Traditions that we might call 'fundamental' propose that politics is a matter of organising society according to divine commands. In Iran, for example, the highest court in the land is a religious one, drawing its principles from the Shia branch of Islam – the second largest Islamic tradition worldwide after the majority Sunni tradition. This court has the power to veto laws of parliament and decide who can hold power. Likewise, in Myanmar (formerly Burma) an influential group of religious monks has started a movement intent on imposing Buddhist principles on the whole country, including non-Buddhist minorities. Thus, some religious politics is based on 'fundamentals' that, in the view of adherents, cannot be changed without the standards of society also being compromised.

By contrast, traditions that adopt a 'contextual' approach hold that politics is a matter of influencing society according to divine principles but as part of a wider tapestry of influences. For example, religious development organisations such as the Aga Khan Development Network (also from the Shia branch of Islam) work in areas of health care and education in countries of Africa and Asia without seeking to control entire political systems. Likewise, in Myanmar, the so-called Saffron Revolution of 2007 saw Buddhist monks stand with the poor against the ruling military dictatorship and support the beginnings of multi-party democracy. In these examples, religious politics is adapted to changing circumstances and takes into account diverse interests and beliefs across society.

What is common to both fundamental and contextual religious traditions is an understanding that politics is in some sort of interactive relationship with the intentions of, or traditions shaped by, gods (or God) and spiritual forces. This contrasts strongly with secular approaches that demote, and sometimes deny altogether, a role for religion in political affairs.

Do you believe that religion has a role to play in public debates or should it be confined to private spirituality only? From an individual point of view, we could address this question by asking what it would be like to live in societies that are either entirely controlled by religion, or entirely without religion. What would the benefits and losses be in each situation? It can be strongly argued that neither scenario exists in pure form. When religion has been used to dominate the public square, a diversity of groups (non-religious and religious) have risen in opposition. Likewise, when religion has been expelled from the public domain, religious actors and interests go underground waiting for a chance to re-emerge.

2. Sacred symbols (re)defining what is real

The second element of religion are rituals that re-order the world according to religious principle. Although the word 'faith' can be associated with belief in unseen realities, humans throughout time have needed to see, touch and smell the sacred. Our senses are portals to the spirit. Therefore, rituals function as tangible symbols of the intangible realm. For examples of different studies that consider the public rituals of Judaism, Islam and Hinduism respectively see Beck (2012), Bronner (2011) and Haider (2011). While some religious rituals are private or hidden, many are performed in public spaces or in ways that are openly accessible to wider society. As such, they are a part of public life – which is one of the original definitions of the word politics.

For religious adherents, rituals symbolise spiritual truths but they can also redefine how power can be understood in the material world. Thomas Merton once described his experience of watching Trappist monks perform the rituals of the Catholic Mass in very political terms. He wrote:

> The eloquence of this liturgy [communicated] one, simple, cogent, tremendous truth: this church, the court of the Queen of Heaven, is the real capital of the country in which we are living. These men, hidden in the anonymity of their choir and their white cowls, are doing for their land what no army, no congress, no president could ever do as such: they are winning for it the grace and the protection and the friendship of God.

> (Merton 1948, 325)

Merton's experience of redefining power and influence through sacred symbols is true for millions of people practising thousands of different religious rituals each day. Beyond the experience of individuals, states also seek divine blessing. For example, over one-fifth of states today have a monarch (such as a king, queen or emperor). Although monarchs differ in the extent of their powers – from figureheads controlled by parliaments to absolute rulers to variations of these – they all draw their power from some form of religious or spiritual authority. The elaborate rituals of monarchies worldwide are understood by their subjects to symbolise divine blessing for the realm and its citizens, redefining where the real power lies.

3. Sacred stories connecting past, present and future

The third element of religion is teaching traditions based on stories of significant figures, events and ideas from the past and beliefs about the future of time itself – like a spoiler alert about the end of the world. For some religions, however, time itself is an illusion and the main focus is living in the now according to sacred ideas rather than the connection of past–present–future. These elements – interpreting the past, projecting the future, living now – are basic to the development of political ideologies also. Therefore, sometimes religious and political groups can appeal to the same stories or ideas even though the interpretation or intent may differ significantly.

For example, both Jews and Christians uphold the idea of 'Jubilee' as central to understanding the story and/or future promise of a Messiah who would usher in a new era of justice with peace (or 'shalom'). In the 1990s members of both communities appealed to one aspect of Jubilee – a tradition of debt cancellation found in the Hebrew Bible – as the basis for addressing the debt crisis facing developing nations. Only a few years later, this sacred story was used for very different purposes by US president George W. Bush, who celebrated the 2003 invasion of Iraq by quoting a Jubilee text from the Book of Isaiah: 'To the captives come out, and to those in darkness be free' (Monbiot 2003). Sacred stories, ideas and teachings from the past have a richness and power that can influence political affairs today and the aspirations we hold for tomorrow. It is no wonder that the anthropologist Talal Asad once observed that what we today call religion has 'always been involved in the world of power' (2003, 200).

4. A community worshiping and acting together

The fourth element common to most religions is the need for believers to belong to a faith community in order to practice sacred rituals and reinforce the truth of sacred stories. Some religious traditions could be described as high demand, requiring strict adherence to rules and standards in order to maintain membership of the faith community. Other traditions are low demand, adopting a more flexible approach to the requirements for belonging faithfully to the community. Both forms of faith commitment are expressions of religion as 'identity politics' connected to who we are (that is, who we understand ourselves to be) and how we live.

The connection between religion and identity politics can have individual and international significance. For instance, empowered by belonging to a faith community, individuals can act in ways that they might not otherwise have done in isolation. Rosa Parks, an African American woman who famously refused to obey American racial segregation laws and sparked a nation-wide civil rights movement in the 1960s, is often lauded as a heroic individual. This may be true, but as a member of a religious community that affirmed human dignity and the divine principles of racial equality, Rosa Parks was never acting in isolation (Thomas 2005, 230–240). This can be understood internationally also, as many (if not most) faith communities have a transnational membership, and some of these exert significant influence on political issues varying from religion-inspired terrorist action against 'Western' values (after all, not all religious politics is peace-orientated) to faith coalitions for environmental sustainability.

The four elements of religion described above – the significance of gods and spirits, the power of holy rituals, the telling of sacred stories and belonging to faith communities – seem in their own ways to be a core aspect of the human condition in the twenty-first century. Although many dimensions of the religious experience can be 'politics-free', both history and contemporary events remind us that these combined elements of religion can have a political impact on individuals, nations and international society.

Elements of culture

We can approach the term culture in the same way we have considered religion. There are many proposed meanings of culture, and these vary from the simple to the complex. While each approach has real value for understanding the social world around us, we will opt for a simple version that still gives us plenty to work with. As such, we begin with an understanding of culture as the combined effect of humanly constructed social elements that help people live together. We will explore four elements of culture, illustrating each element through individual and international political experience.

1. Common life practised in society

The first element of culture has to do with common or shared life. While media reporting seems to constantly prioritise stories of war, conflict and controversy, it is equally the case that local, national and international society requires a remarkable degree of cooperation. How do we live together? Common bonds can sometimes be forged through family ties (as the saying goes, 'you can choose your friends but you are stuck with your relatives'), economic interests ('what matters most is the colour of your money') or security concerns ('the enemy of my enemy is my friend'). Yet, there are other bonds that are forged at the social level as peoples of difference find ways to live together in the same space by forging common beliefs, habits and values. It is from this practice of common life that culture often emerges.

Sport provides good examples of culture as common life. Let us think about football (also known as soccer). Local football clubs can be founded on distinct community identity. For example, local Australian players from a Greek background can play for a team sponsored by the Hellenic Association. Clubs can equally represent a locality rather than a particular group. For example, the Smithfield Stallions of Sydney might have individual players from Greek, Ethiopian, British and Turkish background. Regardless of background, at the international level all players in these clubs have a loyalty to the Australian football team. Football is the common bond – a sporting pastime but also cultural practice. Think about the way entire nations can be said to embody the activities of its national sporting heroes. Supporters from different countries will identify their team as playing in a certain style, even if these are stereotypes and not entirely accurate: do all Eastern European teams play with structure and discipline? Do all South American sides use flamboyance and spontaneity? The larger point, for both individuals and nations, is the tangible power of a sporting pastime to generate common bonds from the local to the international (Rees 2016, 179–182). That bond is an expression of culture.

2. Symbols of group identity

The second element of culture are symbols of identity. Constructing and interpreting 'signs' is a basic activity in any society. The kinds of sign I am referring to are tangible reminders in modern societies of who we are as a people. They include styles of architecture (such as bridges or religious buildings), land or waterscapes that influence the activity of life (such as in harbour cities), monuments, flags and other identity banners, styles of clothing and habits of dress, distinctive food and drink – and so on. These signs are more than a tourist attraction, they are symbols that inform members about who they are as a group and that help the group live together cohesively.

Consider, for example, the individual and international significance of national flags as cultural symbols. For individuals, a flag can be so powerful that citizens are prepared to die on the fields of battle fighting for its honour, representing as it does the 'way of life' of the nation. The Star-Spangled Banner as the anthem of the United States of America describes the power of a national flag to inspire individual and national devotion. Written by Francis Scott Key in 1814 after he spotted the symbol of America still flying following a night of fierce British bombardment, Scott's moving ode to freedom includes the famous words, 'O say does that star-spangled banner yet wave; O'er the land of the free and the home of the brave?'. The answer for Key was yes, the flag symbolising defiance and the promise of victory.

Equally, persecuted communities within a country might see a national or regional flag as a symbol of oppression rather than freedom, symbolising a dominant way of life that excludes them. In all regions of the world nationalist groups fight for autonomy or independence from a country or countries that surround them, and do so under alternative flags that represent their own cultural identity. The flag of the Canadian province of Quebec, for example, employs religious and cultural symbols reflecting its origins as a French colony in the new world. Quebec nationalists campaigning for independence from Canada have employed the flag in the promotion of French language, cultural preservation and Quebecois identity. National separatist groups worldwide are similarly inspired by symbols of culture they are trying to preserve.

3. Stories of our place in the world

The third element of culture is the power of story. Like the cultural use of symbols, societies need to tell stories. These may be about individuals and groups, of events in the distant and recent past, of tales of victory and defeat involving enemies and friends – and so on. Such stories are told to reaffirm, or even recreate, ideas of where that society belongs in relation to the wider world. As such, stories are performances designed to influence what we understand to be real (Walter 2016, 72–73). Sometimes cultural difference can be most starkly understood by the different stories societies tell about themselves. It is no surprise, therefore, that 'culture change' often involves a society accepting a different story about itself (or struggling to do so) in order to embrace a new social reality or accept a new view about its own history. Likewise, what is sometimes referred to as a 'culture war' occurs when different stories clash and compete for public acceptance (Chapman and Ciment 2013).

For example, indigenous (or 'First Nations') peoples readily, and with significant justification, contest the stories of settlement in countries like the United States, Australia, Canada and elsewhere. In such places, national holidays can be mourned as commemorating invasion and dispossession. New Zealand offers somewhat of a contrast, with the story of the nation including the drawing up of the Treaty of Waitangi signed in 1840 between the British colonisers and the indigenous Maori tribes. Although the terms of the treaty are still debated, particularly in relation to 'the lack of Maori contribution' to those terms (Toki 2010, 400), they did grant Maori peoples rights of ownership of their lands, forests, fisheries and other possessions. Such ownership, as an attempt to uphold the sovereignty of the Maori nation(s), was central to the preservation of their cultural story. Sadly, this is not the history recounted by Australian indigenous nations or most Native American tribes in the United States and Canada. Taken together, these depictions of preservation and loss illustrate the importance of language, ritual, place and tradition in the cultural story at the individual and international level.

4. Agreement on what is 'good'

The fourth element of culture is the way a society decides what it means to have 'a good life'. Like living organs, societies experience growth and decline, health and decay, fitness and injury. Extending the analogy, we could say that culture is a way to measure the psychological and emotional health of society.

The United Nations Development Programme regards 'wellbeing' and the 'pursuit of happiness' as fundamental to the sustainable health of a society. The United Nations Educational, Scientific and Cultural Organization regards 'building intercultural understanding' via the 'protection of heritage and support for cultural diversity' to be a priority for international peace and stability. These descriptors reflect what individuals and international societies believe is a healthy culture. As such, culture involves agreement on the kind of things that are good for society and can make it flourish. 'Culture clash' occurs when different societies prioritise different understandings of what those 'good' things are.

One of the leading frontiers of culture clash worldwide involves the campaign for gender equality in areas such as education, employment, reproductive and marital rights. The story of Malala Yousafzai from northwest Pakistan reminds us of the power of one individual to inspire an international response on the vital issue of education for girls. When Malala was 12, and inspired by her teacher father, she began to speak out for the right to education, something that was becoming increasingly restricted due to the influence of the Taliban in Pakistan. In 2012, although critically wounded, Malala survived an assassination attempt at the hands of the Taliban and, on her recovery, became a brave advocate for the many millions who were being denied education due to certain cultural perceptions about girls and their place in society. In 2014 she was co-recipient of the Nobel Peace Prize and dedicated her prize money to the building of a secondary school for girls in Pakistan. Malala's story reminds us that culture is about the way individuals and societies define what the ideal 'good' is and the extent to which individual citizens like Malala, the global networks inspired by her story, and even those like the Taliban who oppose this vision are willing to campaign for what they consider to be cultural rights.

Religion and culture: difference and similarity

We have explored elements of religion and culture and offered various brief examples from an individual, national and international perspective. While it has been important to consider each concept separately, highlighting the particular ways that religion and culture influence international relations, there are clear interlinkages between them. Theorists have long drawn such links and these are useful for our consideration here. For example, the anthropologist Clifford Geertz famously described religion as a 'cultural system' composed of myths, rituals, symbols and beliefs created by humans as a way of giving our individual and collective lives a sense of meaning (Woodhead 2011, 124). Consider the similarities between the elements of religion and culture described in this chapter such as the role of symbols and stories in both accounts, and the pursuit of life according to what either faith or culture determine to be the higher standards of living.

An important question to ask is whether 'culture' should be necessarily understood as the larger more significant category in international relations, always casting 'religion' as a subset within it. Such a view makes sense because no one religion encompasses an entire society in the world today, and no society lives entirely according to one set of sacred rules and practices. On the other hand, in some contexts religious authority and identity can be more significant than any other cultural element. For example, when American soldiers moved into the Iraqi city of Najaf in 2003 to negotiate security arrangements, it was not the town mayor or the police chief that had most influence. Rather, it was the reclusive religious leader Grand Ayatollah Ali al-Sistani, whose authority influenced not only the city but much of the fracturing nation itself. Taking another example, when Communist authorities confronted striking dock workers in Poland in the 1980s, it was not only unions that opposed them but also the Catholic Church, whose priests performed sacred rituals and stood in solidarity with strikers in open defiance of the government. In both these examples, the elements of religion are equally – if not more – prominent than the elements of culture. Perhaps the most useful approach, therefore, is to see the elements of religion and the elements of culture in constant interaction with one another.

We have explored just four elements for each category. What might some other elements be and what are the impacts of these elements on individual and international life? There are some excellent resources to assist us in exploring such questions. These include an introduction to religion in IR by Toft, Philpott and Shah (2011), an examination of religion in a globalised world by Haynes (2012), a large compendium of essential readings on religion and foreign affairs edited by Hoover and Johnston (2012), and E-International Relations' edited collection *Nations Under God* (Herrington, McKay and Haynes 2015). However, the simple outline we have provided so far will enable us to begin answering the 'what' and 'how' questions about religion and culture in global affairs and draw some connections between them.

Can we all live together?

One of the most pressing questions related to our study is whether religious and cultural actors and agendas have more of a positive or negative effect on global affairs. As we have seen above, these elements relate to some of the deepest levels of human experience, both individually and internationally. Should policymakers try to release the powerful energy of religio-cultural identity for the sake of a better world, or should they try to 'keep a lid on it' for fear of unleashing forces that might damage our capacity to get along with others?

The value of a 'both/and' approach

The study of international relations shows that the answer may be to draw on both strategies, since religio-cultural identity inhabits a space somewhere between the problems of conflict and the possibilities of cooperation. This approach can be seen as an adaptation of Appleby's influential idea of the 'ambivalence of the sacred' (2000) in which the elements of religio-cultural politics we have explored above carry simultaneously the potential for both violence and peace. The usefulness of this approach is that it helps us to break free from the restrictions of an 'either/or' logic about religion and culture (i.e. *either* conflict *or* cooperation). Instead, we can focus on a 'both/and' analysis which allows individual and international examples of each (i.e. *both* conflict *and* cooperation) to inform us about the politics of religion and culture at the global level. The influential scholar Martin E. Marty (2003) would add that such an approach helps us to deepen our understanding of world politics as it really is.

Therefore, with a 'both/and' logic in mind, we consider comparative examples of religio-cultural identity in world politics that emphasise conflict and cooperation respectively. The number of alternative examples in IR is potentially unlimited – so as you read on, keep in mind other instances where the elements of religion and culture contribute to violence and peacemaking.

Religion and culture create a 'clash of civilisations'

When Soviet Communism finally collapsed in 1991, US president George H. W. Bush heralded the beginning of a 'new world order'. In many ways this was an accurate description because the conflict between the Soviet Union and the West had shaped the dynamics of global affairs for half a century. But, what would this new order look like? One answer was offered by Samuel P. Huntington (1993), who suggested that world politics would no longer be shaped by a clash of ideologies (e.g. capitalism and communism) but rather by a 'clash of civilizations'. With this hypothesis, Huntington still assumed that global politics would be shaped by conflict as much as the Cold War before it had been. The significant shift in thinking was the prominence that religious and cultural identity would play in shaping the conflict. For Huntington, a civilisation was understood as 'a cultural entity ... defined both by common objective elements such as language, history, religion, customs, institutions, and by the subjective self-identification of people' (1993, 23–24). Significantly, the descriptors Huntington gives to the major civilisations have a cultural or religious link: 'Western, Confucian, Japanese, Islamic, Hindu and Slavic-Orthodox, Latin American and possibly African' (1993, 25).

Thus, the central tenet to Huntington's controversial idea is that those elements of culture and religion that we have studied in this chapter contribute to fundamental differences across the globe. This creates fault lines between individuals and peoples who will inevitably fall into serious conflict over these deep and abiding differences. Not surprisingly, Huntington's ideas have been both criticised and embraced. The phrase 'clash of civilisations' came to popular prominence in 2001 as a way to interpret the 9/11 attacks as a conflict between Islam and the West. Although it is worth noting that the administration of George W. Bush did not apply the notion in the way Huntington proposed, scholars were using the phrase well prior to 9/11 and today its applications vary considerably, from commentary on Turkish politics to describing the tension of multicultural policy in Western regional cities. Whatever the merits of these examples (and hundreds like them) they illustrate how Huntington's thesis has become a way for politicians, commentators and academics to frame conflicts in a changing global landscape. Religion and culture are central to this framing.

Religion and culture create a dialogue of civilisations

At the end of the Cold War, rather than assuming the continuation of a conflict-driven world as Huntington did, some saw the new world order as an opportunity to redesign the way international affairs was conducted. What would such a politics look like? Some policymakers imagined a world where multiple actors – not just powerful states – could contribute to a collective process of stability and accountability. Religio-cultural voices were increasingly considered an important part of this conversation.

Accordingly, an alternative approach to that of Huntington came from a United Nations consultative group known as the World Public Forum, which began an initiative in 2002 called the Dialogue of Civilizations. Influenced by a 1997 proposal from Iranian president Mohammed Khatami, the objective of the Dialogue is to 'combine the efforts of the international community in protecting humanity's spiritual and cultural values ... bringing the spirit of cooperation and understanding into the daily lives of people from different cultures'. Thus, in stark contrast to the clash of civilisations assumption that religion and culture are causes of conflict, the Dialogue of Civilizations deploys the same broad elements as resources for building bridges between individuals and peoples in the development of sustainable peace and cooperation.

What is the value of such a change? The 'clash' emphasises religion and culture as an extension of politics based on power, and one of the abiding problems of world politics is that some states are (much) more powerful than others. The Dialogue of Civilizations potentially offers a more equalising approach, whereby religion and culture become an extension of politics based on shared interests. Noting that religio-cultural communities are often transnational rather than state-based, the Dialogue's emphasis on 'spiritual and cultural values' helps to create an open-ended space for international cooperation beyond the defensive power interests of states.

The importance of precise thinking

Which framework makes more sense to you? Does the rise of religion and culture in international affairs encourage clash or a dialogue? Do religious and cultural elements of politics enable us to live together in cooperation or do they disconnect us in ways that lead to conflict? Applying the logic that we introduced at the start of this section, one answer is that elements of religion and culture contribute to *both* clash *and* dialogue, to *both* conflict *and* cooperation.

The benefit of this approach is twofold. First, it encourages us to look closely at specific elements of religion and culture – as we have done in this chapter – instead of forcing such complex phenomena into a singular assumption about conflict or cooperation. As Reza Aslan once commented, 'Islam is not a religion of peace and it is not a religion of war. It is just a religion' (PBS, 2009). This kind of ambivalent outlook allows us to consider how the precise elements of religion and culture are used in violent and peaceful ways.

Second, applying a 'both/and' logic requires us to consider specific examples of international relations – as we have attempted throughout the chapter – without stereotyping religious and cultural traditions by pinning them to singular events. When the shortcomings of religion were once brought to the attention of the Hindu mystic Ramakrishna, he remarked that 'Religion is like a cow. It kicks, but it also gives milk' (Tyndale 2006, xiv). For every cultural symbol of hate, we see as many cultural symbols of healing and peace. For every religious movement of violence, we see as many religious movements for reconciliation.

This 'both/and' understanding of religion and culture has become influential among policymakers working with individuals, local communities, and national, regional and international organisations, marking a significant shift in our understanding of world politics as a whole. Beyond the issue of peace versus violence, it has also helped us understand the need for particular consideration about the extent of religious and cultural influence on politics throughout the world. For example, on religion, Jonathan Fox (2008, 7) writes:

> A fuller picture of the world's religious economy would show secularisation – the reduction of religion's influence in society – occurring in some parts of the religious economy, and sacralisation – the increase of religion's influence in society – occurring in other parts.

Cultural factors are similarly dynamic, both in influence and in the forms they take. As James Clifford wrote, '"cultures" do not hold still for their portraits' (1986, 10), and as such the influence of culture on individual and global politics requires precise thinking.

Conclusion

In this chapter we set out to draw a diagram of religion and culture in world affairs. The aim was to show that religious and cultural factors matter if we want to deepen our understanding of international relations. The method has been to define elements of each concept and consider the impact of these elements on aspects of our individual, national and international experience. Hopefully, you are convinced that understanding religious and cultural issues is necessary if you want to join some of the most important discussions about world politics today. There is little that concerns IR today that does not involve elements of religion or culture, or both. Equally, it is important to recognise as a final thought that we have only just begun to explore these issues and we need to go deeper in our consideration of the importance of religious and cultural actors and interests. Understanding them will help us better understand an ever more complex and divided world.

Part Two

GLOBAL ISSUES

10

Global Poverty and Wealth

JAMES ARVANITAKIS & DAVID J. HORNSBY

Poverty and wealth are often found side by side. They are two dimensions in our world that are interrelated because they affect each other and influence both the willingness and capacity of states to ensure a stable global system. Traditional approaches to IR are premised on the notion of state sovereignty. But, sovereignty as an absolute concept that reinforces separation between states has been tempered through the many processes of globalisation, including economic agreements and the establishment of international organisations, as well as with the emergence of human rights thinking as captured through the Universal Declaration of Human Rights. With respect to the emergence of human rights thinking, the premise goes that in the context of a common set of universal rights based on the individual, the sovereignty of the state can be challenged if a government does not respect or maintain these rights. Here, sovereignty means that a state does not only maintain rights, it also meets its responsibilities. In relation to poverty, globalisation raises the question of the obligation the wealthy owe to the poor and vulnerable. One of today's most pressing international problems is what to do about poverty and the approximately one billion people living in such a condition. As we start our scan of key global issues, it is appropriate to open this second section of the book by addressing an issue of this magnitude.

Poverty matters as a subject for reflection in IR on many levels, one of which is a prominent set of ideas around global justice that considers what states owe each other in the process of international cooperation. After all, it can be said that those with the power and ability to assist have a moral and ethical obligation to try and solve problems like poverty. This stems from what Peter Singer (1972) calls the 'rescue case', noting there is an obligation for someone to assist an infant drowning in a shallow pond if the child can be saved with minimal effort or inconvenience. In the context of global poverty, the logic flows that developed states have an obligation to help poor states because they can, with minimal effort. However, the obligation of developed states to help alleviate poverty is not just relevant because they can assist; it is also because they are very often implicated in creating the conditions for its existence. For example, Thomas Pogge (2008, 2010) argues that poverty exists due to a coercive global order – which includes international governmental organisations such as the World Bank and the International Monetary Fund – that disadvantages the poor and reinforces a context of poverty. This means that developed states and multilateral institutions contribute to the persistence of global poverty due to both the way they have structured the international system and how they operate in it. These perspectives indicate that a global problem like poverty requires a global solution that developed countries have both a moral, and strategic, responsibility to address.

Defining poverty

Defining poverty begins with a consideration of conditions that prevent regions, states and peoples from having access to wealth. Though there are many elements to this, there are four key structural conditions to consider.

1. History of exploitation

Many of today's poorest nations were previously exploited through colonialism and/or slavery. These actions have had lasting impact through entrenching inequalities between socio-ethnic groups within states. A prescient example is South Africa, which, under British and Dutch rule, restricted the rights of indigenous African groups in the areas of education, land ownership and access to capital. At the same time there was a concentration of wealth in the hands of the white colonising minority. Such actions were eventually enshrined in the creation of the apartheid system of racial segregation. However, even since its dismantling in 1994, poverty amongst the indigenous population is disproportionately high in comparison to white groups due to the fact that capital and land continues to be concentrated in the hands of a select few. Of course, some former colonial nations have emerged from their exploitation to become some of the world's leading economies – consider the US and Australia. Yet, even in these 'Western' societies there remains a legacy of colonialism that often affects indigenous peoples disproportionately. In more absolute terms, as decolonisation unfolded in the second half of the twentieth century, many new nations, particularly in Sub-Saharan Africa, were left with inadequate or weak political structures that soon gave way to other types of exploitation via dictatorship or corruption. In these cases, the bulk of the population experienced exploitation. In some states, these problems still persist.

2. War and political instability

When thinking of the fundamental conditions for economic development to take place in a state, security, safety and stability often come to mind. This is because peaceful conditions permit a government to focus on developing natural resources, human capacity and industrial capabilities. War and political instability often act as significant distractions as efforts are directed at combating violence or insecurity. For example, think of the conflict in Syria that began in 2011. This has led to a mass flow of millions of refugees seeking to escape the conflict, leaving behind a war-torn state that lacks the human and economic resources to govern itself effectively. It is a pattern that has been seen before – for instance, in the 1990s in Somalia, where instability still persists. The outlook for Syria in the years to come could well be even worse. It is also something that can be seen in the developed world, though to a different degree. Consider the United States: it spent upwards of $3 trillion on the invasions and occupations of Iraq and Afghanistan as part of its 'Global War on Terror' while, simultaneously, relative poverty and inequality increased within its own society, in part due to the government prioritising public spending on warfare. It is no surprise, then, that when surveys on citizens' qualities of life are undertaken, stable nations which do not typically engage in warfare – such as Switzerland and Denmark – are often top of the list.

3. Structural economic conditions

The way in which the international economic order is structured can either reinforce or ease poverty. Institutions like the World Bank and the World Trade Organization are dominated by wealthy nations. This has placed them under scrutiny due to embedded practices that often place developing countries at a disadvantage. For example, before the World Bank issues a loan to a low-income nation, certain conditions must be met. These are known as conditionalities. They can include policy changes such as the privatising of public services – for instance, the provision of water, sanitation and electricity. Imposing such conditions, or structural adjustments as the World Bank calls them, have frequently been shown to cause more harm than good.

4. Inequality

Inequality is an important contributor to poverty as it can reinforce divisions between the so-called 'haves' and 'have-nots'. In a relative sense, it can result in certain elements of a population lacking the tools and resources needed to counter the challenges they face. In an absolute sense it can render a whole state unable to rescue its citizens from dire circumstances because it lacks the financial resources. For example, in the United States approximately 16 million children live in poverty. This is despite the fact that it is one of the richest countries in the world. Inequality can be measured by looking at how much income a family has relative to the cost of living in that society. It is not the same as the absolute poverty a child living on less than $2 a day would experience in the Democratic Republic of the Congo, one of the world's poorest nations. Yet, it is still poverty when viewed in a relative sense through the lens of inequality. The nature of the problem is thus extensive since it is something that exists at both the domestic level (inequalities within states) and the international level (inequalities between states). Although there is a vibrant international charity system and a range of international assistance programmes, inequality remains a key structural condition associated with poverty.

Measuring and reducing poverty

Since the end of the Second World War states have come together to find ways to reduce poverty through prompting economic growth. As discussed earlier in the chapter, concepts of global justice underpin international poverty-reduction strategies, giving focus to approaches that seek to enhance the rights of the marginalised. The extent to which these efforts have been successful is highly debatable – but the intent has certainly been there. States have attempted to address the challenges of poverty at a global level in various ways. We discuss four approaches below.

1. Official development assistance (aid)

Typically, aid comes from developed states and is either channelled bilaterally (or directly) from one state to another or diverted multilaterally through international organisations like the United Nations. It is one way in which wealthy nations have attempted to meet their moral obligation to assist poorer nations. Indeed, developed countries have spent a great deal on official development assistance over the years. In 2014 alone, states spent over $135bn on aid according to a report from the Organisation for Economic Co-operation and Development (OECD). However, the success of such efforts has been inconsistent, and in some cases poverty has actually got worse. The reasons for this are complex but some examples may be helpful.

First, inappropriate types of aid can be sent. Instead of sending money that a developing country can use to address poverty, developed states sometimes provide goods that may or may not be helpful. For example, in Gambia a number of oxygen devices were donated to a hospital, but unfortunately they were not compatible with the local electricity voltage. This rendered the devices unusable, highlighting how aid needs to be properly thought through. Second, corruption in some countries has seen aid syphoned off into the offshore bank accounts of the political elite. For example, the New York Times claimed that over $1 billion in foreign aid intended to help Bosnia rebuild itself after years of destructive war was stolen by Bosnian officials for personal gain (Hedges 1999).

Aid has also been used for the political purposes of the providing state. For example, during the Cold War the United States and the Soviet Union used aid to prop up states that were sympathetic to their own political cause. In many of those places this did little to address poverty; rather, it helped fund regional wars that led to further instability and poverty. For example, the 1975–2002 civil war in Angola saw the Soviet Union and the United States provide aid in the form of military assistance to opposing forces. Aid has also come from developed countries or international institutions with specific conditions for use ('conditionalities') that have only served to make things worse. As already mentioned, such aid requires the receiving nation to restructure its economy in ways that may not benefit the most vulnerable people. For example, during the structural adjustment programmes of the 1980s in Latin America, income per capita fell in 18 countries. During similar programmes in sub-Saharan Africa, income per capita fell in 26 countries over the same period (Stewart 1991).

2. Trade and investment

The trade in goods and services together with foreign direct investment by private corporations can play an important role in poverty reduction. One of the ideas behind free trade and reducing barriers to investment between countries is to provide opportunity for states in the international system to grow economically. International trade in goods and services has risen significantly since 1945. Investment between states, or so-called foreign direct investment, has been a major source of that economic growth. But these global activities frequently hide an inconvenient reality: developing countries are often only involved in a minor way in global trade and investment activities. This is due to a number of reasons ranging from inadequate infrastructure such as roads, rail, and ports to limited access to financial capital. In comparison to developed nations, many developing countries have a higher proportion of lower skilled or undereducated workers in their workforce. As a result, investment opportunities that require high-skilled and high-income employment are more often found in developed countries and investment by corporations in developing nations typically targets a low-skilled and low-wage workforce. This reality is difficult to overcome. Although nations such as China and India are investing heavily in an attempt to level the playing field, they are more fortunate than others due to their comparative wealth and high historic levels of economic growth. Despite some notable exceptions, the general picture is that trade and investment have not assisted poverty reduction to any significant extent.

3. Money lending

A third poverty-reducing strategy is lending developing countries money, or capital, so that they can invest in areas that will help them develop economically. Money lending is different from aid as loans need to be paid back, with interest. Loans can be provided for key infrastructure projects like bridges, roads, electricity lines and power plants. These can typically act as catalysts for economic development, but they require significant access to capital. The importance of access to capital resulted in the establishment of the World Bank in 1944. Its mission was to lend developing countries money at below market interest rates and also provide expert advice on the establishment of sound economic policies. On paper, the idea is a good one. However, the practices of the World Bank are not without controversy. As we explored earlier in the chapter, there has been criticism of the conditions attached to the loans. Although the most censured of the policies have been abandoned, damage has been done. In addition, the provision of interest-bearing loans to developing countries has created a huge problem of indebtedness. Many developing countries cannot afford to invest in important domestic programmes such as education and healthcare due to the burden of their debt repayments. This has sparked calls to cancel the debt of developing countries and allow them a fresh start. To date, although some debt has been cancelled, the larger challenges caused by the nature of outstanding loans and how they were imposed remain.

4. United Nations' goals

In response to the many failings noted above, a new approach emerged in 2000 when the United Nations and its member states moved to eradicate extreme poverty by 2015. The United Nations Millennium Development Goals (MDGs) consisted of eight categories or areas of focus for states to engage in:

1.   Eradicate extreme hunger and poverty
2.   Achieve universal primary education
3.   Promote gender equality and empower women
4.   Reduce child mortality
5.   Improve maternal health

6.   Combat HIV/AIDS, malaria and other diseases
7.   Ensure environmental sustainability
8.   To develop a global partnership for development.

A cross-section of approaches was employed for achieving these goals, including harnessing elements of the three strategies outlined above. The key thing however, was to have a coordinated approach to a set of agreed targets. However, the initiative proved a mixed bag in terms of results. For example, some goals related to education and child mortality have seen real – if uneven – progress, while rates of hunger and malnutrition have actually worsened in some cases. Exacerbating this further, the aftermath of the 2008 financial crisis has reduced the projected amount of money (and jobs) available to many governments. Anthony Lake, Executive Director of the United Nations Children's Fund (UNICEF), accounted for the mixed picture of success and failure as follows:

> In setting broad global goals the MDGs inadvertently encouraged nations to measure progress through national averages. In the rush to make that progress, many focused on the easiest-to-reach children and communities, not those in greatest need. In doing so, national progress may actually have been slowed.

> (UNICEF, 2015)

Given these unsatisfactory results, the international community agreed that a more robust initiative was needed and the Sustainable Development Goals (SDGs) were adopted at the United Nations in 2015. They have 169 clear targets spread over 17 priority areas, all to be achieved by 2030:

1.   No poverty
2.   No hunger
3.   Good health
4.   Quality education
5.   Gender equality
6.   Clean water and sanitation
7.   Renewable energy
8.   Good jobs and economic growth
9.   Innovation and infrastructure
10. Reduced inequalities
11. Sustainable cities and communities
12. Responsible consumption
13. Climate action

14. Life below water
15. Life on land
16. Peace and justice
17. Partnerships for the goals.

Like the Millennium Development Goals, the Sustainable Development Goals can be described as aspirational. Although the newer targets have their critics, one reason that they may offer greater hope in reducing poverty is that the planned interventions are more detailed. The target is not only reducing poverty, but addressing the many conditions that feed and cement conditions of poverty, including poor (or negative) economic growth. And the most vulnerable are now being targeted proactively, addressing one of the criticisms of the Millennium Development Goals.

Globalisation and the wealth–poverty dynamic

Globalisation is an important concept to add to the discussion of global wealth and poverty. It refers to a perception that the world is increasingly being moulded into a shared social space by economic and technological forces. Developments in one region of the world can have profound consequences for individuals and communities on the other side of the world. Central to the idea of globalisation is the perception of intensity. As a concept, globalisation is thus said to be ever increasing in scope, scale and speed to the point that it is effectively irrevocable. As such, globalisation is multi-dimensional. For example, globalisation is more than the goods that flow between geographically diverse communities. Globalisation includes not only the what, but also the how and the why, the frequency with which something occurs, the social consequences of this process and the range of people involved. Although the concept of globalisation is contested and subject to many different interpretations, it has clear relevance to the subject of this chapter.

It can be said that the process of becoming more interconnected as a set of nations has worked towards reducing poverty. Certainly the World Bank argues that globalisation has improved the material circumstances of those who have engaged in the global economy. Though such an analysis is accurate at one level, it fails to account for the structural conditions that influence poverty. An alternative view is that globalisation actually causes poverty by further entrenching inequality and concentrating any gains in the hands of those who are already wealthy and in powerful positions. For example, the internet has allowed many individuals to establish successful businesses and sell their goods all over the world. But how can you take advantage of this technology if you live in an area without access to the internet due to poor infrastructure, poverty or war? These citizens get left further behind and the inequalities that already exist are aggravated. Certainly, any analysis of the impact of globalisation on the wealth–poverty dynamic must recognise both of these perspectives. But, globalisation is a complex issue. If globalisation is only viewed in terms of 'good' and 'bad', we will not appreciate the multifaceted nature of global processes.

For the purposes of our analysis, globalisation has opened up many (primarily economic) opportunities, and this is evident in the reduction in numbers of those living in extreme poverty. This has dropped from over half the world's population in 1981 to within reach of ten per cent today. This figure, from the World Bank, takes into account issues like inflation. But, it can also be said that globalisation has entrenched power relationships and inequalities and this has had material effects on poverty and inequality. A common critique relevant to our discussion on poverty is that globalisation is another word for 'Americanisation'. According to this critique, many of the economic policies that supposedly 'open up' international markets are of benefit to US-based multinational corporations and create fertile ground internationally for American foreign policy objectives. On the other hand, globalisation can also be seen as hybridisation. This view was initially based on the creation of 'new' cultures and identities due to colonisation and the destruction of traditional indigenous groups. Applied to the processes of globalisation, hybridity has taken on a more positive character – framing globalisation as a series of processes that serve to benefit all sides involved in the exchange by promoting intercultural development and harmony.

Globalisation and neoliberalism

One reason that poverty has remained a key characteristic of the global economy is a suite of policy initiatives based on the economic philosophy of neoliberalism that have arguably failed the world's poorest and most vulnerable. Since the 1970s, according to Stewart Firth (2005), the priority of the state has been to create and implement policies that promote a neoliberal economic agenda. That is, the opening up and deregulation of markets and the privatisation of essential services. In his book *Globalization and its Discontents* (2002), former World Bank chief economist and Nobel laureate Joseph Stiglitz provides a number of examples that highlight how the free market neoliberal agenda has driven the agenda of international institutions such as the International Monetary Fund and the World Trade Organization since the 1970s. This has seen trade deals and reforms that minimise the role of government, the removal of trade barriers – even ones that protect workers' rights – and a reliance on the flawed belief that economic growth and increases in wealth will eventually trickle down to all segments of society. These organisations have fundamentally altered the traditional role of the state, whose priority has been more with the promotion and protection of an open, market-orientated system. States focused on the market often fail to meet the needs of the majority of the population and address poverty. Hence, the philosophy of globalisation, if viewed through the lens of neoliberal policies, has resulted in the welfare of citizens being diminished at many levels.

The global financial crisis of 2008 highlights a bigger challenge for globalisation in addressing the poverty issue. This event began in one nation and quickly reverberated across the world. Due to the interconnected nature of the global economy, what started out as a collapse of the American subprime mortgage market ended up having implications for markets outside the United States. Efforts to reduce poverty were impacted as recession and wealth contraction led to less money being available. Nations prioritised spending at home and foreign direct investment fell as corporations delayed or cancelled projects. These events had negative outcomes with regard to poverty levels in developed nations, but even more so for citizens in developing countries. While significant economic events like this are not common, the risk always remains that in an interconnected global economy the poorest will suffer the most when economic shocks occur.

Conclusion

It is one of the major conundrums of our world that poverty still exists amidst extreme and growing wealth. Today, the richest 1 per cent of the world's population hold half the world's wealth. In contrast, the bottom 80 per cent owns just 5.5 per cent. What is worse, statistics like this seem to be getting worse over time with regard to inequality and wealth distribution. It seems that while economic processes have helped lift many out of poverty, they have largely failed to mitigate income and wealth inequality. This result poses serious moral and ethical questions. What cannot be disputed is that the interdependence of our economies is best accompanied by an equal measure of ethical concern. That is, we owe each and every person a debt of responsibility for the actions we take and the policies we promote within our own states. Hopefully the recognition of this, perhaps best marked out by the United Nations 2015 Sustainable Development Goals, will lead to a more just world in the years ahead.

11

Protecting People

ALEX J. BELLAMY

The United Nations (UN) was established in 1945 with a charter that set out to 'save succeeding generations from the scourge of war' and 'uphold faith in fundamental human rights'. Three years later, the Universal Declaration of Human Rights was signed at the United Nations, calling for states to work together to ensure that everyone enjoys 'freedom from fear' and 'freedom from want'. Added to the issues of global inequality and poverty addressed in the previous chapter, finding ways of protecting people from harm is a major contemporary debate. While the picture overall might be improving, too often the international community does too little, too late to protect people from atrocities, civil wars, and other human-made ills. In the twentieth century tens of millions of people were killed in wars between states, while an even higher number were killed by their own governments. Facts like these pose a major challenge for the way we think about world politics. Our contemporary international order is based upon a society of states that enjoy exclusive jurisdiction over particular pieces of territory and rights to non-interference and non-intervention that are enshrined in the United Nations charter. This system is in turn prefaced on the assumption that states exist primarily to protect the security of their citizens. In other words, the security of the state is considered important, and worth protecting, because states provide security to individuals. But, as countless examples show, not every state protects the wellbeing of its population. From recent examples like Syria to examples from the past century, threats to individual security have tended to come more from one's own state than from other states. Facts like this pose a major challenge to international peace and security and raise questions about whether there are circumstances in which the security of individuals should be privileged over the security of states.

Key positions

The debate about human protection hinges on the issue of whether a state's right to be secure and free from external interference should be conditional on its fulfilment of certain responsibilities to its citizens, most obviously protection from mass violence. We might plot various responses to this question along two axes – the first relating to our conception of whether moral progress is possible in world politics (more optimistic or more pessimistic) and the other relating to which actors should be privileged (states or individuals). The first axis refers to the way we understand the potentiality and limits of world politics. Some approaches are prefaced on an optimistic vision that dialogue between communities makes moral consensus and shared purposes possible (Linklater 1998). The alternative is a fatalistic or 'tragic' conception of world politics based on the view that the world is composed of culturally distinct units with different values that pursue their own, distinct goals with limited possibility for cooperation (Lebow 2003). This account is sceptical of progress, doubts that morality does (or should) play a role in world affairs, and predicts that efforts to spread moral values will prove costly and counter-productive. The second axis relates to what sort of actor should be privileged – states or individuals. It is common for theories of International Relations to privilege the state on the grounds that it is the principal actor in world affairs, the main source of order, and the bearer of international rights and responsibilities. An alternative perspective privileges individuals as the only irreducible actor. Individuals cannot be means to an end; they must be seen as ends in themselves. From these two axes, we derive four ethical positions.

1. Optimistic and state-centred: a rule-governed international society

This accepts that progress in international affairs is possible, but that in a world characterised by radical difference the basis for progress should be voluntary cooperation between states in a rule-governed international society of states. Perspectives housed in this quadrant hold that the common good is best served by privileging the rules of co-existence found in the UN charter. This focuses especially on the legal ban on the use force and ensuring that the two exceptions to that ban are not abused (Articles 42 and 51). According to this view, allowing states a free hand to promote human protection in other states would create disorder by allowing wars to protect and impose one state's values on others. Disorder would weaken the international system, undermine human development, and make cooperation between states more difficult. This view dovetails with the commonly held legal view that there is a general prohibition on interference except when authorised by the UN Security Council. This account is unnecessarily pessimistic about the capacity of states to reach consensus about shared moral principles. There is relatively little evidence to suggest that the incremental expansion of collective action into new areas of peace and security, such as human protection, has given rise to greater disorder. This account also overlooks the flexibility built into the Security Council to redefine its role in international peace and security to take account of changing conditions, should it decide to do so.

2. Tragic and state-centred: the realities of life in an international state of nature

This perspective espouses a communitarian view about the diversity of communities and the relativity of values, but rejects even basic claims about the capacity of states to agree meaningful rules of co-existence, let alone substantive rules. This account suggests that norms and rules are irrelevant as causes of behaviour when set against material factors such as economic gain, territory and the national interest. To paraphrase a prominent realist, Edward Hallett Carr, international interference for 'protection' would in fact be nothing other than the interests and preferences of the powerful masquerading as universal morality. This account counsels against humanitarian activism. It doubts the capacity of states to be altruistic and thus sees all state action as exercises in the self-interested use of power that undermines world order. Few, if any, states openly subscribe to this approach. Accepting that states tend to do only what they perceive to be in their interests does not get us very far analytically. To understand why states act in certain ways we need to understand variation in the way that states (even similar states) construct their interests and this requires a deeper understanding of the factors that guide national decision-making.

3. Optimistic and individual-centred: defending humanity and our common values

The third perspective is the one most positively disposed to advancing human protection. It is usually associated with liberalism and a broader cosmopolitan view that all humans belong to a single world community. It holds that states have positive duties to protect foreigners from tyranny as well as a right to do so since human rights are universal rights that ought to be defended everywhere. According to theorists in this tradition, states have agreed certain minimum standards of behaviour. As such, action across borders to support human protection is not about imposing the will of a few powerful states but about protecting and enforcing basic values and/or the collective will of international society. While this view is on strong ground when it comes to the theoretical right of the UN Security Council to mandate enforcement action, when it comes to a more generalised right to intervention the theory is contradicted by strong bodies of legal thought and state practice that counsel against it. Not surprisingly, therefore, liberal cosmopolitans tend to be divided on whether there is such a general right of intervention outside the boundaries of existing international law.

4. Tragic and people-centred: the distinctiveness of humanitarian action

These accounts tend to privilege traditional forms of humanitarian assistance and exhibit deep scepticism about military intervention on the grounds that it tends to make situations worse and reinforces the militarist ideals that are among the chief underlying causes of humanitarian crises in the first place. Precisely because of this scepticism, however, these accounts help to widen our understanding of the tools that might be used to protect populations. In exposing some of the intrinsic limitations of forcible action to promote human protection, these approaches emphasise that interventions are selective, partial and never solely humanitarian. That said, critics question how suffering can be alleviated let alone prevented without taking a political stance and so there are real limits to the physical protection that can be afforded by humanitarian action alone. This 'individual-centred' approach is vulnerable to many of the criticisms levelled against the 'tragic' conception. Notably, its prescriptions often fall well short of what is needed to protect vulnerable populations.

Emerging norms of human protection

Since the end of the Cold War, the practice of human protection has evolved through at least eight interconnected streams of norms, rules, practices and institutional developments. Each of these emerged to address the problem of civilian suffering, especially during war and will be addressed in turn.

International humanitarian law

International humanitarian law had its origins in the nineteenth century with the development of the US Government's 'General Orders No. 100' (better known as the Lieber code), which were military laws designed to limit the conduct of soldiers – and the emergence of the Red Cross movement. After the Second World War, international humanitarian law was developed and codified in a series of international treaties. In 1948, the newly established UN General Assembly approved the Genocide Convention, which prohibited the crime of genocide and assigned all states a legal duty to prevent it and punish the perpetrators. The International Court of Justice (ICJ) was established as the judicial arm of the United Nations and is responsible for adjudicating on disputes between states and other legal matters. It judged that as a result of this convention, all states have a legal responsibility to do what they can, within existing law, to prevent genocide.

The laws of war were further codified in the four Geneva Conventions (1949), two additional protocols (1977), and in a range of protocols covering the use of Certain Conventional Weapons. Of particular importance was Common Article 3 of the 1949 Geneva Conventions, which committed parties to respect the human rights of all non-combatants; and the Convention on the Protection of Civilian Persons, which offered legal protection to non-combatants in occupied territories. The Geneva Protocols (1977) extended the legal protection afforded to non-combatants to situations of non-international armed conflict. They also insisted that armed attacks be strictly limited to military objectives and forbade attacks on non-combatants or their property. These principals provided the legal and moral foundation for subsequent campaigns for conventions banning weapons, such as landmines and cluster munitions, that were considered inherently indiscriminate. International humanitarian law has thus created a normative standard of civilian protection that not only prohibits attacks on non-combatants and restricts the use of certain weapons but also calls for the prevention of particular crimes, such as genocide, and the punishment of perpetrators.

Protection of civilians

The UN Security Council's formal engagement with this theme dates back to 1998 when, at Canada's request, it adopted a presidential statement calling for the Secretary-General to submit periodic reports on how the UN might improve the protection of civilians. Since then, it has held a series of open meetings on the protection of civilians, establishing it as one of its major thematic interests. In 1999, the Security Council unanimously adopted Resolution 1265 expressing its 'willingness' to consider 'appropriate measures' in response 'to situations of armed conflict where civilians are being targeted or where humanitarian assistance to civilians is being deliberately obstructed'. In addition, the Security Council expressed its willingness to explore how peacekeeping mandates might be reframed to afford better protection to endangered civilians. In 2006, it adopted Resolution 1674, which built further on this progress by demanding that parties to armed conflict grant unfettered humanitarian access to civilians.

As it has developed its thematic interest in the protection of civilians, the Security Council has also developed and strengthened its practices of protection. In doing so it has broken new ground. In Resolution 1973, passed in 2011, the Security Council authorised the use of force for human protection purposes in Libya. This was the first time in the history of the Security Council that such an action had been passed without the consent of the host state. Through this resolution, and the one that preceded it (Resolution 1970) the Security Council utilised the full range of the collective security powers granted to it by the UN Charter. Three years later, Resolution 2165 authorised the delivery of humanitarian assistance into Syria without the consent of the

Syrian government – the first time that the Council has done this. Hence, two very important issues of precedent were established, built on a new understanding of the need to protect civilians.

Before the turn of this century, civilian protection was typically not considered a core part of peacekeeping. Starting in 1999 with the UN mission in Sierra Leone, the Security Council has invoked Chapter VII of the UN Charter with increasing regularity to authorise peacekeepers to use all means necessary to protect civilians. Chapter VII of the Charter gives the UN Security Council the authority to authorise whatever means it deems necessary, including the use of force, for the maintenance of international peace and security. By design, it was intended as a key deterrent to international aggression. Today, civilian protection and the authorisation of 'all means necessary' to that end are core aspects of UN peacekeeping and central to many of its new mandates. In the Democratic Republic of the Congo (DRC), the Security Council went even further by tasking a 'Force Intervention Brigade' to take the fight to non-state armed groups that were employing mass violence against civilians. Today, the bulk of the UN's 120,000 peacekeepers are deployed with mandates to use all necessary means to protect civilians from harm.

Addressing specific vulnerabilities

Since the end of the Second World War, international society has periodically recognised groups that are exposed to particular vulnerabilities and has established mechanisms aimed at addressing or reducing those vulnerabilities. Of these, the best developed is the international refugee regime, which is governed by the 1951 Refugee Convention and subsequent 1967 Protocol. It is overseen by the UN High Commissioner for Refugees (UNHCR). This system grants people facing persecution the right to claim asylum and receive resettlement in third countries and mandates the UNHCR to ensure that refugees have access to protection and durable solutions to their displacement. During the 1990s, it became apparent that this system was unable to cope with a new displacement crisis – that of internal displacement. Internal displacement occurs when people are forced from their homes by mass violence and other ills but remain within their host country. As a largely domestic issue there was little appetite for an international convention governing the displaced. Instead, the UNHCR extended its mandate to cover the protection of all displaced persons and United Nations officials developed 'guiding principles' for their treatment.

Another longstanding facet of mass violence that gained political prominence only in the 1990s was sexual and gender-based violence. The use of rape as a weapon of war in various cases pushed the UN Security Council to establish the protection of women and girls as one of the principal elements of its 'Women, Peace and Security' agenda adopted in the year 2000 via Resolution 1325. Since then, the United Nations has created the post of Special Representative of the Secretary-General to give permanent focus to the issue, and has instituted a series of annual reports that identify where these crimes are committed and advocate for steps to be taken in response. The United Nations has also begun to 'mainstream' the protection of women and girls through, for example, the deployment of women's protection advisers. Beyond the United Nations, the British government launched its Preventing Sexual Violence in Conflict Initiative which, amongst other things, has helped persuade two-thirds of the world's states to support a 'Declaration of Commitment to End Sexual Violence in Conflict'. These developments have been paralleled by a range of initiatives focused on protecting children in armed conflict. Also led by the Security Council, the United Nations has appointed a Special Representative for the protection of children, which reports on the unique protection challenges facing children and related issues such as the recruitment of child soldiers. In 2014, the UN's ambassador for the promotion of education, former UK prime minister Gordon Brown, launched a global initiative to establish a contingency fund to support the provision of education to children during humanitarian crises, be they caused by natural disasters or mass violence.

Human rights

While human rights as a whole are subject to a great deal of questioning, their higher profile has undoubtedly made an important contribution to human protection. Two aspects in particular stand out, but they are illustrative rather than definitive since the overlap is extensive and complex. First, emerging principles and practices of peer-to-peer review, where states evaluate and comment on each other's performance (mainly through the compulsory review process of the UN's Human Rights Council), create expectations about the type of steps that states ought to take in order to protect their populations from various forms of abuse, including mass violence. While the most intransigent states remain largely unmoved, there is increasing evidence that peer review activities are influencing many states and pushing them towards greater compliance with their human rights obligations due to the pressure that being 'watched' places on them. Second, over the past two decades, international society has made increasing use of permanent and ad hoc arrangements for human rights monitoring and reporting in its decision-making on mass violence. Through a variety of different mechanisms, such as independent commissions and inquiries, special rapporteurs and fact-finding missions, international society is increasingly utilising human rights mechanisms to monitor and prevent mass violence. Most obviously, this reporting helps support decision-making on mass violence by furnishing key institutions with reliable information. It also encourages states to respect human rights by raising international awareness of domestic human rights practices.

International criminal justice

The idea that some crimes are so serious that the prosecution of perpetrators should be universal has advanced significantly in the past two decades through the activities of the International Criminal Court and a series of special tribunals. These institutions have proliferated since the mid-1990s and contribute to individual perpetrators being held accountable for their actions. Proponents argue that by ending impunity such institutions help deter would-be perpetrators and also give some legal protection to the victims. The first tentative steps were taken in the mid-1990s when the Security Council established tribunals to prosecute the perpetrators of grave crimes in Bosnia and Rwanda. The Rome Statute establishing the International Criminal Court in 1998 held that the Court's jurisdiction could be invoked when a state party proved unwilling or unable to investigate evidence pointing to the commission of widespread and systematic war crimes, crimes against humanity and genocide. The Court's prosecutor can initiate proceedings in cases where he or she is able to persuade a panel of judges that a case fell under the Court's jurisdiction, where a complaint was made by a signatory state, or when a case was referred to the prosecutor by the Security Council. To date, the Court has indicted 39 individuals and counts 124 states as members – though importantly the United States, Russia and China have yet to join. While it is important to state that developments like the International Criminal Court are still embryonic, the evidence suggests that transitional justice measures make reoccurrence less likely and improve general human rights within states. It also has a deterrent effect that spills over into other countries, including those that are not (yet) members of the International Criminal Court.

Humanitarian action

The notion that civilians ought to receive humanitarian assistance in wartime dates back to the nineteenth century and was integral to the development of the humanitarian idea of providing lifesaving assistance to whomever needed it. Those rights and expectations were incorporated into international humanitarian law but their applicability gradually expanded during the 1990s. The UN Security Council began authorising peacekeeping missions to support the delivery of humanitarian aid and, in the cases of Somalia and Bosnia, authorised the use of force to achieve this end. Since then, the Security Council has regularly authorised force for these purposes. What is more, however, in successive resolutions on the protection of civilians and in substantive resolutions on crises, the Security Council has demanded that parties to armed conflict grant unfettered access to humanitarian agencies.

Regional initiatives

The foundations for Europe's engagement with civilian protection were laid in the 1970s with the Helsinki Accords. Over time, these provided the basis for a Conference on Security and Cooperation in Europe mechanism that by the 1990s incorporated specific references to protection issues, including the protection of children and protection against torture. When this was transformed into the Organisation for Security and Cooperation in Europe in 1995, it was given additional responsibility and capacities to protect human rights including the post of High Commissioner for National Minorities.

As part of its common foreign and security policy the European Union also started to develop a civilian protection role, exemplified by the French-led multinational force in the Democratic Republic of the Congo in 2003 and a range of other operations. The African Union has established a comprehensive regional system for crisis management and response that includes a specific focus on the protection of civilians from mass violence. Article 4(h) of the Union's Constitutive Act enshrines its right to intervene in the affairs of its member states in issues relating to genocide and mass atrocities. Although this article has not been formally acted upon, owing to African leaders' continuing commitment to sovereignty, the African Union's peacekeeping operation in Darfur included a civilian protection mandate and its missions in Mali, the Central African Republic and Somalia have also supported civilian protection. In Latin America, states have established a comprehensive regional human rights mechanism. Even the Southeast Asian region, which is formally committed to the principle of non-interference in the domestic affairs of states, has begun to develop its own mechanisms for promoting human rights and protection through the ASEAN Intergovernmental Commission on Human Rights. These mechanisms might not understand or pursue 'rights' in precisely the same fashion, but they do rest on a shared understanding of atrocity crimes as grave human wrongs and a commitment to the prevention of these crimes.

Responsibility to Protect

In late 2005, world leaders unanimously adopted the Responsibility to Protect (R2P) in paragraphs 138–140 of the UN World Summit Outcome Document. This commitment was subsequently reaffirmed by both the UN Security Council and the UN General Assembly, which also committed to ongoing consideration of its implementation. The Responsibility to Protect rests on three pillars. The first is the responsibility of each state to use appropriate and necessary means to protect its own populations from genocide, war crimes, ethnic cleansing and crimes against humanity (hereafter referred to collectively as 'atrocity crimes'). The second pillar refers to the commitment of the international community to encourage and help states exercise this responsibility. The third pillar refers to the international responsibility to respond through the United Nations in a timely and decisive manner when national authorities are manifestly failing to protect their populations from the four atrocity crimes. The principle was initially considered to be controversial, as it countenanced the potential use of force and other transgressions of sovereignty. Over time, however, international consensus on the principle has widened and deepened.

More tellingly, the Responsibility to Protect has become part of the working language that frames international engagement with political crises and the Security Council has referred to it in more than forty resolutions. It has reminded governments of their protection responsibilities (e.g. Resolution 2014 on Yemen); demanded active steps to protect civilians (e.g. Resolution 2139 on Syria); tasked peacekeepers with assisting governments to protect their own populations (e.g. Resolution 2085 on Mali) and demanded that perpetrators of mass violence be held legally accountable (e.g. Resolution 2211 on the Democratic Republic of the Congo). The Security Council has also connected its work on the Responsibility to Protect with its international efforts focused on preventive diplomacy and conflict prevention through such measures as the control of small arms and light weapons, the prevention of genocide, counter-terrorism and international policing. With this changing focus, debate amongst states turned to focus less on the principle of the Responsibility to Protect and more on its implementation.

Problems and challenges

The world is more likely to respond to human protection crises today than it once was, but as Syria shows we are nowhere close to solving the problem of human insecurity. Even when the normative and political context allows for it, the effective protection of populations from atrocity crimes confronts significant practical challenges. It is important to be upfront about what these challenges are.

The first point is to recognise that there are significant limits to what outsiders can do to protect people in foreign countries. Many internal conflicts are not readily susceptible to outside mediation as they are so complex and fraught with danger that they can defy easy resolution. Concerted international action can sometimes protect populations or prevent mass atrocities, but the primary determinants of violence or peace typically rest within the country itself and the disposition of its leaders. From the United Nations' perspective, this problem is compounded by the fact that it tends to be confronted only by the world's most difficult cases. Situations usually reach the UN Security Council only when others have tried, and failed, to resolve them. As a rule of thumb, where conflicts have an easy remedy, solutions tend to be found at the local, national or regional level. The world body tends to assume the lead only on those crises for which others have found no solution. In such circumstances, a modest success rate might partly reflect the sheer difficulty of the cases presented to the United Nations system.

A second challenge is that human protection operates in a world of finite global capacity and competes with other cherished norms and values for attention and resources. This problem of limited resources is compounded by a climate of financial austerity arising out of the 2008 global financial crisis. Many major donors have cut their own national budgets and have imposed austerity measures on their own populations, putting pressure on their support for the protection of people in other countries. The harsh reality, therefore, is that in the near-term, the cause of human protection will not be able to call upon significant new resources.

A third challenge is to recognise that the pursuit of human protection is politically sensitive. Human protection is both enabled and constrained by politics and can generate acute controversies and disputes by, for instance, requiring that some states be identified as being at risk of a crisis and demanding actions that some governments might object to. Often, even long-term preventive measures entail a significant degree of intrusion into the domestic affairs of states, which is not likely to be always welcome. States jealously guard their sovereignty and are sensitive to perceived incursions on their rights or criticisms of their conduct or domestic conditions. As such, they rarely invite assistance or look kindly upon external efforts to prevent atrocities within their jurisdiction. It is important to remember that the United Nations' activities are overseen by political (as opposed to judicial) organs comprised of sovereignty-wielding member states. One facet of the problem is that states sometimes judge that their own interests are best served by *not* preventing atrocity crimes. This can be seen over a wide range of cases, but perhaps none have been as striking as the Syrian example, where from 2011 the Security Council failed to act decisively as hundreds of thousands were killed and millions displaced. Historically, the United Nations has struggled to assert its primacy in such situations where the interests of powerful states, especially permanent members of the Security Council, are engaged with competing aims.

Another facet of the problem of 'political will' is that states are self-interested actors that prioritise the wellbeing of their own citizens. As such, they are generally reluctant to commit extensive resources to prevent atrocity crimes in other countries. The issue here is not whether governments support atrocity prevention as a goal, but the depth of their support relative to their other goals – including cherished domestic objectives such as healthcare and social welfare. Political and diplomatic capital is also a finite resource. Sometimes, states may judge that trade-offs have to be made to achieve the greatest good or least harm overall. For example, at the outset of the crisis in Darfur in 2003, several states decided not to press the government of Sudan too hard, fearing that this might jeopardise negotiations to end the government's war with rebels in the south – who eventually seceded and founded their own state in 2011 with the creation of South Sudan.

Conclusion

Whichever position one holds on the virtue and practicality of international action to protect humans from imminent peril, it is indisputable that the past few decades have seen a proliferation of mechanisms, institutions and practices aimed at improving protection. This has gone hand in hand with a global decline in both armed conflict and mass atrocities. Through at least eight distinct but connected streams of practice, we have seen the codification of norms of acceptable behaviour, the establishment of responsibilities for third party states and international institutions, and the emergence of a range of practices aimed towards the protection of vulnerable populations. As a result, mass violence today is typically met with complex – if not always entirely effective – responses from a range of different types of actors. Nevertheless, international practices of protection have improved markedly over the past few decades, contributing to an overall decline in both the incidence and lethality of atrocity crimes. The most important point is that this all remains unfinished business. Not only are there a number of political issues left to address, we have barely begun to scratch the surface of the practical issues connected to implementation. Questions of which strategies offer most protection in what kinds of circumstances will need to be addressed if the promise of protecting people globally is to be turned into a lasting reality.

12

Connectivity, Communications and Technology

ANDREAS HAGGMAN

In the words of Rucker (1983, 108) 'the human race is a single vast tapestry, linked by our shared food and air'. In this sense, it is correct that the entire human race is connected through the material world. It is wrong, however, to assume that such connections create any kind of unity. In international relations, when we think of humanity, we do not think of a single, homogenous, peaceful body, but of a number of distinct factions competing, coercing and cooperating to achieve their own end goals. These factions may be groupings such as ethnic, racial or religious divisions or they may be nation-states. They can also be anywhere on a scale from very large to very small. Importantly, however, none of these groupings exist independently of the individual humans within them. The individual is the basic unit at which humanity exists. In this way, individuals are symbiotic with the wider system, with each playing a role in shaping and influencing the other. Humanity consists not only of human bodies, but also of the ideas, the convictions, and the wills contained within human minds. Given this definition, what does it mean for humanity to be connected? In a physical sense, a disconnection has always been present. Each human mind is contained within a human body that exists separately from all others. It is, however, on the metaphysical plain – that of ideas, convictions, and wills – that humanity can be connected. The uniting of many individuals for a common cause, for example, represents a connection of minds leading to action. Such unity can of course arise by complete chance or through non-conscious actions. However, more powerful connections arise when the unity stems from conscious interaction. Central to the concept of connectivity, therefore, is the ability to communicate with others, which we do more and more today via digital means.

The internet

The internet is a collection of connected computer networks, linking tens of billions of devices across the globe. These include servers, personal computers, mobile telephones and video game consoles. Increasingly, other devices are also being connected to the internet, such as cars and domestic appliances. Devices connected to the internet are connected to each other through network links. These links can be either physical cables or wireless connections. Physical cables come in an array of shapes and sizes, ranging from small cables used to directly link two computers together, to large undersea cables connecting continents. Wireless connections, though not visible, work on similar scales, from Wi-Fi networks in the home to links to satellites in space. Communications on the internet may traverse any combination of these network links, and they have become a hotly contested topic in international relations.

Though often used synonymously, the internet is not the same as the 'world wide web' (www). The web is just one of many services operating on the internet, accessed through a web browser to display documents containing text, images and other media. Examples of other services on the internet include email, voice and video communications and online gaming. The distinction between the internet and the web is important as conflating technological concepts can have severe repercussions in the area of laws and regulations where precise wording is paramount. Throughout this chapter, the internet should be envisaged as the whole gamut of connected digital devices and services. When individual devices or services are discussed in detail, it will be made explicitly clear which device or service is being talked about.

Digital commerce

Commerce is a cornerstone of human interaction. Throughout history the trade of goods and services has provided opportunities for humans to connect and necessitated methods of communication. Bartering, agreements and contracts have been made possible through verbal, written and visual means. With the exponential growth of the internet, it was inevitable that merchants and private traders would adopt this channel for commercial purposes. The shift of commerce from offline to online has repercussions for human interaction and communication. In the modern economy, commerce involves a long supply chain and multiple agents that affect the production and transport of goods. To take a product from idea to conception to finally reaching purchasers requires first raw materials, then a manufacturer, a distributor, a seller and a customer (with possibly a marketer or two thrown in for good measure). Each step in this process requires individual human beings interacting with one another, especially at the point of sale. Through digital commerce, however, many of the middlemen in the process can be eliminated. Customers can purchase goods directly from the manufacturer with a few clicks or taps without ever (directly) interacting with another human being. To buy a television, for example, would previously have required a person visiting a more generalised retail outlet such as an electronics store, speaking with a sales representative and making the purchase. The retail store would in turn have procured the television from a distributor, who would have acquired it from the manufacturer. Thanks to the internet, however, a prospective buyer can now simply visit the manufacturer's web page, purchase the television and have it delivered to their door, effectively cutting out most of the traditional commerce chain and with very limited interpersonal communication.

In some ways this method of conducting commercial activities is reminiscent of trade before the advent of mass production. From the days of the ancient Athenians gathered in the Agora, a central square for meetings and business, commerce was typically a highly personal affair. The public marketplace as a central site for commerce has now been re-enabled by the internet through websites like Amazon and eBay. Here, manufacturers and producers can reach customers directly, without requiring an established long chain of suppliers and agents. Though Amazon may be analogous to the Agora, a perhaps better example of how digital commerce affects international relations is the Silk Road. In ancient times, the Silk Road was a 6,000-kilometre trade route connecting Europe and Asia. It not only facilitated commercial trade but also enabled the flow of ideas, and even religions, between cultures. It was in effect a widely dispersed network of traders and outposts through which flowed both goods and information. Importantly, these flows were embodied through personal interaction between those who travelled along the Silk Road.

The ancient Silk Road shares its name with a modern digital counterpart. First established in 2011, Silk Road was an online marketplace that could be accessed and operated using software provided by the 'Tor network' in the form of a special web browser that preserves users' anonymity. This allowed shoppers to make purchases without revealing any personal information, including bank card details, as payments were made in bitcoin – a decentralised digital currency. Vendors operated under pseudonyms. The anonymity aspects of the transaction process differentiate the modern Silk Road from the ancient one, exemplifying the depersonalisation of commerce in the internet era. Silk Road and Tor are also emblematic of the growth of a part of the internet called the 'dark web' that can only be accessed by specific software, or specific means such as access passwords. The effect of this in the sphere of international relations is most starkly evident in the police operation that eventually shut down Silk Road. A holding page displayed after the seizure of Silk Road's website was emblazoned with the crests of a number of US and European law enforcement agencies, bordered by the flags of 13 countries between them speaking 11 languages. The internet has provided a place for shady activities, and the task of combating these has in turn taken on an international scope.

Digital communications

At least as old as the idea of commerce is the idea of communicating with other humans across geographical divides. A primary means for doing so is through the written word. The most direct of these means is the letter, because it is sent from one individual to another individual carrying a specific message. As such, letters represent a key connection between humans. In the digital age, email and instant messaging have usurped letters as the primary means of written communication, with hundreds of billions of digital messages sent from one person to another each day. The process of mailing a letter resembles the protracted commercial chain described in the section above. There is a sender who authors the letter and drops it in a post box. A postal worker then collects the letter and brings it to a sorting centre where a machine (though previously a human) directs the letter towards the right address. The letter is then transported by land, sea and/or air to a distribution centre where more sorting happens. Finally, a delivery person deposits it at the stipulated address, where the receiver accepts and reads the letter. Through a convoluted series of middlemen, the sender and receiver can thereby communicate with each other. With email and instant messaging, the human middlemen are completely removed from the process. The only step between sender and receiver is some technological wrangling that ensures the email or message arrives intact at the correct destination. In this way, sender and receiver can communicate directly and, importantly, with near instantaneousness. A written letter can take anything from a day to a week, or more, to arrive at its destination. By comparison, an email usually takes a matter of seconds, regardless of how much of the planet it has to traverse. Even emails to the International Space Station take only a few seconds to transmit.

You may take the speed at which you can message others for granted. But it is worth putting this in perspective with a historical comparison. According to legend, when Martin Luther set in motion the Protestant Reformation in 1517, he did so by nailing a polemical document to a church door in Wittenberg. This act began a process of violent upheaval that culminated in 1648 with the end of the cataclysmic Thirty Years' War. The full effects of Luther's public posting thus took some 130 years to come to fruition. The modern equivalent of his document would be a social media post. Given that digital communications travel with almost no delay, messages can be quickly delivered to millions of people to spread ideas and organise movements. Perhaps the best example of this is the Arab Spring, also called the Twitter Revolution due to the widespread use of social media to propagate ideas and organise a response. While the Thirty Years' War took over a hundred years to materialise and play out, the revolution in Tunisia took just a few weeks. It is clear that digital communications have played some role in speeding up such events.

Reach

One important theory, only made possible by the digitisation of commerce and communications, is that of the 'long tail' (Anderson 2004). In a nutshell, the theory suggests that because products can be distributed and sold more cheaply, vendors can now stock a broader range of goods each of which appeals to a small customer base (the tail), rather than focus on a narrow range of goods that appeal to a large number of customers (the head). For example, the virtual shelves of Amazon contain almost every type of product conceivable, whereas the physical shelves of a retail outlet are limited by the space available. Through the internet, niche products can appear alongside mainstream ones. With a literally global audience reachable through the internet, even the most obscure ideas (about, for instance, political ideology, religious convictions, business ventures) can find someone to appeal to. There are both benefits and drawbacks to this phenomenon.

On the one hand, people living under repressive regimes may be limited in their ability to communicate both within and outside their country. With digital technologies this repression can be sidestepped, allowing the expression of grievances and bringing to light issues that might otherwise be shrouded from view. The Arab Spring, as discussed above, is a case in point. In Egypt, the Mubarak regime even switched off the country's internet services in acknowledgement of the role they were playing in the organisation of protests. The fact that protesters were nevertheless able to bring down Mubarak's regime shows how the internet can empower people to overcome repression. This is also true in cases where communication is not actively repressed, but simply ignored or lost. With a 'long tail' to communicate to, people have a greater chance of making themselves heard. With greater reach of communications, the presentation of a novel idea is more likely to garner support, dissent, or comments than an idea presented to a smaller audience. Consider, for example, 'crowdfunding' platforms, where budding entrepreneurs can present their ideas to the public and appeal for funding to make them a reality. The idea does not have to be a physical product, it can also be the manifestation of a political or religious conviction. The internet makes it possible for ideas to gain traction that in the past might have fallen by the wayside. In this way, digital communications can increase shared knowledge and foster conversations that lead to the reformulation and improvement of ideas.

On the other hand, the long tail also gives a voice to unsavoury constituents of society. Just as the repressed can make themselves heard, extremists may find a foothold in the murky depths of the internet where bad ideas can be picked up and amplified. Perhaps the most notorious beneficiary of this has been the Islamic State group (also known as ISIS, ISIL and Daesh). Much has been made of their mastery of the internet to radicalise and recruit new members and spread propaganda – particularly through social media. There is no shortage of people, including Muslims, who renounce the group and actively seek to combat its message, but in the online world the majority view does not necessarily eliminate others being expressed. Previously, a bad idea might have faded into obscurity for lack of an audience, but with a long tail even the most heinous ideas can find adherents.

Affordability

More people than ever before are partaking in commerce and communications thanks to digitisation lowering the barrier to entry. The traditional lengthy logistics chain to move products adds more cost. At each step along the chain the handling party requires a fee, which will be passed on to the customer by increasing the price of the product. By shortening the logistics chain and cutting out middlemen, manufacturers make cost savings. Although the cost of producing a product might stay the same, savings can be made when it comes to distributing, selling and marketing the product. These savings can be passed on to customers in the form of a lower price, with the manufacturer maintaining the same profit margin. This lower price can potentially attract customers who were previously barred by high prices. The digitisation of commerce can thus open up markets by making products more affordable.

The digital communications chain has been shortened in similar ways, with the same sort of cost benefits. However, the monetary cost of communications was never really high enough to pose a barrier to entry. The benefits of the digitisation of communications are not primarily price, but rather the lowering of the skills required to partake. Communicating via letters as outlined above requires the ability to both read and write. Until the spread of mass education in the twentieth century, these skills were limited to a relatively small subset of humanity. Now, since literacy levels are high in most developed states, digital communications have the power to make a difference for people with learning difficulties or in areas where education is limited. Courtesy of video messaging applications, real-time long-distance correspondence can be achieved via face-to-face communication. This bypasses any need to be able to read and write, requiring only the interpersonal communication skills every person has. It does of course require a device, such as a laptop or smartphone, on which to run the application. However, devices are becoming cheaper, and a single device can be shared and passed around. Shared ownership not only spreads the initial cost of purchasing the device, but is in itself a means for people to connect with one another. The ability of a family to gather around a laptop and video call with relatives on the other side of the world is a powerful way to maintain relationships otherwise challenged by distance and time.

Those previously separated by geographical distance and/or access to means of communication are now able to reconnect with lost acquaintances and even forge relationships with strangers on the other side of the globe. In this way, digital communications have the potential to increase humanity's homogeneity. If everyone is connected, divisions between locations, races, nationalities, classes and wealth can be blurred. Rather than emphasise the things that have traditionally separated humanity, it is possible to concentrate on those things that unite us: the shared values that make us human.

Reliance

Digital devices are inseparable from the new logistics and communications that are increasingly underpinning human activity. Devices come in a wide array of shapes and sizes and have an equally wide range of functions. Probably the most ubiquitous and familiar devices are personal computers and smartphones. For many people it is impossible to imagine life without the instant connectivity and wealth of information provided by the internet and accessed through such devices. Devices have thus become an integral, perhaps indispensable, part of human life. As these devices permeate society, it is conceivable that humans cede some of their humanity to the digital realm. Using the internet for many of our basic human functions, both individual and societal, effectively requires the internet to make up part of what it means to be human. In 1945 Vannevar Bush introduced his idea of a 'memex', which he described as

> a device in which an individual stores all his books, records, and communications, and which is mechanized so that it may

be consulted with exceeding speed and flexibility. It is an enlarged intimate supplement to his memory.

(Bush 1945)

Eerily prescient, Bush's description accurately describes smartphones. The implication of this is that, thanks to such a device, the limited human mind can be freed up to perform the uniquely human capacities to imagine, associate and experiment.

Of course, such reliance on technology can have negative consequences. If the technology was to disappear or be denied to us, we could potentially lose some of our humanity. The example of Egypt's internet services being cut off demonstrates the large-scale vulnerability of the technology, as do the cyber-attacks on Estonia in 2007 that lost citizens access to essential services such as banking. Consider Facebook, a social networking platform with over one billion users. Facebook, and its subsidiary Instagram, are used today as photograph repositories. Hundreds of millions of people upload photos as they are taken, effectively replacing the physical photo albums that older generations typically kept in their homes. Facebook thereby becomes an archive of visual memories. If the internet malfunctioned, Facebook, and the memories it contains, would be inaccessible. Memories, both individual and societal, are a key constituent of what makes us human: losing them would amount to losing some of our humanity. The example of memories shows how over-reliance on technology for important human functions may be unwise.

Control

The issue of internet control has recently come to the fore, chiefly due to revelations in documents leaked by the whistle-blower Edward Snowden in 2013. The documents showed the extent of the United States' intelligence capabilities in cyberspace, many of which were predicated on the fact that most internet traffic originates from, terminates in, or transits through servers based within America. This of course gives the United States a huge advantage, as it enjoys unprecedented access to the flow of information on the internet. Recognising this disparity, and also reacting to alleged infringements of their own citizens' rights, several countries have called strongly for the nationalisation of the internet. By this they mean moving to a model in which countries ensure data stays within their own borders. Where this is not possible, data should be handled in accordance with the law of its origin state, backed up by an international governance framework. Though this could redress the imbalance of power, it also has the potential to Balkanise the internet. Many of the benefits of the internet rely on the technology being uniformly functioning and accessible across disparate geographical areas. A Balkanised internet would inevitably produce a range of operating standards that might well be difficult to integrate. China is an example of a country that does operate a national internet policy, although for different reasons to those expressed above. Through the 'Great Firewall', the Chinese government blocks access to sources of uncensored information such as foreign news outlets and prominent websites like Facebook, Google and Wikipedia. The full benefits of the internet are clearly not available to the bulk of Chinese users, showing how control of the technology can be a powerful tool for controlling a population.

Conclusion

The internet is a truly revolutionary technology which has empowered individuals to connect with other individuals, systems to connect with other systems, and individuals to connect with systems on scales previously unknown. Though issues such as those around reliance and control demonstrate that modern technology is still a work in progress, the key point to remember is that through participation in logistics and communications, digital or otherwise, each person has the potential to affect the process and progress of international relations. Interacting with other humans through the written and spoken word and through trade is what makes humanity flourish. The internet has made this possible for more people, in more locations, more of the time, more quickly. We are therefore connected not merely by shared food and air, but also by a shared capability to meaningfully shape both our own lives and those of others.

13

Voices of the People

JEFFREY HAYNES

The people referred to in this chapter are those citizens who want more say in what their rulers do and are not content with current political arrangements – even in the context of an existing democracy. Popular protests have been an issue in international relations for a very long time. An early example was the French Revolution of 1789 when the old order was overturned and replaced, at least for a while, with a popular, revolutionary government. Today, popular movements are not only growing in frequency but also in importance due to how they shape international relations. When considered alongside the availability of instant communication via the internet, as explored in the previous chapter, the phenomenon of ordinary people mobilising to bring about meaningful – and sometimes abrupt – political change raises important questions for IR about how change occurs at the domestic level and the wider implications of that change at regional and global levels.

Change in a globalising world

In today's world there are numerous examples of popular demand for political change. They generally arise at a time when politicians seem unable to deliver on their promises. Take, for example, the year 2008 – described by Amartya Sen (2009) as 'a year of crises'. First, there was a food crisis that impacted on poorer consumers, especially across African states, as the staples of their diet often became unaffordable. Second, there was a spike in oil prices that raised the cost of fuel and petroleum products globally. Finally, in the autumn of 2008, there was an economic crisis in the United States that quickly spread, compounding prior issues, and the global economy faltered. What does economic downturn have to do with the 'voices of people'? The answer lies in the newly interconnected nature of our world.

For the bulk of the world's population, daily life is characterised by easy and speedy communications. Of course, some areas of the developing world still suffer from poverty and infrastructure issues and so lack the benefits of global communications. That said, it is not uncommon to find mobile phones, which are ever cheaper, proliferating in the poorest regions of the world – such as across sub-Saharan Africa. Improved communications are a fundamental aspect of a wider phenomenon: globalisation. Globalisation enables us, via the communications revolution, to learn quickly and consistently about events all over the world, almost as soon as they happen. Globalisation has in a real sense shrunk the world and made it interactive. When something happens in one country, it can quickly affect others. This may be an economic matter, such as the global economic downturn referred to above, but terrorism is also an issue.

The era of deepening and sustained globalisation coincides with global events following the end of the Cold War. When the Soviet Union dissolved in the early 1990s it gave way to a range of newly independent post-communist states that redrew the map from central Europe to central Asia. Fifteen new states were created, including Russia. It also initiated a dynamic phase of globalisation which affected our understanding of international relations in a number of ways. First, the end of the Cold War threw the study of international relations into a state of flux. Soon after the Cold War ended, there was talk of a new international order. This reflected a widespread optimism that there could be improved international co-operation and a fresh commitment to strengthening key international organisations, especially the United Nations. The aim was to achieve various goals, including better, more equitable development; reducing gender inequalities; defusing armed conflicts; lessening human rights abuses, and tackling environmental degradation and destruction. In short, to manage multiple global interdependencies it would be necessary to improve processes of bargaining, negotiation and consensus-seeking, involving both states and various non-state actors, including the United Nations.

It soon became clear, however, that there was a lack of ideas as to how the desired international improvements might be achieved. During the 1990s there were serious outbreaks of international conflict. Many were religious, ethnic or nationalist conflicts that spilled over into neighbouring states. When these events occurred, local or national issues quickly spiralled into regional or international crises. Examples of these include conflicts in Africa – in Burundi, Haiti, Rwanda and Somalia – and also Europe, where Yugoslavia tore itself apart during the 1990s, eventually splitting into seven states. All these led to serious, and in many cases still unresolved, humanitarian crises requiring external intervention. These conflicts showed how difficult it is proving to move from the problems of the old international order that had characterised the Cold War to a new era marked by international peace, prosperity and cooperation.

'Colour' and 'umbrella' revolutions

Between 2000 and 2005, a series of popular protests, which later became known as 'colour revolutions', swept away authoritarian and semi-authoritarian regimes in Serbia, Georgia, Kyrgyzstan and Ukraine. The common trigger for these revolutions was an attempt by leaders to falsify election results in their favour. Via various non-violent regime-change strategies, the protests sought to change political configurations in a democratic direction. The 'Orange Revolution' in Ukraine was archetypical. In 2004–2005, the Orange Revolution – so called because this was the colour worn by many protesters to illustrate their solidarity – helped bring to power a pro-Western president, Viktor Yushchenko, who defeated his rival Viktor Yanukovych in a repeat run-off election. Protesters claimed that the integrity of the initial election, which Yanukovych 'won', was undermined by massive corruption, voter intimidation and direct electoral fraud. Subsequently, thousands of protesters demonstrated daily, in events characterised by widespread civil disobedience and labour strikes.

Events in Ukraine echoed wider examples of vote rigging, voter intimidation and electoral irregularities that characterised many countries in Central and Eastern Europe following the collapse of Communist governments in the 1990s. In addition, the colour revolutions demonstrated the increasing volatility of international relations, the spread of ideas and the associated demands by citizens for political and economic change. In some countries, the colour revolution swept away the authoritarian or semi-authoritarian regime. In others, it did not. Thus, the issue of the 'voices of the people' is not just about success but also failure and the causes of failure. Today's political and economic protests tend to have both longevity and wide ramifications. At the very least they change the relationship between ruled and rulers. If harnessed fully they can lead to profound political upheaval.

In other Central and Eastern European states, attempts to replicate successful strategies in the earlier colour revolutions, such as peaceful protests, public demands for democratisation, the use of election monitoring and post-election mass protests to contest fraudulent elections, failed. Moreover, in those states where no serious attempt to launch a colour revolution was made, governments took action to avoid the possibility of regime change by espousing policies sometimes referred to as 'anti-colour insurance'. For example, rulers in Russia, Belarus and Azerbaijan adopted strategies such as strongly attacking local, independent civil society and political activists as 'foreign agents', unfairly limiting electoral competition and portraying colour revolution ideas and techniques as subversive and alien to the country's culture and traditions. Thus, to understand why some protests succeeded and others failed, we need to take into account the ability of authoritarian regimes to prevent democratisation and significant economic reform. This amounted to the ability of the regimes to study democracy promotion techniques at the heart of protests and directly combat these techniques. As there was variation in activists' choice of strategies across the various protesting nations, rulers' responses also differed according to the perceived seriousness of the threat to regime survival and the regime's strength in relation to the opposition it faced.

Although not connected by geography, time or culture to the colour revolutions, Hong Kong's 'Umbrella Revolution' (also known as 'Occupy Central' and the 'Umbrella Movement') in 2014 similarly involved popular protests against authoritarian rule and lack of democracy. The name 'umbrella' refers to the fact that many activists held umbrellas as a symbol of protest during the events. Hong Kong is a semi-autonomous island territory and a former British colony. It passed from British to Chinese control in 1997 and part of the deal was that China would allow at least a measure of democracy to continue. China, of course, is ruled by a Communist government and is a one-party state that strictly limits political competition. Protesters believed that the Chinese government was going back on an agreement to allow Hong Kong to have open elections and was progressively governing Hong Kong more like mainland China. There were also underlying economic issues, with Hong Kong's citizens experiencing some of the highest levels of wealth and income inequality in the world. For several weeks, Hong Kong's ultra-modern business centre was transformed into a conflict zone, with up to 200,000 protestors confronted by police in riot gear. The protests eventually fizzled out, with the protesters not only failing to persuade the government of China to accede to their demands but also experiencing dwindling support as people grew tired of the disruption to their lives. As was the case in some Central and Eastern European countries, this highlights the ability of entrenched rulers to stay in power without making significant concessions. Yet it is also clear that the protests have had an impact on how many Hong Kong citizens view their political future. This may be significant in years to come as a large proportion of the protesters were students and young people.

Although separated by a decade, the colour and 'Umbrella' revolutions were both indicative of a wide sense of disconnection from power. When this is matched by an ability for people to use their voice to influence political and economic outcomes, mass action can quickly follow. Here, we can see the double-edged impact of globalisation at work. On the one hand, the end of the Cold War unleashed the forces of democratisation and economic reform that many authoritarian elites did their best to prevent – sometimes with success. On the other hand, ideas set free by the end of the Cold War found resonance in diverse cultural contexts and expression in the form of street protests that reflected the power of the voice of the people. In fact, so extensive was the spread of such thinking that even established democracies in the West were affected.

The Occupy movement

The United States is a country that allows its citizens full participation in politics – a place where the people determine the direction of the nation via their mass participation in elections. Such slogans as 'land of the free' and 'anyone can be president' come to mind. But, like many other similar political regimes it faces degenerating into a system that favours the rich. In the US today, the top one per cent of people are in receipt of 21 per cent of national income. Over time, this proportion has been changing for the worse. In the 1970s the top one per cent's income share was 'only' about 10 per cent. The issue became acute following the 2008 financial crisis, which laid bare the degree of inequality in American society and the lack of influence over public policy felt by the majority of the population (see Picketty 2014). Two million Americans lost their homes in the so-called 'sub-prime mortgage' collapse, which then spiralled into a much bigger crisis affecting the entire financial system. The US government bailed out some large corporations and banks to the tune of hundreds of billions of dollars to prevent the whole financial system from collapsing. This was accompanied by austerity measures that eroded benefits and public services as the government had less money available due to the economic crash. This general pattern was also seen in other liberal economies, including the United Kingdom. Hence, a picture emerged in some circles that the government had given money to the richest and taken money from the poorest. The Occupy movement was a diffuse and diverse reaction to this perception. It was a reaction against the ineffectiveness of the traditional tools of democratic politics and government such as political parties, elections and lobbying.

The Occupy movement protested against Wall Street, home of the US financial industry, as a symbol of 'unearned' privilege and wealth – even though it was politicians who were coming up with and implementing austerity cuts. The movement began in Zuccotti Park, near Wall Street, on 17 September 2011. Critics noted the activists' lack of a clear set of demands and their tendency to only highlight grievances. However, a clear set of values did emerge:

- Solidarity – society's institutions should aim to maximise mutual benefits.
- Diversity – diverse solutions to pressing problems.
- Equity – in terms of solutions and distribution.
- Control – especially self-management, freedom and autonomy.

Following the emergence of the Occupy movement, there were hundreds of similar occupations all over the world – though mainly in the United States and Western Europe. Years later, it remains clear that the problems that prompted these protests have not gone away. However, much of the energy has dissipated from the movement. This is partly because the protesters could not develop and articulate a common platform that would enable a clear pathway to action to be advanced (which would have been the priority of a political party or revolutionary movement). Instead, they just produced a slogan, 'We are the 99%', highlighting the growth of inequality since the 1970s that disproportionately affects women, young people and minorities. The Occupy movement splintered following the decision of the mayor of New York to break up the protest in November 2011. Without leaders or specific demands, it turned into an unfocused protest against everything that was 'wrong' with the world.

While the Occupy movement's social critique resonates with many people, the question remains whether it offers a practical and achievable means to accomplish goals. How best to mobilise people to alleviate poverty? Many would argue that action aimed at poverty alleviation – for example, building public housing projects or preventing cuts to food stamps – has to involve mainstream politics. Critics claim that the new generation of activists may have forgotten, abandoned or overlooked the progressive ideal of a reform-minded government raising up the poor and mitigating discrimination. What is clear is that the Occupy movement has given voice to concerns about systemic divisions in the economic and social structure in the United States and other Western states. These concerns have touched a nerve that continues to resonate – much like the aftermath of the Umbrella Revolution in Hong Kong. And, also like Hong Kong, the adverse reaction of certain political leaders and senior police officers suggested to some the hypocrisy of those with power. Post-2008, it is now common for politicians seeking election in the United States to profess their support for 'main street' rather than Wall Street as a means of rallying popular support.

The Arab Spring

The Arab Spring is a collective term for a series of political protests that began in late 2010 in Tunisia. Over the next few years, a number of countries saw their political situation greatly affected as protests broke out across the Middle East and North Africa against the corrupt and authoritarian leaders that were typical of the region. While Arab peoples live in very different states, the protesters were united by a feeling of alienation from political power. Despite this, it is unclear whether the Arab Spring events will lead to more democracy in the region. That is, there has been no uniformity in what subsequently occurred. In some cases, old dictators remain in power, while in others new leaders acquired power via the ballot box. In Egypt, things are more complex still as there have been several changes of power. What is clear is that rebellions occurred that have reshaped the region. Libya's Gaddafi regime was overthrown by rebels aided by international intervention in the form of a NATO bombing campaign. There were also major political upheavals in Syria and Yemen and smaller, though still noteworthy, expressions of dissent in other states such as Bahrain, Algeria and Morocco.

The events of the Arab Spring highlighted the importance of stability, security and regime longevity. They also directed attention to the prospects for democratisation and economic and social improvements for 'ordinary' citizens. The pressing question is whether governments can deal with the challenge of fast-growing populations demanding more jobs and improved welfare. This is almost certainly the key concern of the tens of thousands of people in the Middle East and North Africa who were active and vocal in the Arab Spring protests. Such people – like their counterparts elsewhere in the world – expect political change that improves their lives. However, while Arab peoples have been lumped together in accounts of the Arab Spring due to their apparently common political and economic plight, it is important to note that widespread divisions characterise the region. This involves conflict between different religious expressions, including intra-Muslim struggles (Iraq, Syria, Bahrain) and Muslim–Christian (Tunisia, Egypt) tensions. Despite the coming together of people of all faiths in the Arab Spring protests, sectarian tensions and conflict have followed. The stand-out case here is Syria, which in 2011 spiralled into a deeply polarising sectarian conflict that has since been fuelled by regional (Iran–Saudi Arabia) and also global (US–Russia) rivalries. The conflict has caused the deaths of hundreds of thousands and the displacement of millions. It represents the extreme edge of what was unleashed by the Arab Spring.

Not since the end of communism a generation ago has the role of religion in democratisation and post-authoritarian political arrangements been so centrally and consistently to the fore. The Middle East and North Africa are regions often characterised as places where religion – especially Islam – is a key component of demands for political and social change. However, it is not obvious what the role of religion has been in the Arab Spring. Across the

Middle East and North Africa, identifiable religious actors have been, and continue to be, conspicuous in anti-authoritarian and pro-democratisation movements. But there appears to be no clear pattern in terms of outcomes related to democratisation. What we do know is that rebellions in Egypt and Tunisia unseated incumbent governments and initially ushered in recognisably democratic elections which, in both cases, Islamists won. Yet, we saw an apparent transition to a recognisably democratic regime only in Tunisia. In Egypt, the primary struggle was between democrats and non-democrats. Over time, this shifted to a fight between secularists and the Islamists who had triumphed in a popular election. As things became polarised the military felt emboldened to crack down on the Islamists, who were perceived by the secularists as following a more extreme version of political Islam than was tolerable for Egyptian society at large. Eventually, the elected president Mohamed Morsi was ousted from power in a coup led by military chief Abdel Fattah el-Sisi. Sisi was subsequently elected as president via the ballot box in June 2014, receiving a popular mandate.

Overall, evidence suggests that the likelihood of the Arab countries of the Middle East and North Africa taking a clear path to democratisation is currently poor and the chances of widespread democratic consolidation still worse. In this midst of the picture is the serious proliferation of transnational terrorism that is explored in the next chapter. The unwelcome but most likely outcome is a gradual slide into entrenched and long-term political instability culminating in some cases in state failure, with serious ramifications for regional and international instability. The plight of Syria is a worrying case in point. In this context, the voices of the people of the Arab Spring can be seen to have had a very mixed set of results.

Conclusion

The aim of the chapter was to show how, in various parts of the world, the voices of ordinary people – intensified and encouraged by globalisation and the attendant communications revolution – challenged the status quo. In some cases this resulted in significant regime change; in others, rulers were able to hang on to power. While the picture may appear more gloomy than cheerful in terms of evidence of change, it is important to understand that none of the examples of the protests covered in this chapter are definitively concluded. Unlike earlier revolutions – for example, those in France, Russia and China, all of which ushered in definitive regime changes – none of the examples covered in this chapter amount to clear-cut jumps from one political system to another. What we can observe is the connectedness and shared ideas that collectively characterise today's popular protests. We can expect to see more such protests in the years to come as people across the world raise their voices and demand change.

14

Transnational Terrorism

KATHERINE E. BROWN

As had been explored in previous chapters, globalisation has brought with it not only unprecedented opportunities and progress in human development but also greater risks. Events in one economy can quickly spiral to others and the same can be said of social, cultural and political events. One theme that we have not explored in detail is how terrorism has evolved in the era of globalisation. Rather like the way in which the dark web piggybacks on the internet, a shadow side of globalisation gives criminal and violent groups the ability to spread their message and widen their operations. The impact of this shadow form of globalisation alters not only the organisation, resources and methods of such groups but also their reasoning and motivations. Under these conditions we have seen the proliferation of transnational terrorist groups with globalised agendas whose operations involve many countries or have ramifications that transcend national borders.

What is transnational terrorism?

Terrorism, whether transnational or not, is a highly contested arena. To date there is very little consensus regarding its definition. Disagreements emerge over the purpose and function, the perpetrators, the victims, the legitimacy and the methods and targeting of terrorist actors. Perhaps the most widely accepted attribute of the term 'terrorism' is that it is derogatory and a sign of disapproval. Typically, labelling a group as terrorist negatively affects our perception of the group's legitimacy, legality and how they should be addressed. Therefore, how we differentiate a terrorist group from any other group is important. For the purposes of this chapter, terrorism is understood as the use or threat of violence by non-state actors to influence citizens or governments in the pursuit of political or social change. This is not only a semantic or academic debate; the label gives states considerable power to act and use violence against a group and it significantly guides how a state should act. Wrong definitions can lead to flawed counter-terrorism strategies.

Moreover, as states cannot agree on the definition, they argue over both the nature and the cause of terrorism as well as who can be called a terrorist. With no agreed international law governing state responses, they struggle to work together to remove the threats. According to Acharya (2008), this permits states to act like vigilantes, or cowboys in the Wild West, on the global stage.

Rapoport (2004) divided the history of terrorist groups into four successive waves, each characterised by the global politics of the day. He noted that nationalist and anti-colonial groups emerged with a force at the end of the first and second world wars, while anti-communist and anarchist movements proliferated during the Cold War. Today it is argued that a new, or fifth, wave of modern terrorist groups are both products of and challenges to key ideas associated with globalisation, thereby giving terrorism a transnational character. It is important to note that some terrorist groups in the past had transnational goals, but they lacked the tools of the modern world to widen and deepen their message. Today's transnational terrorism is seen to operate in many states, utilising the 'shadow globalisation' flows of people, weapons and information to further their cause. The causes of this new type of terrorism reflect the deepening of human interconnectedness worldwide. Peter Mandaville (2007), writing on one of the first groups to be designated as a 'fifth wave' terrorist group, Al-Qaeda, argued that their initial success was because they operated a global technology, mythology and ideology. Specifically, it was the mythology of military success against the United States in the form of the spectacular attacks of 9/11 and then drawing it into costly military activities abroad. Combined with the franchise-like nature of their organisation, they were able to claim responsibility for attacks all over the world by financially, logistically and materially assisting smaller groups that affiliated themselves to the organisation. Such affiliations were possible because Al-Qaeda promoted a global ideology that linked local causes together via an image of world politics that presented Muslims worldwide as victims of Western oppression. These components enabled them to function and replicate on a global scale.

Today's terrorism is therefore transnational in cause, operation and effect. Its essential features ensure its importance within international relations because it represents a whole new security concern for states: the risk of attack does not just come from other states (war) but from mobile criminal groups that move between states and are dispersed globally (transnational terrorism). States perceive this new wave of terrorism as threatening core elements of their sovereignty – their capacity, legitimacy and autonomy within a particular jurisdiction. This all-encompassing threat has led to a range of responses. These have included the creation of new criminal offences, broadened legal definitions of terrorism, the granting of greater powers of detention and arrest, as well as improving funding for state agencies involved in countering terrorism. In light of the transnational elements, states have also sought closer cross-border cooperation between government agencies, most notably in policing and intelligence, in order to prevent the spread of terrorism. States have also reacted to the new threats by seeking to prevent or disrupt the emergence of ideas that might support terrorist violence through anti-radicalisation initiatives. These are sometimes referred to as 'soft measures'. Overseas these include supporting development goals of other countries to facilitate their stabilisation and the production of moderate voices in politics. Within domestic jurisdictions, 'soft' counter-extremism policies include placing greater emphasis on challenging particular extreme ideas in schools and universities, monitoring citizens for signs of radicalisation and making illegal the ownership and distribution of material that glorifies violence. These forms of intervention bring the state more directly into contact with the everyday lives of citizens, often regardless of any laws broken. Such efforts demonstrate how terrorism is a concern for human security as well as state security because of the manner in which it affects everyday life.

Motivation and goals

Individuals join terrorist groups for a variety of personal and political reasons. They may join because most of their friends have, or for the feeling that membership of the organisation brings benefits. For example, the group Islamic State (also known as Daesh, ISIS and ISIL) seeks to establish a new theologically driven state in the Middle East and promises fighters from all over the world better living conditions and pay than they might achieve in their home countries. The ability to travel across borders more freely because of globalisation and the economic resources available to Islamic State in the form of oil make this possible. Individuals may also join a terrorist organisation because they strongly empathise and identify with the group even if they are not directly affected by the cause. Global online media can facilitate this identification by giving a cause a global appeal. It is important to note that what motivates individuals to join and remain in transnational terrorist organisations is not necessarily the same as the wider goals of those groups.

A key way of understanding why individuals join and remain part of transnational terrorist groups is radicalisation theory. Radicalisation is understood to be 'everything that happens before the bomb goes off' (Neumann 2013). It suggests that there are pathways to becoming a radical or terrorist and that it is a dynamic and very individualised process. Because of its individual nature, there is no single terrorist profile in today's transnational world, even in particular countries. Terrorists may be female, married, old, rich, have children – or not. Attempts to profile behaviours have therefore not been successful. The New York Police Department produced one of the early guides for 'spotting' radicalisation, which led to some seemingly bizarre characteristics (inability to grow pot plants, enjoying camping out) being identified as 'signs' of radicalisation (Silber and Bhatt 2007). The signs were problematic because they were so broad in their scope that almost everyone was potentially a suspect. What radicalisation research does show is that a quest for identity and greater significance in the world together with empathy for those who are suffering makes an individual more vulnerable to terrorist messages that appear to offer solutions (Silke 2008). Research also shows that an individual with friends or family involved with terrorism or supportive of terrorist views is more likely to join a terrorist organisation than someone with no connections at all (Wiktorowicz 2006). As a result, transnational lone-wolf actors are extremely rare despite their high profile and the media attention they receive.

At the group level, goals are also transnational. This is best illustrated by looking at Al-Qaeda and Islamic State. These groups utilise a global religious language to create an understanding of global politics that divides the world in two. On one side is the world of Islam. This is a place of goodness, where religious laws are upheld and Muslims are not oppressed. On the other side is the world of war where Muslims are oppressed by unjust and tyrannical leaders. They argue that, because of the global connection Muslims have with each other as a community of believers (Umma), all Muslims should join them in their fight against the 'Oppressors', regardless of where they live. They also argue that because the 'Oppressors' are everywhere and attack Muslims everywhere, their cause and fight is global. They refer to the 'near enemy' (local governments) and the 'far enemy' (governments of global powers) as possible aggressors against whom a member of their organisation might fight. This enables them to tap into local political grievances and give them a global religious veneer, or to highlight global incidents and claim that they are related to their local cause. What is notable is the degree to which such an understanding of the world replicates (or is replicated by) some Western governments' thinking that also sees the world as 'either with us or against us'.

It is important to note that the logic of worldwide oppression that shapes Islamic State and Al-Qaeda thinking is not representative of the bulk of the world's Muslim population and is widely condemned by Islamic scholars. It is also important to note that while most of the coverage of terrorist events seems to focus on high profile events in Western states, the majority of those killed in terrorist attacks worldwide since 2001 have actually been Muslims, living in Muslim-majority countries. This is because of a range of factors. First, it is easier to target less well-protected and defended sites in poorer Muslim-majority countries. Second, ideologically, Muslims that resist jihadist violence are demonised as unbelievers by those groups and therefore become 'enemies' who can be killed. Finally, violent actions are often targeted to alter the relations between governments and citizens in the Muslim world and improve the strategic position of the terrorist group (Mustafa and Brown 2010).

Activities

Despite the consequences of transnational terrorism primarily being felt in Muslim majority-countries, fear and awareness of the threats is felt strongly in Europe and North America. Terrorism is a 'communicative act', by which we mean it seeks to send a message that goes beyond the actual destruction caused to life and property. That message is to be heard by three groups of people. The first are civilians either local or globally who witness the events. The second are governments which are called upon to respond to the terrorist violence. Finally, the third are potential supporters who are attracted to join by the terrorist actions. We will now look at each of these three groups in turn.

Transnational terrorist groups focus on the location of attacks as much as, if not more than, who is attacked in order to generate a wide message. The importance of location is demonstrated by the attacks in Paris in 2015 by the Islamic State group. Paris is one of the most visited cities in the world and the group targeted 'everyday' places – bars, a football stadium and a rock concert. This signalled the idea that anyone and anywhere is a target, increasing fear of and publicity for the group's actions. This targeting strategy is in contrast to that of groups which may act across borders – such as the Tehrik-e-Taliban, working in both Afghanistan and Pakistan, or Boko Haram, operating in Nigeria and neighbouring countries – but for which the local political scene remains key. With the Tehrik-e-Taliban, their actions, while linked to a global cause of 'jihad', are local. They target beauty shops, police stations and market squares because they see these as opposed to the way of life they want to establish in their lands. Boko Haram too targets villages across different countries' borders and punishes those who don't conform to their new laws, which are about 'everyday living' even as they claim allegiance to a wider global political cause. However, this is not to say these groups do not target individuals. The Tehrik-e-Taliban tried to kill the activist Malala Yousafzai because of her support for girls' education and Boko Haram kidnapped hundreds of Christian schoolgirls in Northern Nigeria. Schools are targets because they are seen to promote state agendas, and schoolgirls are targets because these groups wish girls to have an Islamic education that focuses exclusively on domestic responsibilities and learning the Quran. Malala Yousafzai has gone on to campaign against this understanding of

Islamic education and promote women's schooling the world over, winning a Nobel Peace Prize for her efforts. In addition, the Nigerian military was forced to take a more active stance against Boko Haram due to global outrage over the kidnappings. Thus, while these are 'local' causes and local targets, they are global and transnational in their wider effects.

The second feature of transnational terrorism is that activities are sometimes designed to provoke states into action as well as generate fear in populations. Attacks are frequently symbolic in purpose and often have a high casualty rate for maximum shock value. It was inconceivable, for example, that the United States would not respond to the 9/11 attacks or that France would not react to the Paris attacks. Here, attacks are designed to provoke states into doing something to prove they are protecting civilians, even when that action may undermine the values they live by or end up being so costly that popular support for government is eroded. This terrorist strategy was first formulated by Che Guevara, a leader of revolutionary communist movements in Cuba against the American-sponsored authoritarian Batista government. The approach is known as 'focoist' (or focoism), whereby terrorists imagine themselves as the 'vanguard' of popular revolutions. The Uyghur ethno-separatist groups (which now have links to regional Islamist terrorism) operating in China's north-western provinces have been applying this strategy for over a decade. Their attacks are seen to have provoked ever-greater Chinese crackdowns on the civil liberties of people living in affected provinces in order to provide security and to demonstrate the strength of the central government. Yet the government has failed to reduce the number or severity of the attacks and also failed to stop people joining the separatists. Some have argued that European counter-terrorism policies are more reactionary than effective because they follow the same pattern of government suppression of human rights in the name of security as the Chinese example. The disproportionately felt impact of counter-terrorism legislation on Muslim communities across Europe is, critics argue, providing more propaganda for the Islamist groups' recruitment campaigns.

The expectation of many terrorist groups is that, in time, ever greater numbers will realise they are oppressed and join resistance groups or that, with sufficient coverage, the international community will come to support their cause. The example of Palestine underlines this well, since, despite decades of political struggle – which has included terrorist tactics – to establish Palestinian independence from Israel, the Palestinian cause remains relatively popular domestically and internationally. On the other hand, rather than *creating* something (an independent Palestine), this tactic may also be used to *destroy* something. Here, we can point to the 9/11 attacks and the many years of terrorism that followed as bait to lure the United States into engagement in the Middle East as a means of undermining their political and economic stability. By this logic, first Al-Qaeda and later the Islamic State group pursue strategies that aim to grind down the global power and image of the United States so that it may no longer be willing or able to interfere in Muslim lands.

In the past, countries have managed to resist reacting to these sorts of violent action by terrorists. Consider Italy's reaction to the assassination and kidnapping of the popular prime minister Aldo Moro by the socialist Red Brigades: during the investigation of Moro's kidnapping, General Carlo Alberto Dalla Chiesa reportedly responded to a member of the security services who suggested torturing a suspected Brigade member, 'Italy can survive the loss of Aldo Moro. It would not survive the introduction of torture' (Dershowitz 2003, 134). However, with public and media scrutiny operating at speed and levels not previously encountered, the ability of governments, especially democratically elected ones, to resist pressure is significantly reduced. The crossover with popular culture is interesting too, with military ethicists reporting a 'Jack Bauer effect' – referring to the tendency of this character in the TV series '24' to torture individuals as time runs out to stop a terrorist attack. Bauer's tactics often reflect (albeit in dramatised form) the enhanced interrogation tools that many governments have used in response to terrorism. Pressure is also placed on governments by allies and neighbours demanding support and action. For example, there has been a considerable chilling of relations between Thailand and Malaysia since 2004 because Thai authorities believe Malaysia to be turning a blind eye to Thai Muslim separatists operating across the border.

Finally, the third reason for terrorist violence is to recruit members and reinforce loyalty and membership among existing supporters. Extremely violent or highly technical attacks demonstrate the capability and will of the group carrying out the attack and its overall support. We see support for Islamic State coming from citizens in nations of every region because their attacks are dramatic and spectacular, which raises the profile of the group and demonstrates their military mastery. Mandaville (2007) calls this the myth of success. Islamic State group videos and propaganda frequently assert the weakness of the opposition as demonstrated by their deaths. The videos dehumanise their opposition, treating them like cattle or computer game characters in first-person shooters. The use of videos that mimic computer game imagery is supplemented by Islamic State creating its own 'skins' or 'maps' for popular computer games. In its version of Grand Theft Auto, the city is Baghdad and the people opposing you are the police and the military. As one British supporter said of their life in Syria under Islamic State, 'it's better than that game, Call of Duty'. Members say how they will 'respawn in Jannah' – 'respawn' being a gamer word for 'reincarnation' or 'being reborn', and Jannah is paradise in Islam. This is clearly designed to recruit and sustain membership by linking to Western masculine experiences (Kang 2014).

Organisation and resources

Managing such a transnational organisation and connecting to multiple locations and identities requires considerable logistical and organisational capability. The practice of tapping into the local and the global can be described as a 'plug and play' approach. Transnational terrorist organisations not only have an ideology that 'plugs' into local grievances, their organisational structures and resources also operate in this manner.

One of the main claims about transnational terrorist groups is that they are not hierarchical in structure but rather cell-like and even anarchical, lacking a formal leader. This led Marc Sageman to talk about a 'leaderless jihad' (2008). He characterised Al Qaeda as a loose-knit amorphous organisation, a position which was hotly contested by Bruce Hoffman (2006). Hoffman seems to have lost the argument, as terrorist organisations are becoming increasingly decentralised as they take advantage of new technologies, forms of communication and other aspects of globalisation. Consequently, communicating with transnational terrorist groups can be difficult. Negotiators cannot be sure the people they are talking to are representative of the group or have sufficient leverage to influence other members of the group, and splinter groups are more likely under these conditions. There are risks and vulnerabilities for terrorist organisations associated with this approach, notably in relation to information and operational security, coordination issues and resilience. There are also advantages in terms of longevity: the lack of central leadership gives them a greater scale and scope of operations and makes opposing or destroying them very difficult.

Rather than focusing on individuals, it is more helpful to focus on processes. One of the key processes within transnational terrorist organisations is the distribution and acquisition of money and equipment. Here we see the connections to transnational crime – particularly the smuggling of human organs, drugs and guns and human trafficking. Criminals can provide terrorist groups with whatever they require, provided the price is right, and terrorists will engage in or tolerate criminal activities when it serves their needs. Failed states offer fertile ground for possible and profitable connections between terrorism and criminality. The US government's National Strategy for Combating Terrorism (2006) contends that terrorists exploit failed states, using them to 'plan, organize, train, and prepare for operations'. However, some scholars disagree, noting that few international terrorists emerge from failed states (Simons and Tucker 2007) and most failed or failing states are not predisposed to exporting terrorism (Coggins 2015) – though they generate significant security problems for their own citizens and neighbouring states. What is worth noting is that states that are weakly governed, rather than failing, are also implicated. Pakistan is one such example – and was where Al-Qaeda's leader Osama bin Laden was living when he was killed by the US military in 2011 during a covert operation. This occurred, incidentally, without Pakistan being informed: the United States could not assume that he was there without the knowledge of elements of Pakistan's government, which is often accused of having state links to terrorism.

Countering transnational terrorism

The consequence of terrorism operating transnationally is that states have been presented with a number of decision points about when and how to intervene, and these are intimately connected. The first set of decisions is about where to intervene. Some Western states have been tempted to intervene internationally in order to prevent the emergence of terrorist groups or minimise the efficacy of existing terrorist groups in 'frontline' states. Such intervention comes in the form of international aid, military advice and training, and financial and military support to governments. This has entailed the risk of supporting undemocratic governments and engaging in militarised activities in contested spaces. The use of drones by the United States in Pakistan is one instance that has given rise to considerable controversy. First, because of the transnational element potentially undermining Pakistani sovereignty. A second point is that it imposes a state of fear on ordinary civilians, who find themselves under threat of strikes termed 'surgical' or 'targeted' by those operating them but which feel and are perceived as random by civilians in these areas (Coll 2014). Such operations can actually help terrorist groups by giving them a narrative to spin their agenda around, reinforcing local fears of an aggressive Western intervention in their societies that must be opposed.

A parallel approach has been to intervene at home by increasing state powers to minimise the effects and capability of terrorist groups to attack in Western societies. The consequence however, whether at home or overseas, has been to reduce civil liberties and restrict human rights. It is presumed that there is a necessary balance between human rights and human security and that protecting citizens, namely their security, is the first duty of government. However, a counter-argument is that failures to uphold these basic principles reward terrorist behaviours by treating them as 'outside' usual criminal processes, while at the same time punishing law-abiding citizens. Indeed, the human experience of counter-terrorism and counter-radicalisation policies and processes has been overwhelmingly negative. We can see this in the crackdown on protestors in Egypt, including journalists and civil rights groups, in the name of fighting terrorism. Human Rights Watch (2015) has reported that Egypt is undergoing the most serious human rights crisis in its modern history, with the government invoking national security to muzzle nearly all dissent. Egypt has attempted to justify these policies in light of transnational terrorist actions and the existence of opposition groups that appear to have overseas links with terrorist organisations. Similar patterns are seen in Turkey, especially following a failed coup attempt in 2016.

In Western nations, state attempts to impose security have often disproportionately affected certain groups – especially Muslims. The transnational element is perhaps most keenly felt at airports. Blackwood, Hopkins and Reicher (2013) found there was a 'prototypical' Muslim story of travelling through airports that was characterised by discrimination, humiliation and fear because of the actions by airport and border authorities. The ability of states to use violence so that a 'state of fear' is produced for (a section of) a population even when in the name of countering terrorism has even led some to call for the definition of a terrorist actor to include states (Jackson 2011, Blakeley and Raphael 2016). Those researching in the field of critical terrorism studies advocate this approach, arguing that the only significant difference between terrorism by state and terrorism by non-state actors is the agent carrying out the act of violence. For example, when the Israeli military attacks a Palestinian group this is commonly seen as 'defence' or 'national security'. But, when a Palestinian group attacks an Israeli troop convoy, which they perceive as invaders or occupiers, they are commonly deemed 'terrorists'. If we remove the binary of state and non-state actors, we might see this instead as a conflict between two opposing forces – both sharing legitimate aims and objectives. Due to examples such as this, complex and emotive as they are, there is often a failure to fully examine state actions that critical scholars blame for a significant cause of human insecurity worldwide. It is also important to look beyond the state toward civil society and everyday acts of resistance.

Conclusion

Terrorism, and terrorists, are transnational in three ways: their goals, their actions and their organisational form. However, we must be cautious before assuming that this is the new, and only, form of terrorism. Not all terrorism is transnational. Terrorist groups like the Irish Republican Army (IRA) and Euskadi Ta Askatasuna (ETA) still operate at the national level, targeting just one state. States too have shown themselves capable of inflicting forms of terrorism. Furthermore, while examples of transnational terrorism since 2001 may appear to be mostly religiously inspired, one cannot conclude that there is anything inevitable about this, or that Islam specifically is the significant factor. Rather, it is in this instance that Islam provides a framework for some marginal groups to construct a convincing worldwide counter-narrative to that of a world dominated by Western political, social and economic models. For that reason, it is perhaps no surprise that Islamic terrorism, over and above other types of terrorism, has become a sustained issue of concern in international relations. An important note to conclude on is that countering terrorism does not fall exclusively to the state: civil society and everyday acts by ordinary people also have a role. These can include examples of popular culture, inter-faith dialogue and moments of solidarity that break down the oppositional and binary world view that dominates transnational terrorist ideology. Nevertheless, terrorist groups are products of their time and, just like us, live in a globalised world. They are both shaped by globalisation and contribute to it by their actions.

15

The Environment

RAUL PACHECO-VEGA

Today, our planet carries over seven billion people. Yet its capacity to provide for each one of these individuals is threatened by population growth, climate change, deforestation, collapse of fisheries, desertification, air pollution and scarcity of fresh water. The full extent of our shared global environmental problems goes far beyond the well-publicised challenge of global climate change (or global warming). In fact, one of the elements often forgotten is the complicated relationship between human beings and their environment. In the early years of the conversation around environmental protection, some argued that the planet's resources were there for our collective consumption. However, there are limits to growth and this raises a range of important issues for international relations. Our population quadrupled between 1900 and 2000. This growth, coupled with abrupt climate change events and further compounded by rapid industrialisation and fast urban expansion, have combined into a perfect storm of negative environmental processes that put pressure on the capacity of Planet Earth to sustain life. As students of IR, we ought to recognise that the environment is one of the areas where much work remains to be done, particularly because cooperative approaches to environmental protection have had a very mixed record despite the grave implications of failure.

The relationship between international relations and environmental problems

It is often hard to assess whether international cooperation efforts have had any real effect on society's wellbeing, the quality of our environment, or even the construction of long-term relationships between states. One form of evaluation takes place through the study of environmentally focused 'megaconferences'. These large-scale events bring together representatives of national governments, intergovernmental secretariats, non-governmental organisations, academics and industry actors to engage in conversations about the state of the environment. They usually focus on a particular issue at hand. What makes these megaconferences interesting is that their goal is to engage in productive collaborative efforts to reach agreement and consensus on specific strategies to protect the environment and solve global challenges.

Historically, the two environmental issues that have gained the most attention have been climate change and biodiversity. Both of these issues came up at the Earth Summit in Rio de Janeiro in 1992 – formally called the United Nations Conference on Environment and Development. Nevertheless, most scholars will recall the 1972 United Nations Stockholm Conference on the Human Environment as the first large-scale environmentally focused megaconference. The Stockholm Conference was also the starting point for the first global coordination mechanism for environmental protection, the United Nations Environment Programme (UNEP). This conference was also the first one where participants explicitly linked human health with environmental and ecosystem health in their discourses.

The second milestone in global environmental governance is the publication of the Brundtland Report in 1987. This report outlined the need for a new model for development that brought into play the notion that we cannot simply use (and misuse) the resources we have at our disposal. The new model, coined sustainable development, became an enduring part of the global conversation about environmental protection. The Brundtland Report defines sustainable development as having three main components: economic, environmental and social – an idea that was then put forward for implementation at the Earth Summit.

The third milestone was the 1992 Earth Summit. A major outcome of this meeting was the recognition of two of the most important environmental issues – the loss of biodiversity and rapid climatic change – and the need for intergovernmental secretariats and agreements to respond to these twin challenges. The bulk of the world's states, 161, signed a declaration on the need for a model of global development that enabled future generations to live within their means but also facilitated current generations' livelihoods. The fact that so many states reached an agreement on the concept of sustainable development, and the need to operationalise it, became the key contribution of the Earth Summit. Activist involvement became the norm in international conferences on environmental issues starting with the Rio Summit. Non-governmental organisations were considered part of the negotiations from the very beginning and over 2,000 non-governmental representatives attended.

The fourth milestone was the 2002 Johannesburg World Summit on Sustainable Development. The goal was to establish collaborative intergovernmental, cross-disciplinary and cross-sectoral partnerships. In theory, this would strengthen the way in which environmental activists interact and partner with national governments. Different types of partnerships were elucidated and non-state actors were considered from the design stage up to implementation. However, following the summit there was a widespread perception that there had been very little progress on the implementation side, leading to a feeling of megaconference fatigue. To remedy this, the 2012 UN Conference on Sustainable Development (also known as Rio+20) created mechanisms for follow-up of commitments to sustainable development. It also highlighted the relevance of specific targets for development and the need for transition towards broader-reaching sustainable development goals. Moreover, the outcome document of this conference defines specific regional initiatives towards the implementation of sustainable development.

The 2015 Paris Agreement represented consensus among a number of countries that something needed to be done to maintain the level of global warming below two degrees centigrade. The fact that an agreement was reached was groundbreaking for the global climate negotiations community. Prior negotiations were marked by disagreements and lack of consensus on a strategy to compel nations to reach internationally agreed targets in their carbon emissions. This is important as carbon dioxide, released primarily by burning fossil fuels such as oil, natural gas and coal for energy, is the main cause of global warming. Nevertheless, Paris showed that many countries were able to agree on specific goals, targets and policies needed to combat rapid and impactful global environmental change. The process it established is yet to be fully realised, but in the years to come the expectation is that states will comply.

Climate change isn't the only ecological issue facing our planet. But its role in catalysing global action to protect the environment cannot be overstated. One of the most neglected issues is water. While the earth is two-thirds covered by water, the proportion that is fresh (drinkable and useable for agriculture) is sometimes highly contested by neighbouring states and in short supply for growing populations. When added to the effects of climate change, access to water is an issue of real concern. While many other challenges remain in the areas of climate and environment, it is likely that a framework for global water governance will be a major issue on the agenda in the near future.

Common pool resource theory

With a brief history of megaconferences now complete, we can move on to discussing the substance of the debates on climate and the environment. The notion of public goods comes from the original definition of a good that is non-excludable and non-rivalrous. Think of it as something that anyone can access at any point in time without making it any less available for anyone else to consume. The best example of a public good is knowledge; in this case we can use the example of information that we find on the internet. All knowledge, once freed and put online for public consumption, is non-excludable and non-rivalrous in consumption. You cannot exclude anyone from consuming knowledge and learning, unless they do not have access to the means for knowledge transmission, which may be the case in some countries where specific websites are banned. You also experience non-rivalry in consumption. Air is another example of a public good. Under normal circumstances nobody can stop you from breathing air into your lungs, and the fact that you breathe air does not stop someone else from having the opportunity to enjoy it. This is the definition of a perfect public good: one that is always non-rivalrous in consumption and non-excludable in access.

Common pool resource theory derives from Garrett Hardin (1968), who said that if left to our own devices we would exhaust all the resources available for our consumption. Imagine if you were a shrimp fisher. You need to fish and sell your catch to sustain your family. Let's say that there are 10,000 shrimp in the small catchment that you fish in. But there are 99 other fishers in the sea at the same time as you. If everyone cooperated and consumed only 1/100th of the total available shrimp, each would have 100 shrimp to sell. If at any point any fisher catches more than 1/100th, there will be other fishers negatively affected. Hardin used a similar metaphor to make the point that if resource consumers behave selfishly, they would exhaust the resources they were supposed to preserve. Hardin called this the tragedy of the commons. Closed bodies of water, plots of land and large-scale areas of forests are all common pool resources. They are rivalrous in consumption, but non-excludable.

One can summarise the theory of common pool resources by placing goods in four specific categories: private goods, common goods, club goods and public goods. This categorisation framework has two dimensions. The first dimension is excludability. If you can prevent someone from accessing a good, that good is excludable. The second dimension is rivalry in consumption. Goods that are depleted are rivalrous in consumption. If I consume an apple, you cannot consume that same apple because I have already eaten it. Private goods, such as food, clothing and other material objects, can be purchased and acquired because they are tradable. As a result, these goods are both rivalrous in consumption (if I buy a car, nobody else can buy that exact same car) and excludable (you cannot buy a car unless you have the money to purchase it).

Goods that are non-rivalrous in consumption and non-excludable are called public goods. These are the things that everybody can enjoy. Consuming them does not reduce the possibility of someone else having the same opportunity of consumption. Air is a public good. Everybody can breathe air without worrying that at some point they will not be able to breathe simply because somebody else is also breathing. Finally, common goods, which are also called common pool resources, are those goods that are non-excludable but rivalrous in consumption. Fish in a fishery, trees in a forest, water in an aquifer or a lake. All these natural resources are common goods and, therefore, common pool resources. What makes common pool resources so interesting is that the theory, developed by Elinor Ostrom (1990), argues that despite the fact that humans are supposed to be selfish, faced with conditions of scarcity we are able to self-organise and govern our common pool resources (our 'commons') in a sustainable manner. One of the reasons why Ostrom's work had such an impact was because her theory of cooperative approaches to resources governance contradicted Hardin's tragedy of the commons model. Instead of being so selfish that they would want to fish all the shrimp (for example), Ostrom found that fishers would build a shared agreement to reduce their own consumption for the wellbeing of the collective. Obviously, this is an example on a relatively small scale. What remains to be seen is whether we can achieve global cooperation to protect our global commons. One way to think about this is through the lenses of global public goods, as discussed below.

The global environment as a global commons

Perhaps you would agree that a shared environment would be a resource community and individuals would work collaboratively to protect. But there is another view, which is that responsibility for care of the environment rests with governments. One way of thinking about this is to use the concept of the global environment as a global commons. After all, global environmental problems are by their very nature global. However, international cooperation is hard to achieve. As the example of the US shows, there are powerful countries that will avoid cooperation for various reasons. For many years the US refused to sign the international agreement on climate change, the Kyoto Protocol (the forerunner to the 2015 Paris agreement), thus blocking many international efforts to reduce global carbon emissions. There are several other examples that can be cited, but suffice it to say that a powerful country's refusal to collaborate to solve a global issue is concerning. It is hard to make countries commit to specific conservation goals (in forest policy) or emission-reduction targets (in climate policy) or standards for pollution in rivers (in water policy) because each nation has its own national development objectives that may conflict with other countries' goals, thus making it hard to find common ground for collaboration.

Given that cross-national collaboration is so difficult, we create international environmental agreements that build a framework to help these countries talk to each other and agree on specific targets for environmental protection. Some of the most popular international environmental agreements are specific to the area of climate change (like the Kyoto Protocol), but other, less well-known examples – such as the Aarhus Convention on Access to Information, Public Participation in Decision-Making and Access to Justice in Environmental Matters – are equally relevant. One of the biggest problems for human beings acting at the individual level on environmental issues is the lack of information. Countries that are signatories to the Aarhus Convention make an agreement to share data that will enable citizens of a country to understand the potential risks that they face with regard to chemicals' processing and emissions. This information also helps environmental activists bring industries to account and ensure that they reduce their polluting emissions.

Global rights and domestic environmental politics and policy

The right to a healthy environment and the global commons are ideas that suggest that it is our shared duty to take care of our collective environment because everyone has a right to enjoy their environment and use some of its resources for their survival. It is possible to link human rights with global environmental regulation through the implementation of the international norm of a right to a healthy environment. This is a new avenue of research for scholars of international relations, and it is founded on the basis of a popular idea, or norm, that every individual on the planet has a right to a healthy environment. Despite states having different abilities and varying degrees of technical expertise to implement the norm, the number of countries with constitutional environmental rights has expanded radically (Gellers 2015). Eighty states now have such legislation in their constitutions, but we are still quite a long way away from having this norm as a fundamental human right.

There are also, of course, many other concerns that divert government focus from environmental issues. Increasing regulation on certain heavy-polluting industries, such as steel and coal, can have a negative effect on jobs. Setting 'green' taxes, either directly or through such things as energy tariffs, can also cause a burden on taxpayers and businesses. Thus, there has sometimes been a tendency to see environmental legislation as damaging to economic growth and prosperity. By extension it can also be unpopular in domestic settings, making legislation difficult to pass – or even propose in some cases. It is consequently encouraging to see so much domestic legislation gaining traction. The number of countries where the human right to a healthy environment is enacted constitutionally may help build collaborative transnational networks to protect the global commons. The starting point would be a shared understanding of the need to reduce human impact on national and global ecosystems. Sharing a paradigm that pushes the human right to a healthy environment may also induce national governments to actively seek participation in international environmental agreements. Nevertheless, it is important to find a way to coordinate these agreements, and this challenge raises the question of whether we need a global environmental organisation to make sure states comply.

The best situation for Planet Earth's citizens are solutions that are made not just in each state, but internationally. And, most importantly, complied with. IR is often concerned with the phenomenon of states cheating on, or withdrawing from, agreements. Perhaps nowhere is compliance more important for our long-term prosperity and security than in the areas of climate and environment.

Do we need a global environmental organisation?

Who is in charge of protecting our global environment? To answer this question, you may recall from previous sections that there is now a consensus regarding one specific tool that may help achieve the lofty goal of providing global public goods: international environmental agreements. These agreements, often produced at megaconferences, help protect our global commons by requiring nations to acknowledge and respect the human right to a healthy environment. However, the next big question is an equally important one – who is in charge of implementing these international environmental accords? Some have argued that in order to force countries to cooperate in the protection of our shared environment, we need a global intergovernmental secretariat. This would take the form of a far-reaching international institution whose sole purpose would be coordinating efforts to improve environmental quality.

For many years there was a collective belief that the United Nations Environment Programme had been tasked with the challenge of protecting our global network of ecosystems and shared resources. This may have been true in the early stages of its creation following the 1972 Stockholm Conference, but protecting our global environment has proved to be an impossible task for a small agency with a limited budget and no power to compel states to act in a particular way. The reality is that even though there is increasing interest in strengthening international cooperation across countries to protect the global environment, it is the number of institutions, agencies and programmes dealing with environmental issues at other levels that grows in size and complexity. Regrettably, the frequent mention of abrupt climate change events, increasing deforestation and growing levels of pollution in oceans, rivers and lakes makes it clear that we have yet to solve these complex global environmental problems. And while there is still no agreement as to whether the United Nations Environment Programme is the agency that should be tasked with protecting the global environment or whether we should create a new global environmental organisation (see Biermann 2000), we must ensure that we focus on collective solutions at the international level rather than state, regional or local level – we all share the earth.

To strike an optimistic note, we can find at least one instance of global environmental cooperation, the Paris Agreement of 2015. This was led by the chair of the United Nations Framework Convention on Climate Change Secretariat, Christiana Figueres, and is an example of what can be achieved in global cooperation for environmental protection by just one intergovernmental secretariat. The fact that the majority of the world's states were able to reach agreement on the specific tactics and strategies that every state needs to undertake in order to reach the stated goal of holding increases in the earth's temperature below two degrees centigrade is to be lauded. Even more important is that the agreement has secured the support of the world's two biggest state polluters, the US and China. The Secretariat is probably not the global environmental organisation we need right now, but it played a pivotal role at a crucial time.

The debate around whether or not we should have a global environmental organisation may never be settled. However, if we were to establish such a thing it would need full and complete cooperation from all states to stand any chance of success. The example of Paris, which built on the example of earlier megaconferences and movements, suggests that international collaboration to protect our environment is on the rise. This offers hope for the future despite rising political tensions in some nations over the nature of climate agreements.

Conclusion

It is clear that we still have a lot of work to do with regard to our shared understanding of what constitutes strong, robust, effective and efficient global environmental governance. We need to better integrate regional and transnational initiatives with domestic policy strategies to tackle environmental problems. This means creating the conditions for a model of governing the environment that is flexible and cuts across different levels, from the local to the global. It is also clear that frameworks based on ideas of global public goods and global commons are very useful. However, at the same time they are daunting, since collective action on any scale is clearly an enormous challenge. Trying to find mechanisms, models and strategies to ensure cooperation across different levels of government, across a broad variety of issue areas and across a range of political and policy actors is a problematic and difficult process, as experience has shown. Today, the world's states have been able to find common ground in relation to certain goals for environmental protection, including the flagpole issues of global warming and climate change. The hope is that this trend continues so we can continue to live healthily and happily on Planet Earth.

16

Feeding the World

BEN RICHARDSON

How should we think about global food politics? It is tempting to start with big moments on the world stage such as the United Nations discussing famine in Ethiopia or Syria. But this approach can be alienating. It locates global politics far away from daily life and sees food as just another issue that international leaders address on our behalf. So rather than this top-down approach, this chapter offers a bottom-up approach, beginning with everyday people like you and me. Through this perspective we can better appreciate the meaning of 'big' statistics like the estimate of the United Nations that 795 million people in the world are undernourished. What kind of lives do these individuals lead, and what is it like to go without food? We can also see that it is not just problems of hunger that food politics concerns itself with, but those relating to food safety, nutrition and livelihoods as well. Being attentive to everyday voices shows that these issues affect people in developed countries just as much as those in developing countries. Who in the world gets fed, with what, and by whom are fundamental questions that concern us all.

The bottom-up approach

When I started writing this chapter I was sitting in my local café, a Cuban-themed place with Latino music on the stereo and pictures of Communist revolutionary Che Guevara on the wall. In the newspaper was a story about the multinational drinks company SABMiller avoiding taxes in Africa. Visiting the supermarket later on with my family, we picked up sausages from Ireland, tinned tomatoes from Italy and peppers from Morocco. For dinner we cooked up a casserole, a dish with French roots, and sat in front of the television to eat. A celebrity chef was presenting a programme about diets in Japan and how the British could learn a lot from their healthy lifestyles. We wondered whether we might try sushi for our next family meal.

These encounters with national cultures, current affairs and global supply chains can be thought of as the social foundations of international relations. They are foundational in two senses. First, they create the cross-border flows of ideas, people and goods that make international relations, or how people in different nations see and relate to one another. For example, debates about how to govern the international trade of food wouldn't exist if people didn't buy foreign products to begin with or care about the effects of doing so. Second, it is through these interactions that individuals come to know their political community and form opinions about what is best for it, helping to construct 'the national interest'. This happens through multiple subject positions. In the story above, for instance, I was sometimes thinking from the perspective of a consumer, but at other times as a worker, a citizen, a cook, or a family member. This is important because different subject positions create different political priorities. Thinking as a consumer, I would prefer supermarkets to stock a wide variety of foods and keep prices as low as possible. But thinking as a citizen, I would prefer them to supply more food from local farmers and make sure everyone earned a decent living out of it. The bottom-up approach thus provides an alternative way of thinking about global food politics by analysing its social foundations. It recognises that important political decisions do not happen 'above' society, separately from it, but rest on the beliefs, opinions and actions of those who would be governed.

Sudden food shortages and the disenfranchised citizen

In 2007/8, and again in 2011, the world market prices of cereals, meat and dairy products, vegetable oils and sugar all began to increase rapidly. This was blamed on a variety of causes. These ranged from poor harvests in agricultural producing countries like Australia and Russia; policies in the United States and Brazil that encouraged food crops to be replaced by biofuel; rising gas prices that pushed up the cost of fertilisers; and financial speculation leading to volatile prices. Commentators spoke of a 'global food crisis' as the effects were felt in every country, albeit to differing degrees. In the United Kingdom (UK) the average cost of a loaf of bread doubled from £0.63 in January 2005 to £1.26 just four years later; an increase way ahead of inflation and an unwanted burden for those on lower incomes. In states with greater dependency on food imports and higher levels of poverty, though, the impact was felt even more deeply. These states could mainly be found in the Middle East and Africa, and in city after city riots broke out as people found it difficult to access basic staples at prices they could afford.

One of these cities was Algiers, the capital of Algeria. As elsewhere, people took to the streets not simply because food was hard to get hold of but also because of the injustice they perceived in the way their country had been run.

Demands for affordable food ran alongside calls for jobs, political freedoms and an end to government corruption. Banners were written saying things like 'Give us back our Algeria' and 'No to the police state'. At first the Algerian government responded to these events with repression. The police fired tear gas and water cannons at youths who had angrily taken to the streets and set up roadblocks. Football matches were suspended as it was thought the crowds might turn political and become a threat to public order. However, aware of the Arab Spring revolutions and fearful that the uprisings seen in Egypt and Tunisia would be repeated in Algeria, the government soon relented. Import taxes on sugar and cooking oil were slashed and prices capped for flour and vegetables. The government also renounced the 19-year-old State of Emergency law that had prohibited peaceful protest in the country. The forcible removal of long-standing president Abdelaziz Bouteflika was thus averted, although widespread disapproval of his autocratic regime continued to simmer.

What effect did these food riots have on international relations? First of all they created the sense that there was a 'global food crisis' to resolve. It is important to note here that if a food crisis were to be simply defined as the existence of widespread hunger, then the situation would have been nothing new. Throughout the 1990s and 2000s there were consistently between 800 million and 1 billion people in the world who were chronically undernourished. Living largely in rural areas in Asia and Africa, these people suffered away from the spotlight. However, based on the position of the disenfranchised citizen, the food riots that broke out in volatile urban areas directly challenged the legitimacy of political leaders and forced a response (Bush 2010). This kind of hunger could not be ignored.

Attempting to manage the food crisis, world leaders gathered at the United Nations' High-Level Conference on World Food Security. They produced a declaration to provide more emergency aid, prevent international agricultural trade from being disrupted, and increase global agricultural production. Critics saw this as a conservative response that did not address the root causes of the crisis. Instead of ensuring people had decent incomes and accountable leaders, reflecting the demands of the protestors, the focus was simply on bringing down world market prices. This also reproduced the misleading idea that hunger is best dealt with by growing more food rather than changing existing power relations. Oxfam, a confederation of charitable organisations, made this point when they said that there was already enough food to feed everyone. For Oxfam the problem unveiled by the riots was not so much lack of supply but unequal distribution (Oxfam 2009). During 2008, the height of the food crisis, there was a global average of 2,826 calories produced, per person, per day according to official United Nations data. The recommended intake for an adult is between 2,000–2,500 calories. So, if the data is taken at face value, there was no actual shortage of food. Rather, political decisions had created a situation where some people could acquire food more easily than others.

Chronic hunger and the civic participant

A different approach to governing hunger can be seen in Brazil. Although the country was for a long time a net exporter of agricultural products, it also had huge numbers of undernourished people living within its borders. This reaffirms the point that, in and of themselves, food surpluses do not prevent hunger – even at state level. So, when the left-wing Workers' Party was elected to power in 2003, their leader Luiz Inácio Lula da Silva made the Zero Hunger programme a cornerstone of his government's social policy. He declared in his inauguration speech: 'We are going to create appropriate conditions for all people in our country to have three decent meals a day, every day, without having to depend on donations from anybody' (cited in da Silva et al. 2011, 9).

This commitment came out of the country's re-democratisation process in the 1990s, when civil society began to exert a greater influence in national politics after two decades of oppressive military dictatorship. The Council on Food and Nutritional Security, which was supported by Lula, was a particularly important institution in this respect. Composed of 54 representatives, two-thirds from civil society and one-third from federal government, the Council drove forward a number of policies, including increased funding for school meals and support for family farmers. It also promoted the National Law on Food and Nutrition Security, which obliged the federal government to uphold people's right to food and create food councils at more localised levels. Along with cash transfers given to poor mothers and an increase in the minimum wage, these reforms lifted millions of people out of chronic undernourishment. The Zero Hunger programme could claim real success. In contrast to Algeria, diverse groups in Brazilian society – including teachers, farmers, clergy and health professionals – were able to play a more proactive role in national food politics. Indeed, their collective contribution also reshaped international policy. When the minister for food security in the Lula government, José Graziano da Silva, was elected to the head of the UN's Food and Agricultural Organisation in 2011, he began to promote many of the same policies that had been developed in Brazil. A twin-track strategy based on investments in rural areas to boost the incomes of farming families and basic welfare payments to protect the most vulnerable in society was advocated.

Backed by other United Nations agencies and the UN Secretary-General, Ban Ki-moon, over the next three years Zero Hunger Challenge programmes were launched in a number of countries including St. Lucia, Laos and Zambia. This approach also informed the 2015 UN Sustainable Development Goals, which set out a roadmap for the end of world hunger by 2030. That said, it is a lot easier to make policies and plans than to achieve them. Key in the Brazilian case was the mobilisation of national civil society, which brought forward people willing to play a role in political affairs. In countries where this is not encouraged, it is hard to see plans for the reduction of poverty and hunger taking effect. Moreover, Brazil itself is far from perfect, with mass protests and political upheavals in 2016 reflecting the nation's slide into ever-deepening recession. Chronic hunger may have diminished but temporary hunger and poor diet remain, especially in the impoverished areas of Northeast Brazil and among indigenous communities. Ensuring their right to food is an ongoing struggle, and one that will have to overcome the significant domestic political and economic challenges that Brazil faces.

Adulterated milk and the protective parent

In September 2008 news broke that the industrial chemical melamine had been found in powdered milk infant formula in China. Within two weeks, more than 50,000 babies had fallen ill and developed kidney stones. The mass poisoning became a national scandal and within the space of a year the Chinese government had overhauled its food safety laws and inspection systems. Provincial courts also sentenced 21 people involved, ultimately executing two of the traders caught selling adulterated milk. On the face of it this was a sudden crisis that had been swiftly dealt with. In actual fact, the melamine milk scandal was long in the making and slow in the breaking.

Milk consumption had been encouraged in China from the late 1990s by the government and by dairy companies as a way for people to become healthy and 'modern'. Competition to supply this growing market thus intensified. Milk was watered down and melamine was added so as to make the protein content appear normal, but the practice was knowingly covered up – a fact disclosed by company executives in the subsequent trials. Neither the dairy industry nor government officials wanted the public to panic as this would be disastrous for sales and the country's reputation, especially while hosting the 2008 Olympic Games. It was largely thanks to the parents of affected children that the problem was finally acknowledged. Some took to the internet to raise awareness and vent their anger while others held impromptu press conferences to give their side of the story and gain assurances about their children's long-term health. In both instances there were cases of parents being detained or jailed by the police for inciting social disorder.

The scandal had profound international consequences. Government authorities in Asia and Europe began to pull Chinese dairy and baby food products from the shops, while the United States had so little faith in the Chinese food safety system that they installed their own officials in the country to check US-bound exports. Doubts about the safety of Chinese milk also spilled over into diplomatic tensions with Hong Kong and Taiwan. In Hong Kong, there was a public backlash against travellers and smugglers who began buying up infant formula to take back to China, leaving little for local consumption. In Taiwan, demonstrators used the milk scandal to publicly contest the wisdom of plans by the Taiwanese ruling party to forge closer ties with Beijing. Finally, the World Health Organization tried to agree on an international standard for safe infant formula at the same time as its director-general reinforced the message that breast milk is best for babies, implicitly criticising the Chinese government for promoting the use of powdered milk in the first place.

From the protective parent's point of view, then, ways of feeding the infant population had become criticised and politicised. However, Chinese parents should not be treated as a homogenous group. For example, one response by richer parents worried about using unsafe infant formula was to hire other new mothers to breastfeed their children. Most of these 'wet-nurses' were migrants from the countryside and so poor that they chose to sell their breast milk for money, feeding their own babies potentially harmful formula instead. Another class dimension of the scandal was the fact that many of the Chinese businesses involved were part-owned by multinational companies. Sanlu, the Chinese company at the centre of it all, was in fact only able to expand its operations thanks to a large investment by a dairy cooperative based in New Zealand called Fonterra. A political question for global capitalism is thus to what extent such transnational companies should help protect consumers in other countries as well as profit from them.

Childhood obesity and the bad mother

Concerns over food safety can also be extended to include foods high in salt, sugar and fat. These do not cause immediate harm in the same way that melamine-tainted milk does, but their cumulative effects can still be dangerous. The World Health Organization has warned that unhealthy diets are a leading global risk to health because of their link to illnesses like heart disease and stroke. In fact, these are the two biggest killers in the world, each causing more deaths every year than HIV/AIDS, lung cancer and road accidents combined. This aspect of food malnutrition – 'mal' meaning bad rather than insufficient – should be just as worrying as the existence of food shortages. In the United Kingdom, the public debate about malnutrition has paid particular attention to children's diets. Some of the debate has focused on problems experienced during childhood itself. For example, in 2014 it was reported that the consumption of sugary foods and drinks had contributed to 25,000 children aged five to nine being admitted to hospital to get rotten teeth pulled out. But mostly it has focused on childhood obesity and the risk this poses for children later in life. Under pressure from campaigners, including doctors and other health professionals, successive British governments have introduced policies to promote dietary change. Restrictions have been placed on junk food adverts, minimum nutritional standards have been applied to school meals, families have been targeted with healthy lifestyle campaigns, and food manufacturers have been asked to lower the salt, sugar and fat content of their products. To cap this off, a 'sugar tax' on high-sugar soft drinks was announced in 2016.

Despite first impressions, these internal debates have actually had an international dimension. In this respect it is important to remember that the United Kingdom is a nation-state made up of four countries (England, Scotland, Wales and Northern Ireland), with the latter three each having some devolved political powers of their own. As such, policy debates about diet have often become proxy wars over the further devolution of power away from the central state. This happened in 2014 when the first minister of Scotland declared that the Scottish policy to offer more free school meals to pupils showed that Scotland would be better off as an independent country. International data has also been used to defend or discredit domestic policy proposals. The successful campaign to tax sugary drinks, spearheaded by the celebrity chef Jamie Oliver, constantly referred to a similar policy introduced in Mexico to show that what worked there could work in the United Kingdom.

International comparison has also been used in depictions of national identity. British newspapers have run countless stories saying it has become a nation beset by increasing obesity. For some people, especially those with right-wing political views, this has been taken as evidence that the British are becoming lazy and that standards of parenting have worsened. Since childhood obesity is positively correlated with poverty, meaning that children from poorer backgrounds are more likely to be overweight, this interpretation also produced a divisive image of the nation. Put simply, it implied that poor parents were to blame for the country's moral failings. Moreover, since it is women that tend to be the primary caregivers, the figure of the bad parent inevitably assumed a female face.

Low wages and the deserving worker

So far in this chapter we have focused on food consumption, on what people eat. But how that food is produced and exchanged is important in its own right. Indeed, if we include all the jobs involved in providing food – from farming and fishing through processing and distribution, right up to retailing and cooking – then it is arguably the most important income-generating sector in the world. In the United States (US), there has been a long history of struggles over food work. John Steinbeck captured a slice of it in his 1939 book *Grapes of Wrath*, writing about a family of tenant farmers evicted from their home in Oklahoma and who end up working on a peach plantation in California for a pittance. This fictional book based on real events echoes in the lives of farmworkers in the United States today. Jobs like picking fruit and weeding vegetables are still tough and still done by migrants – only now they typically come from Latin America. In 2012, their average pay was less than $19,000 a year. The US government's own statistics would place this income thousands of dollars below the minimum threshold for meeting the basic needs of a family of four. In other words, even though they were living in the world's richest nation, they were living in relative poverty.

There are some differences between Steinbeck's story and contemporary events, though. In *Grapes of Wrath*, a preacher called Casy tries to organise his fellow workers into a trade union and is murdered by the police for his troubles. For the Coalition of Immokalee Workers, a group of immigrant tomato pickers based in Immokalee Florida, their initial meetings in a local church grew into something much bigger. They first used tactics like work stoppages and hunger strikes to demand higher wages from their employers, but as their public profile grew they sought to reorganise the food supply chain itself. In 2011 the Coalition launched the Fair Food Program. Major restaurant and supermarket chains were encouraged to pay a few cents more for a pound of tomatoes and to buy these tomatoes from suppliers who pledged to follow labour law and put the extra money in their workers' wage packets. The Coalition scored its biggest success when the biggest retailer in the world, Walmart, agreed to join the Fair Food Program and to extend it beyond just tomatoes.

But while Walmart made commitments to *these* workers, with its own workers it has been less forthcoming. In 2012 its regular employees like cashiers, cleaners and warehouse assistants were paid on average just $8.81 an hour (Buchheit 2013). This meant that they, too, were paid a poverty wage and thus qualified for additional social security benefits like food vouchers, many of which were then spent by workers back in Walmart stores! This costs the government billions per year and is surely the grand paradox of the American economy. For all its wealth and Wall Street millionaires, the national minimum wage is so low that many people in full-time work still cannot make ends meet. Nor is it just Walmart where this happens. Supermarket cashiers, farm labourers, fast food servers, cooks, dishwashers, bartenders and waiting staff are all among America's lowest paid workers. The price of cheap food in the country has been gross inequality.

In both the Walmart case and that of the Coalition of Immokalee Workers, the position of the deserving worker has been crucial in contesting this inequality. We can see this first in the way that immigration policy has been conducted. For years US farm companies lobbied the government to allow them access to cheap foreign labour, which the government achieved by issuing temporary immigration visas and turning a blind eye to the use of additional undocumented workers. This created tensions with the general public, some of whom were worried about wages being undercut and others about the decline of 'American values'. A 2013 proposal by Republican and Democratic Party senators to offer permanent citizenship to undocumented farm workers thus had to cast them in a particular light. They were not called 'illegal immigrants', as was more usual in political discourse, but portrayed as 'individuals who … have been performing very important and difficult work to maintain America's food supply' (Plumer 2013). What the politicians were implying was that these were honest and hardworking people that could and should be made into Americans.

A second example is the way that trade unions have tried to organise Walmart employees across national borders. The company's takeover of food retailers in other countries has given it a truly global workforce. Walmart now employs over two million people worldwide; only the United States and Chinese militaries employ more. Concerned that the labour standards in its American operations might be adopted in these supermarkets and their supply chains too, groups like the UNI Global Union have thus tried to link people together through the shared subjectivity of the deserving worker and create a sense of international solidarity between them. As a UNI coordinator put it: 'When I can connect a Chinese worker with a Mexican worker then it doesn't become about a Chinese worker taking their job. Workers can see, "Oh they [Walmart] are screwing us both. We have to unite to win"' (Jackson 2014).

Land dispossession and the traditional peasant

The examples from the United States were about waged work, but most of the jobs in the food sector are unwaged. People who farm, fish, herd, hunt or forage for food are effectively self-employed: they sell some of what they get for money and keep the rest to eat. As far as farming goes, there are an estimated 570 million agricultural plots in the world, the vast majority of which are small-scale family farms (Lowder *et al.* 2014). Whether these rural livelihoods will disappear as farming becomes mechanised and people migrate to cities is much debated (see Weis 2007 and Collier 2008). Either way, it is evident that the transition from small-scale peasant agriculture to large-scale industrial agriculture can be extremely violent. This can be seen in a case from Cambodia.

In 2006, large areas of land were granted by the Cambodian government to private holders to transform into sugar plantations so they could export this 'cash crop' to the European Union. However, the plan ignored the fact that many people already lived on the land and didn't want to be evicted. But the protestations of the existing tenants fell on deaf ears. In part this was because they did not have legal title to the land as a previous government, the Khmer Rouge, had banned private property and burned land records. Things got worse still. Financial compensation and alternative land that the current government was meant to provide was either inadequate or not forthcoming. When people resisted, force was used to remove them. Buildings were burned, land was bulldozed and animals shot. Over 1,700 families lost their land (see Herre and Feodoroff 2014). Responding to these events, community groups and human rights organisations formed the Clean Sugar Campaign. Given that the Cambodian government was itself involved in the land sale, the campaign's search for justice took on an international dimension. First of all they tried to pressure the investing companies by filing complaints with the National Human Rights Commission of Thailand. Then they turned their attention to the rules and relationships incentivising sugar export. They pressurised the European Union to suspend the free trade access it gave to Cambodia, began legal proceedings against Tate & Lyle in the UK for importing illegally produced sugar, and publicly shamed the project's financial backers, Deutsche Bank and ANZ Bank, to make them withdraw their money. This can be described as a form of 'boomerang activism' (Keck and Sikkink 1998) – working through institutions in other countries meant that the campaign first left Cambodia but then came back.

In the course of their activism, campaigners did not just point out the breaches of law involved in the 'land grabs' but also made a political argument about why this way of producing food should be opposed. This turned on the fact that it was not just people's livelihoods that were being threatened but also their identity. The land that was lost was used not only to grow rice and collect water but also to worship ancestral graves. It was their home as well as their workplace. This is a common experience of people displaced by commercial agriculture – they are not just victims of dispossession but see their very way of life destroyed. The position of the traditional peasant adopted in the campaign thus gave it a broader resonance in global civil society. For example, the charity Oxfam has used the plight of the Cambodian peasants as an example of the dangers facing rural dwellers the world over, and has lobbied companies like Coca-Cola to make sure they source ingredients like sugar in a responsible fashion. However, there is still a long way to go for full restoration or compensation for the land loss, and unfortunately much of the damage has already been done.

Conclusion

The cases presented in this chapter show that political authority over food is globally dispersed. People in each case were affected by decisions taken in the state, in international organisations and in corporations. This constellation of institutions, sometimes referred to as global governance, reminds us that power does not lie in any one single site, even though in certain situations some actors take on greater significance than others. Thanks to our bottom-up approach, we also saw how individuals outside these central institutions can inform and challenge the way that governance is organised. The chapter demonstrated how professional networks, charities, trade unions, political groups and even celebrity chefs all claimed their own kind of authority on the basis of expertise, morality, membership or personality. This allowed them to speak for large numbers of ordinary people; the kind of people often excluded from top-down accounts of global politics. The chapter also showed how looking at different subject positions can help explain how collective action happens. Some positions were based on political identity (the disenfranchised citizen, the civic participant), some on familial identity (the protective parent, the bad mother), and some on economic identity (the deserving worker, the traditional peasant). What is important about each of these is the way they spoke to people in a particular way, giving them a shared lens on the world and a common language to articulate it. These positions are also important in shaping international relations, along with class relations, race relations and gender relations. They show how global food politics are built from the bottom up, based on contested ideas about who we are and what is in our best interests.

17

Managing Global Security beyond 'Pax Americana'

HARVEY M. SAPOLSKY

We often hear that we live in a world where power and wealth are increasingly decentralised. The world is indeed changing, in some cases rapidly, as prior chapters in this book have documented. Despite this, there has been one constant since the end of the Second World War – the United States of America (US) has been the dominant military and economic power in the world and the manager of global security. The phrase 'Pax Americana' can therefore be used to describe an era without major war post-1945, overseen by the stabilising force and military might of the United States. IR calls actors that are noticeably above others in military and economic terms 'hegemons'. While there have certainly been regional hegemons in the past, there has never been a global hegemon in known history – until now.

Today, the bulk of the citizens of earth would surely be able to identify the sitting American president by name, or at least recognise their face. This cannot be said for any other leader. Many debates in International Relations circle around the question of whether such a situation is desirable or sustainable. In order to address these debates, it is important to assess how dominant the United States is and whether the situation is likely to continue. As we ponder this we must also understand that a debate is underway not just internationally but also within American society over whether it should continue to play a global role. This chapter explores such questions in a direct and sometimes provocative way: the eventual answers, whatever they may be, will determine the next era of international relations. We should therefore not shy away from pondering the implications of a world beyond Pax Americana.

From isolation to global superpower

The Second World War was the hinge point for establishing American dominance. Prior to that war, the United States had focused on continental expansion, making sure its neighbours recognised its regional dominance and pre-empting the influence of European powers in the Americas. George Washington, the first American president, warned in his farewell address that the US should avoid 'entangling alliances'. Another president, John Quincy Adams, said that America should not go abroad searching 'for monsters to destroy' and that its glory was in liberty, not dominion. The United States did, nevertheless, dabble in imperialism during the late nineteenth century, toppling a decaying Spanish empire to help liberate Cuba and acquiring Puerto Rico, Guam and the Philippines in the process. But, having won its own freedom in 1776 from British colonial control, there was little desire in America for it to become a colonial power itself. Even involvement in the First World War could not shake the US out of its preferred isolationist shell. The United States entered the war late, brought its forces home quickly afterwards and refused to help enforce a peace its president helped design due to the US Congress rejecting membership of the League of Nations.

The Second World War was truly global in scope and revolutionary in its impact. The United States was drawn into the conflict, again late, by German submarine warfare in the Atlantic and a surprise attack on its military facilities at Pearl Harbor by the Japanese in December 1941. When the war began in 1939 there were several powers contesting for global leadership, but the United States was not among them. The United Kingdom and France had sizeable empires. Adolf Hitler was determined to create a new German 'Reich' (or empire) that would last at least 1,000 years. Imperial Japan was seeking dominance in Asia and had already occupied parts of China and all of Korea. Finally, the Soviet Union had proved that a communist revolution was possible, and prospects were good that other nations would follow suit and communism would spread globally. By the war's end Germany and Japan were devastated, defeated countries, occupied by foreign powers. Among the victors, the United Kingdom and France were spent powers. Their empires were fragmenting and their economies near-destroyed. The Soviet Union had suffered the most significant losses of all, primarily through battling a German invasion. Despite winning the war, the cost of victory for the allied powers had been high. In contrast, by 1945 the United States had shaken off the effects of the Great Depression, the global economic collapse of the 1930s, and was relatively untouched by the war. It had demonstrated its power by mobilising and equipping a military of over 16 million. As the war ended it had military forces stationed across the globe and was the world's dominant economic power.

The United States took several lessons from the Second World War, the most important of which was that it had to be involved in managing global security in order to protect its own security. It was too big and too powerful for others not to challenge even if it had no interest in challenging them. Because international relations as a system is anarchical, with no ruler, powerful states tend to make other states feel insecure by default. Even if powerful states do not behave threateningly, there is a fear that they may do so in the future. This leads to competition and the risk of future conflict as states seek to maximise their security by attempting to increase their relative power. In the past this was typically done by acquiring territory, as described in chapter one. But in a post-war era characterised by decolonisation and the presence of nuclear weapons, security calculations were in flux. To monitor the situation, the United States chose to be involved globally, designing the international frameworks for commerce and governance at conferences it convened in Bretton Woods and San Francisco, both in America, and joining the United Nations which was headquartered in New York City. Essentially, the Americans created a new system of international relations, both economic and political, and placed themselves in the driving seat. Although the bulk of its forces were demobilised at the war's end, the United States maintained the network of bases it had built during the war and retained a substantial military presence in both Europe and Asia. At home, it created, via the National Security Act of 1947, the governmental framework for coordinating the development and exercise of global power. In short, the United States was now permanently constituted to be a different type of actor.

Having helped destroy fascism in the Second World War, the United States set itself the task of first containing and then undermining the two remaining rival systems of global order – colonialism and communism. The test came quickly with the Soviet Union's push to dominate Eastern Europe and its acquisition of nuclear weapons in 1949. Many American politicians feared that the Soviet Union could dominate all of Europe and Asia – an area with the industrial resources and military potential to match or even surpass the United States. When China turned communist in 1949 and other nations looked set to follow, these fears seemed to have a basis in reality. A series of confrontations and crises that we now call the Cold War became the new normal in international relations. The conflict marked a two-power struggle between the United States and the Soviet Union spanning more than forty years. IR calls this a bipolar system, as two principal actors are responsible for shaping global affairs. In the end, with the Soviet Union's internal collapse between 1989 and 1991, there was one superpower standing – the United States. The question was, would this mean that bipolarity would give way to unipolarity (the dominance of one power) or multipolarity (many centres of power)?

On global watch

Today, the American population of 325 million is the third highest in the world. Still, that total is less than five per cent of the world population and small by comparison with the billion-plus populations of China and India. However, the United States accounts on its own for over 40 per cent of global military expenditures, exceeding those of the next ten nations combined. The current amount it spends on defence per year is similar (adjusted for inflation) to its military spending during the Cold War when it faced a direct military competitor. Perhaps more significant is the legacy effect, as the United States has been investing tens of billions of dollars per year in defence technology since the Second World War. That investment has built a capacity that gives it a peerless military advantage in nearly every aspect of warfare. As we enter a period known as the 'Revolution in Military Affairs', when drones and other types of advanced – and even autonomous – weaponry become the new norm, the United States has a significant head start.

The United States Armed Forces is the only military with the ability to carry out truly global operations. It has a worldwide network of nearly 700 bases and other military-related facilities that supports its overseas deployment of more than 200,000 military personnel. Command and control for these forces is provided by several redundant and protected communications, intelligence and surveillance systems. Orbiting above the earth are dozens of US military satellites. Constantly circling the skies above several of the earth's trouble spots is an air armada of American military drones. Finally, roaming the world's oceans are ten US aircraft carrier groups – perhaps the most illustrative statistic as no other state has more than two. This military is substantially bigger than is needed to defend the American homeland. The United States is a geographically advantaged nation with oceans on two of its sides and non-hostile states (Canada and Mexico) on the other two. It is a nation that is hard to invade because of those oceans and even harder to intimidate because of its scale and wealth. Although reachable by missiles, the United States maintains a formidable nuclear deterrent force that has global reach.

The US military is scaled to maintain what it describes as global stability. In other words, the tempering of regional conflicts via deterrence and engagement. But, no one elected the United States to the position of global security manager. When the Cold War ended, no force stood in the way. It had the global presence, the alliance and aid relationships and the extra military resources to intervene anywhere to prevent conflicts from escalating and to provide assistance when famine or natural disasters struck. Some viewed this as a moral obligation as they believed American leadership was an indispensable force for good in the world. For others, the United States was acting more narrowly and using the opportunity of a lack of a rival to embed its position as the world's dominant power and gain a long-term advantage over any future rivals.

A world full of troubles

The United States has been constantly engaged in military operations of one type or another since the end of the Cold War. The seizure of Kuwait by Saddam Hussein's Iraq in 1990 is an early example. The United States led an international coalition to liberate Kuwait soon afterwards in what was known as the Gulf War. Unlike the second US-Iraq war 12 years later in 2003, the Gulf War of 1991 was authorised by the United Nations Security Council. Another mission for American forces just after the Cold War ended was the humanitarian effort in Somalia. Warring factions there had disrupted the distribution of food, causing widespread hunger and the potential for a major famine. Under a United Nations mandate, a US-led coalition sought to bring relief and stability to Somalia. Fighting among the factions soon spiralled out of control and the aid mission collapsed as the United States and other nations withdrew troops from the chaos to prevent any more of their personnel being killed or wounded. Somalia had become the classic failed state, a land and a people without a functioning government. The United States, chastened by the Somalian experience, has since been hesitant to help in other such cases. It turned away from intervening in the 1994 genocide in Rwanda, as did other members of the international community. However, it has gradually returned to involvement in Africa via training and supporting the regional coalitions acting as peacekeepers in African Union and/or United Nations operations, especially those directed against militant Islamic terrorist groups like Boko Haram. Significant effort has also gone into humanitarian projects related to fighting international piracy off the Horn of Africa and combatting pandemics such as Ebola and HIV/AIDS.

Elsewhere, the nations freed by the collapse of the Soviet Union face continuing problems as Russia seeks to reclaim lost territory and protect the interests of ethnic Russian populations caught on what they see as the wrong side of new borders. Russia annexed Crimea from Ukraine in 2014 and has also intervened in parts of Georgia and Moldova. And Ukraine endures a Russian-supported rebellion in its disaffected eastern regions. Although the United States now rotates combat units through Northern and Eastern European nations, and is constructing a ballistic missile defence system on NATO's eastern frontier, West Europeans have been content to be mostly worried observers, concerned about Russian behaviour but also concerned about their trade with Russia. There seems no strong appetite in Europe to rise to the Russian challenge in any way other than via economic sanctions and punitive diplomacy.

Closer to home, in Latin America, there are constant problems with poverty, drugs and corruption. Haiti, the region's poorest country, has had US troops as frequent visitors – for instance, to help the government survive a coup attempt and to provide relief after a devastating earthquake. Columbia required substantial assistance to suppress a persistent insurgency, fed in part by narcotics traffic. Less visibly, the United States helps Mexico cope with wars among rival drug gangs that have cost thousands of lives and threaten the stability of the Mexican government. Several Central American nations suffer similarly. Through the Mexican border and the Caribbean flows a flood of migrants seeking to escape poverty and crime by heading north into the United States.

More than six decades after the 1953 truce that ended the Korean War, one of the first battles of the Cold War, the United States still keeps nearly 30,000 troops in South Korea to protect it from North Korea. American forces also keep Japan separated from its neighbours, several of whom have territorial disputes with Japan and outstanding grievances tied to Japan's behaviour prior to and during the Second World War. The most significant of the neighbours is China, whose expansive designs in the South China Sea appear to threaten the interests of many Southeast Asian states as well as the right of free passage for shipping through one of the most travelled international shipping routes. The US Navy has stepped up its patrols in the region and other elements of the US military, primarily the Marine Corps, have begun rotating units to Australia in what some have called the 'Pivot', a US military rebalance towards to Asia.

This quick contextual sweep across the globe does not reflect the central concern the United States has when it looks out to the world. Since 9/11, when it was attacked by Al-Qaeda, its main military preoccupation has been in fighting transnational terrorism. This includes a 2001 invasion of Afghanistan, where the leaders of Al-Qaeda were being harboured by the Taliban regime. It also includes drone and other raids in Pakistan where some of the terrorist leadership had fled. Most notably, perhaps, it also includes an invasion of Iraq in 2003 to depose Saddam Hussein, supposedly to eliminate his efforts to develop and stockpile weapons of mass destruction. Both Afghan and Iraqi actions succeeded quickly in removing the offending regimes, but led to ongoing and costly counter-insurgency campaigns that have destabilised neighbouring countries. The so-called 'Global War on Terror' has ensured that the gaze of the United States remains cast widely, especially in those regions where terrorism is prevalent such as the Middle

East and North Africa. This extends beyond traditional military means into areas of intelligence and cyber warfare.

A world full of free riders?

The United States does not always act alone. Often it is in a coalition of one kind or another. Some of the coalitions are authorised by United Nations Security Council mandates such as those in Somalia and Haiti. Others are under NATO auspices, as in Bosnia, Kosovo and Libya. Others are the product of the recruitment of 'coalitions of the willing', such as those formed for the invasion of Iraq in 2003 when the United Nations would not approve the war. Coalitions are important because they add political legitimacy at home and abroad to interventions with a high risk of substantial casualties and long-term costs. The American public typically sees the participation of other nations as an endorsement of its own leaders' wisdom in deciding to intervene. That being said, as Afghanistan and Iraq demonstrated in their initial phases, the United States is perfectly willing to act on its own when it feels there are serious threats to its security. This is also the case when there are complications or delays in gaining international approval and assistance. Acting alone is often referred to as 'unilateralism'. Strong states such as the United States can be prone to acting unilaterally because they do not always feel bound by shared rules or norms. However, this can have consequences and it is more common for states to at least appeal to multilateral principles and practices so they do not incur the wrath of the international community. The issue with the United States is that, arguably, it has the power to withstand any such criticism.

American politicians complain occasionally about the burdens the United States carries, but not often and not with conviction. NATO was created to contain the westward spread of the Soviet Union during the Cold War. The principle of NATO is that it offers a collective security guarantee for all of its members. If one member is attacked, all others are treaty-bound to respond to the aggression. In the Cold War context, this was to deter any communist attack on Western Europe so that communism would not spread any further. However, it has expanded greatly since the end of the Cold War, even absorbing many former republics of the Soviet Union. NATO endures in the post-communist era because collective security is a positive thing for states, especially those newly independent states that fear Russian resurgence. But, few of the newer or older members of NATO meet the alliance's goal of allocating 2 per cent of Gross Domestic Product (GDP) to defence. Instead, they are safe in the knowledge that the United States, which invests nearly twice that, will be there to do the heavy lifting when a crisis arises.

This raises the larger issue, which is that it appears to some in America that other rich states find excuses to do little for global security or even their own defence. Japan and Germany, the world's third and fourth biggest economies, seem to prefer to be on what is now mostly a voluntary parole for their Second World War crimes. Japan spends about 1 per cent of its GDP on defence. Germany does participate in some United Nations and NATO-sponsored operations, but largely avoids a combat role. Both nations are shielded from nuclear threats by a US deterrence policy that promises them protection from challenges by other nuclear powers. The United Kingdom and France, the fifth and sixth largest global economies, do contribute to global security somewhat in proportion to their wealth. Both, however, have found it hard to prioritise military spending as they embark on domestic austerity policies in the wake of the 2008 financial crisis. South Korea has an economy just outside the world's top ten. It is at least 25 times richer than North Korea on a per capita basis and has double the North's population. Yet it leaves the task of defending itself primarily to the United States. South Korea rarely participates in coalitions to help others, and when it does, as in the case of Afghanistan, it sends non-combat troops. The Scandinavian countries, particularly Demark and Sweden, are exceptions, but Spain, Italy and a half-dozen other developed countries seem to prefer to opt out from most of the hard work in international coalitions. Going beyond Western nations and those with historic ties to the United States; China and India are big in many dimensions but both are absorbed with their own security interests. China has the world's second-largest economy and India the ninth. Both are greatly expanding their military power, but both limit their participation in international peacekeeping efforts and global security issues. China's recent focus has been on asserting itself as Asia's dominant power, causing unease among its neighbours who had grown accustomed to a more inward-looking China.

Finding an alternative world order

As the Cold War was ending US president George H. W. Bush and Soviet Communist Party General Secretary Mikhail Gorbachev declared there was a new world order emerging that would be based upon cooperation between the two superpowers. But with the collapse of the Soviet Union, only one super power remained to provide order. Filled with both goodwill and vast hubris, the United States has set itself an unsustainable task of maintaining global security. It is unsustainable because such a world order is in neither America's interest nor in the interests of the world at large. Although it is possible to concoct long causal chains that tie American safety or prosperity to the fate of failing states in Africa or ethnic conflict in the Balkans, most global problems are distant and of marginal importance to the United States. On the contrary, American involvement in these distant problems can be said to threaten American interests. Interventions often produce enemies, with some of those affected assuming it is not altruistic motives that drive the United States but a desire to steal their assets or slander their religion. And there are real costs of blood and resources. Americans (and of course non-Americans) die in these distant fights and domestic needs such as education and healthcare are neglected as vast sums of money are diverted to military operations.

Those challenged by the United States, including Russia, China and many in the Middle East, deny the legitimacy of its actions and see the United States as a neo-imperial power meddling in the affairs of others. Even America's allies worry about the wisdom of its interventions, most especially the invasion of Iraq in 2003. People the world over concern themselves with who is going to be the next president of the United States, even though they cannot vote in its elections, because of the potential impact a presidential choice has on US foreign policy and its readiness to intervene in their states. Some Americans hope that the United States will come to its strategic senses and abandon the quest to manage global security (Gholz, Press and Sapolsky 1997; Posen 2014). Others believe that the expansion of the welfare state, especially with the implementation of national health insurance and the aging of the population, will curtail military spending in the United States and the temptation to be the world's sole superpower (King 2013). The economy too is a potential restraining factor as the American global policing wars of the post-Cold War era have been financed through extensive borrowing that someday will need to be repaid. The United States may be the world's leading economy, but it has debts of approximately $20 trillion.

If not the United States in the lead, then who? The alternatives are not robust. The United Nations makes itself responsible for significant peacekeeping, particularly in Africa. But it is limited in resources and also by the Security Council's veto system whereby any of the five permanent members can reject an action. This can lead to gridlock and indecision in even the most pressing of cases. There are also persistent problems related to member participation, troop training, discipline, equipment and sustainment for UN peacekeepers. And although they have been forced to do some serious fighting at times to separate or suppress warring factions, they cannot conduct sustained combat operations without the military weight of a major power. The United Nations is also dependent on financial contributions from member states to keep it afloat – it does not have an independent income. The United States is the largest donor. Regional organisations such as the African Union and the European Union are also active in peacekeeping, both in conjunction with the United Nations and on their own. Supplementing their work are relief organisations such as the International Red Cross, Doctors without Borders and the International Rescue Committee. All of this is vital, but it is not enough when the United States is removed, financially and militarily.

Serious change can only come about if the United States actually does less international intervening and those states (or organisations) closer to trouble spots are forced to act when their security is at risk. Other large rich nations will have to fill the vacuum if the United States pulls back from managing global security. Test cases are interventions in Libya (2011) and Syria (2013–), where American reluctance to act has been particularly evident, even though both are marked by a degree of US engagement. The vast regions of North Africa and the Middle East are beset by security problems that outsiders can seemingly neither settle nor fully escape (Engelhardt 2010). Colonialism left behind non-viable boundaries. Although there are many natural resources, the most exportable is oil, which usually enriches rulers, not the masses. Sectarian divides and a rising tide of extremism afflict Islam, the dominant faith. It is territory governed weakly or exploitatively but rarely democratically. But the rich nations of the world are responsible for at least part of the chaos as they are all consumers of oil, former colonialists and/or occasional interveners. They also get some of the refugees and see all of the images of the suffering. The United States will likely find its interventionist urges in the Middle East and North Africa tamed by memories of past failed efforts, high casualty rates, wasted assistance and lack of effective international and local partners (Bacevich 2016). Certain former colonial powers may feel a continuing obligation to help, but they too have memories of past failures. Some states in both Africa and the Middle East can defend themselves, but most cannot. The rise of a regional hegemon is possible, but the area is full of competitors marked out by the long rivalry between Saudi Arabia and Iran – which are also the leading states, each representing one of Islam's two major branches. What is left is continuing turmoil and perhaps disaster. And given that scenario, the question should be asked: who will assist if not the United States?

For other regions of the world a post-US framework of security is more readily available or more easily constructed than it is in the Middle East and North Africa. The European Union (or a NATO minus the United States) can easily control security in Europe or even deal with a resentful Russia should it find the political will. The European Union has more people than and is approximately as rich as the United States. It should have no need for or any claim on American troops for the security of Europe. There are more serious challenges relating to security arrangements for South America, Africa, the Middle East, and Asia. For South America the problem some might see is keeping the United States out. But US interest in South America after the Second World War was largely prompted by fear of the spread of communism and the influence of the Soviet Union, both of which are fading from memory. The South American nations themselves have several boundary problems but little inclination to settle them through the use of force, at least in recent years. Most South American nations focus their attention on economic growth, which is sporadic but not non-existent. Fortunately for all concerned, self-restraint has tempered the competition for regional dominance and arms racing. In Asia the prime security issue is how to accommodate the rise of a richer, more assertive China. But many other nations in Asia also have large populations and growing economies. Most advantageous for regional security would be the development of regional institutions that can temper territorial disputes without interrupting the pathway to continued prosperity. Some nations seem to want to keep the United States engaged in Asia to balance an ever more powerful China. No doubt the United States needs to think of ways to adjust to China, but getting involved in regional disputes is not likely to be one of them.

Conclusion

It is important to understand that the United States cannot be taken for granted. This is equally true whether it continues – or tries to continue – the role that it established for itself in the twentieth century or becomes a 'normal' power much as the United Kingdom did following the Second World War. The rivalry of superpowers that we saw in the past was a certain kind of world order. The hubris of one rich and powerful nation, the United States, is another. Should the United States change its priorities, the large, rich nations of the world may collectively find the need and will to create yet another form of order – one in which they share the decision-making and costs of taking necessary actions. If this does not occur, it is likely that dominant regional powers will provide local security – as meagre or brutal as that may be. The North Africa and Middle East regions lack a plausible candidate for this role and will likely remain in turmoil until one emerges. There could be a struggle among potential contenders, in those and in some other regions, that escalates into more serious conflict. Thus, a large part of the world may continue to be torn by instability, with few voluntary interveners for the foreseeable future. The question many will ask is can more stable regions such as Europe and North America isolate themselves from this instability? Or, does peace and security at home require – as those in America who favour intervention abroad claim – a constant foreign military involvement? Considering such issues as the migration crisis in Europe, which has at its roots instability outside Europe, brings real focus to these questions. Another worry is competition among regional powers. Once a nation gains dominance locally, will it have an irresistible temptation to expand as the United States did after the Second World War? Again, this question brings us back to the issue of China's rise. With all of this in mind, some may come to remember 'Pax Americana', for all its faults, as an era of peace and stability.

18

Crossings and Candles

PETER VALE

'It is better to light a candle than curse the darkness'
W. L. Watkinson 1838–1925

An old lesson teaches that endings are more difficult to write than beginnings. This may be so, but I have found it difficult to even begin writing about the world International Relations (IR) makes without reflecting on a near-forty-year career in both the theory and practice of IR. This is because my intellectual engagement in IR is indivisible from who I am. To make the same point in a slightly more elevated mode, although trained in the tradition that a scholar's gaze is objective, my academic pilgrimage has been one of continuous crossings between the personal, the political and the professional. My early professional life was conducted during a particularly nasty period of apartheid in South Africa. Not only was the minority-white-ruled government cracking down on all forms of political dissent, it was also wedded to a fierce anti-communism. In these circumstances it was difficult to exercise academic objectivity when it came to thinking about the world. Those years taught me a valuable lesson in life and learning: to believe that there is a totally objective or value-free view in IR is to call up the old Russian saying that 'he lied like an eye witness!' We all come to understand the world through our own experiences. Because of this, even the most objective person has predetermined understandings about the world.

A standard dictionary definition of international relations runs that the term 'is used to identify all interactions between state-based actors across state boundaries' (Evans and Newnham 1998, 274). This is certainly suggestive of the scholarly field of IR but unhelpful in explaining the international relationships that fall between the cracks of the discipline's many boundaries and the personal anxiety and fear around these issues. After all, at the height of the Cold War there was real fear that the entire planet would be destroyed by nuclear warfare. In these circumstances, it was difficult not to be anxious about the future or fearful for one's family. So we ought to require, perhaps, that a definition does something more than simply demarcate boundaries. A more reflective gaze points to what it is that we, the prospective student or emeritus professor, actually do when we 'do' academic IR and why it matters to us.

The four-minute mile

To understand why it matters to me, I will begin with a story of a crossing – a very recent one – between my colonial boyhood and my late-middle-aged self. This particular one took place not in South Africa, the country in which I was born and of which I am a citizen, but in England.

To explain why the crossing between past and present matters to my own understanding of IR, some personal background is required. Growing up in colonial South Africa, my home was littered with the culture of England – a country that my South African-born mother never visited until she was fifty. In addition, the boarding school that I attended was loosely modelled on the English public school tradition. So, we were encouraged to participate in the forms of organised sport that were England's 'gift' to the world. Understandably then, my earliest thinking about what made the international was set by the cultural authority of England and the political sweep of the British Empire. Given this, the story of Roger Bannister's sub-four-minute mile had a particular appeal for my young self. To explain: the measured mile became an important test in competitive athletics in the early 1950s. It was long believed that no person could run a mile in under four minutes. But, in the aftermath of the Second World War, when physical training and nutrition techniques improved along with the instruments for timing, the four-minute mile came closer and closer to being conquered. Indeed, breaking the barrier became a sort of milestone competitive goal for both individual athletes and the countries they represented.

My initial fascination with the four-minute mile was ignited by an edition of the *Eagle Sports Album*, which had been sent to the school library from London. In its pages, much was made of the importance of Bannister's feat for Britain and Britons like my family, who were located in distant parts of the world. The drama of the event whetted a life-long interest in athletics. Finally, while on a trip to Oxford in October 2015, I visited the field on the Iffley Road where Bannister ran the famous measured mile. Like many a pilgrimage, the visit was exciting, elating and enlightening. As I stood on the 'Roger Bannister running track' – as the field is now called – I looked for the church flagpole that Bannister had spotted seconds before his famous run. When a young man carrying spiked running shoes walked by, I remembered, if only for a fleeting moment, the thrill of competitive running. But more important than the rush was the slow realisation that what had happened on that famous day offered lessons in how I had first come to know and understand the world of IR.

Until the visit, it never occurred to me that what had taken place on the day of the event was a quintessential moment of modernity – the conquering of space by time. In IR, of course, the control of territory through the instruments and techniques of administration and the control that follows is the very essence of the discipline. So, the idea of the international has no meaning unless territory is under the control of sovereignty. As a result, bringing ungoverned places into the idea of the international is the very first order of business in international relations. The notion of sovereignty, which is the enabling force of IR, follows upon this demarcation of space opening towards the exercise of control along a boundary-line between 'the international' and 'the domestic'. Technology, in the form of maps and their making, helped to make 'permanent' such boundaries in the minds of rulers – especially colonial ones (see Branch 2014).

Strictly speaking, without boundaries there can be no IR. But, the divide between the boundaries drawn by the instruments of modernity are not the tightly patrolled frontier with its technology of control – passports, visa, immigration documents and the like. It is a liminal space where inclusion and exclusion is negotiated continuously. So, there were – as there remain – forms of interaction between groups who have resisted incorporation into the command and control that orthodox IR insists is the gift of statehood. This betwixt-and-between space has been a site of great tragedy, as the migrant crisis in Europe that began in 2015 shows. In many places, outside of the authoritative gaze of modern media, frontiers were killing fields. European colonisation, which drew the furthest corners on the planet into a single political whole under the banner of civilisation and Christianity, was extremely violent. If killing was one dimension of this, another was the disruption to the ways of living of millions upon millions. This violent disruption in the lives of people continued into the 1960s as the idea of the international spread across the world.

One example was a 1965 agreement in which Britain gave an archipelago of islands in the Indian Ocean to the United States. The residents of these islands, known collectively as the Chagos islands, were forcibly moved. In the past fifty years, the islanders themselves and their descendants have made numerous unsuccessful legal attempts to overturn this decision. Generally speaking, tragedies like these – which occur at the margin of the world – have been ignored in IR – although anthropologists, historians and international lawyers have explored them.

The second issue that occurred to me was the power of who pronounces on these matters. In literature – and increasingly in social science – this is the issue of 'voice': who gets to speak, how they get to speak and why this happens. At the policy end of IR, alas, the issue of voice is seldom considered a priority issue, notwithstanding the path-breaking insights that feminists have brought to the discipline. They have exposed the multiple ways in which women experience the international differently to men and how they are silenced in the story of the international despite the significant roles they have and continue to play in its creation.

Two signs on Iffley Road declare Bannister's triumph. The first, which is mounted on a stone gatepost, is informational. It reads, 'Here at the Iffley Road track the first sub-four-minute mile was run on 6th May 1954 by ROGER BANNISTER. Oxford University.' The second is positioned above a wooden fence facing Iffley Road. Under the crest of Oxford University, it reads, 'Here, on 6 May 1954, Roger Bannister set a new World Mile record of 3 minutes 59.4 seconds. The first Mile ever run under 4 minutes.' If the first sign informs, the second proclaims Bannister's achievement as truth. Here, in the historical conquest of space by time, there is no room for ambiguity.

Let us be clear about several things. Of course, the Iffley Road field was the site of the first 'timed', 'authenticated' or 'measured' mile run under four minutes. But – and this is why critical questioning is important in IR, as it is in all forms of knowledge – it seems unlikely that nobody else, anywhere else, across human history had ever run this distance in under four minutes. Indeed, medical science today suggests that humans with particular kinds of physiological traits are able to run faster over distance than those without them. For our purposes of understanding my appreciation of IR, this signage – its declaration and its claim to authority – is rooted in a white, Western, male-dominated world. This is the world into which I was born and raised. Outside of this, nothing is worthy of recognition. It confirms that the late-imperial gaze of the early 1950s, when Bannister ran his famous mile, had little understanding of, or interest in, the non-West.

It seems obvious that prejudices like these need to be challenged, but this is difficult because mainstream IR has elevated its denial of the non-Western world to an art form. For many, the business of IR remains mortgaged to the commonsense understandings of race, class and gender that marked the early decades of the twentieth century when IR emerged as a formal academic discipline. As a result, in many corners of the world, IR is called a 'mutant' discipline (Vale 2016a). This is because IR seems to have no conceptual capacity – no grammar or vocabulary, as social theorists might say – to explain the everyday lives of people who live beyond or beneath sovereign borders. And, because it has no adequate category to include them, IR fails to understand them.

Servant of empire

There is an obvious link between the claims of the signs on Iffley Road and how it is that the voice of authority is used to preserve and sustain social orders. In the Iffley Road case, the claims to authority and the making of history aimed to position British authority in a quickly changing world. After the Second World War, the United Kingdom scrambled to reassert its global positioning in the face of the rising post-war profile of the United States. Roger Bannister's achievement and the authority offered by one of the world's great universities, Oxford, was one way to do so. At the time, the four-minute mile was linked to another attempt to reposition the United Kingdom internationally – the summiting of the world's highest mountain (Everest) by a British-led expedition, which had taken place almost exactly a year before events on the Iffley Road track.

The dilemma that the British faced in the world was best captured by US Secretary of State Dean Acheson, who famously pointed out that 'Great Britain … [has] … lost an empire and has not yet found a role' (1962). Although no longer an imperial power, the United Kingdom's hold on the imagination of the world – and how it is organised and studied, through IR – continues via its culture and language. It appears, however, in some quite perverse ways. This outcome was foretold in the late 1960s by Richard Turnbull, the governor of the colony of Aden (now part of Yemen). Turnbull informed a future British cabinet minister, Denis Healey, 'that when the British Empire finally sank beneath the waves of history it would leave behind only two monuments: one was the game of Football, the other was the expression, "Fuck Off"' (Healey 1989, 283). Though a vulgar phrase like this is seldom heard in IR, British cultural imperialism lingers in the discipline, which explains why English is its tongue. In no small part this is because the language of global culture is increasingly English – a fact readily attributed to the global reach not of the United Kingdom but of the United States. This suggests another relationship between IR and modernity. The third instrument of modernity, after time and space, is language. Like the other two, the English language has set the borderlines for inclusion and exclusion in the world and in its study through IR.

The place of language and culture in fostering international relationships is explained by the idea of Soft Power (Nye 1990). This concept helpfully drew the issue of culture towards the centre of IR but was silent on the dimensions of language. This is because, as we have already noted, English has been proclaimed a 'global language' and therefore objective in its views of the ways of the world. But no language is neutral. Two further points suggest the limitations of having a monopoly of one language in IR – and, indeed, in other social sciences. The first draws upon the thinking of the Austrian philosopher Ludwig Wittgenstein – who pointed to the conceptual limitations of language – and is caught in his famous phrase, 'the limits of my language mean the limits of my world'. So, however commanding language is as a tool to access the social world, its vocabulary sets limits on our understanding. Second, if English remains the language of IR, the discipline will not only be the domain of a global elite but will continue its long history of serving and servicing insiders. Those who have no knowledge of English are excluded from IR, or they can only access the discipline by developing a professional competence in the language. This is plainly discriminatory. There is also the challenge of the English language unable to grasp concepts that lie outside of its vocabulary. For instance, the Sanskrit word 'dharma' is translated as 'religion', but dharma in the Hindu cosmology includes a range of practices and conceptions of rights, duties, law and so on, which are not divinely ordained, as in Christianity. Other important terms in the vocabulary of IR – such as 'state', 'civilisation' and 'order' – are sometimes lost in translation.

World-making

One of the great disciplinary shibboleths is that IR is to be celebrated because it is a neutral instrument of restoration – IR does not so much 'make' the world as 'restore' it (Kissinger 1957). According to this logic, the discipline provides helpful tools – and, sometimes, a hopeful heart – that a world devastated by war can be restored by the discipline's science. But here too there is a need for a contrarian view. Largely absent from this optimism are the interlinked questions: who has the right to remake the world and whose interests will be served by any remaking? These questions would not have troubled those responsible for making – or remaking – the international community on three previous occasions: at the end of the South African War (1899–1902); at the end of the First Word War (1914–1918); and at the end of the Second World War (1939–1945). Certainly, each of these moments presented as a time of despair interlaced with feelings of hope for what might come; each was marked by a particular configuration of politics, both local and global; and each was held captive by the vocabulary of the moment. Let's consider each event in turn.

The South African War (also known as the Second Boer War) was fought between the United Kingdom and the peoples of European descent on African soil known as Afrikaners. This is because the Westphalian state – and the diplomatic routines developing around it – had migrated from its European heartland to Africa. It was the culmination of many contestations for the positioning of an alien social form, the modern state, on a new continent. As recent work has shown, the making of the world after the South African War was concerned with reorganising the British Empire, which was then the dominant form of international organisation. The idea of shifting understandings of what constituted sovereign identity away from an imperial setting towards a species of 'inter-nation' exchange, primarily between Britain and its four settler-ruled vassals – Australia, Canada, New Zealand and South Africa – had gained salience in the years following the First World War. If the three other dominions showed that the local and the international could be seamlessly realigned, South Africa – with its diverse peoples – was a harbinger of the messy world to come. Hence, for the theoreticians of the empire, the reorganisation of the colonies in southern Africa into the single state of South Africa foreshadowed a model for the dismembering of empire. Thus, the chosen path was the idea of an 'organic union', a system that gestured towards the importance of sovereignty within the semblance of an imperial brotherhood – in modern terms, it was a particular strain of multilateralism.

The later incorporation of white-ruled India into this organisation would end in the British Commonwealth. Out of this, in the 1930s, grew the idea of a white-dominated 'World Commonwealth', sometimes called a 'World State' (Curtis 1938). The thought crime – there is no other phrase for it – in this world-making was that all the imaginings of the international excluded other racial groups except in the sense of 'trusteeship'. After the First World War, this status was awarded to states that could be 'trusted' to control foreign spaces in the interests of those who were deemed to be lower down the Darwinian ladder (Curtis 1918, 13). The legacy of this move remains the great unexplored story in IR as an academic discipline because it continues to suffer from the arrogance of defining the international by the optic provided by wealth, race and gender.

In the lore of IR, the restoration of the world after the First World War is sacred ground. The discipline's celebrated tale is how the international codified as science would build a better world. The discipline's institutionalisation was the founding of an academic chair, named after Woodrow Wilson, America's twenty-eighth president, at what is now Aberystwyth University in Wales. As Ken Booth (1991, 527–8) has pointed out, 'when David Davies founded the Department for International Politics at Aberystwyth in 1919, he became the midwife for the subject everywhere.' The genuflection to the United States suggests that the establishment of the discipline was in recognition of America's importance in ending the 'war to end all wars'. Not only did Wilson help to deliver victory, he also offered the League of Nations as an instrument for securing a future of international peace. But this was not to be. In the 1930s, the League failed to prevent another war – the idealism of early IR, around which the discipline was founded – was in tatters. The failure of this resolve, both institutionally and theoretically, is well documented in the chronicles of IR.

The construction of a new world was sought mainly through the idea of embedded liberalism, which could marry free trade, strong government and multilateralism (Ruggie 1982). But an inconvenient truth remained: global apartheid was entrenching itself. Absent in the great councils of peace were the voices of those who were situated in the outer reaches of world-making and excluded by IR's founding bargain. The truth was that sovereignty, and the passport it offered to statehood, was only available to those privileged by birth and by skin colour. The scientific task of understanding those who were excluded was for not IR, but for other academic disciplines, especially Applied Anthropology (on this, see Lamont 2014).

IR folklore holds that the international system is indebted to the triumph of American idealism. An end to American isolationism in the 1940s beckoned the world's most powerful country towards a reincarnation of its 'manifest destiny' – rooted in the nineteenth-century belief that settlers were foreordained to spread across North America. It was a belief shot through with understandings of white superiority, as this quote from the Maryland Democrat, William F. Giles, in 1847 suggests:

> We must march from ocean to ocean. ... We must march from Texas straight to the Pacific Ocean, and be bounded only by its roaring wave. ... It is the destiny of the white race, it is the destiny of the Anglo-Saxon race.

> (Zinn 1980, 153)

The call now was towards making 'the international' as it had made the national – with technology, violence and self-belief. Hopes for this future were transmitted through the increased force of culture, especially American. The sense of 'freedom' that this sentiment conveyed was infectious, and it spread increasingly to all spaces – including colonised ones. In doing so, it fostered 'a period of optimism' throughout the world, as the Indian social theorist Ashis Nandy (2003, 1) put it. Interestingly, for all the celebration of the idea of freedom, the discourse suffered terrible amnesia: the story of the Haitian Revolution (1791–1804), the only successful slave revolution in modern history and a powerful example of black people making a state, conducting diplomacy and practising freedom, was excluded from the emerging narrative.

But American optimism and the future it promised arose in the very age when the conquest of nature by science promised to deliver much to the world. It is difficult today to underestimate how 'the endless frontier' – as America's chief scientist, Vannevar Bush (1945), called natural science – was received in the final years of the Second World War.

Demonstrably, the atom bomb, the quintessential product of science, had brought the war to an end – even though the surrender cry from Japan's emperor foreshadowed different understandings of what science had delivered to the people of Japan and to the world. Speaking after the second bomb was dropped on Nagasaki, Emperor Hirohito surrendered with these words: 'We have resolved to endure the unendurable and suffer what is insufferable.'

Conventional IR history has it that both politics and science – acting both on their own and together – speeded the desire of peoples all over the world for liberation, thus ending formal colonialism. This is certainly nominally so, but the reach of this freedom was, once again, to be framed within the sovereign state. If freedom was one dimension of an American-inspired post-1945 world, it was complimented by a series of international bureaucracies that aimed to manage the new world in the making. These drew sovereign states – both newly independent and well established – towards the bureaucratic authority insisted upon by modernity with its technical know-how and techniques of social control. The international community in the making was to be what anthropologists call an 'administered community' – both states and individuals would be controlled even as they celebrated their freedom.

So, the celebrated multilateral structures of post-1945 – the United Nations and the Bretton Woods family; the International Monetary Fund; the World Bank; and the General Agreement on Tariffs and Trade – were controlling institutions even if they were intermittently cloaked within a rights-based discourse. The archetype of this was the UN Security Council where the power of veto was vested in five states – China, France, Russia, the United Kingdom and the United States. This 'override power', which aimed to control any threat to the interest (or interests) of an already advantaged group, remains a symbol of an international structure that is fatally unequal and grossly unfair.

In academic IR, the reconstruction of the world after 1945 is the story of how the United States appropriated and adapted European 'understandings' of the international for the challenges it faced as 'leader of the free world'. The evidence supports this explanation: at least 64 first-generation émigré scholars (mostly from Germany) taught political science and IR in the United States. More than half of them came from law, including figures such as Hans Kelsen, Hans Morgenthau, John Herz and Karl Deutsch, who would command IR. The ways of the world that they transmitted – culture, diplomacy, law – remained essentially white, Western and male. In disciplinary IR, the non-West was deliberately silenced by exorcising two of the most important issues – decolonisation and racism – from its theoretical concerns (Guilhot 2014). It was this legacy that led the late Stanley Hoffman, who was born in Vienna, to declare that IR was 'an American Social Science' (1977).

The ghastly – but truly historical – advent of nuclear weapons certainly raised the question that awakened ethical concerns within IR, the most important of which has already crossed our paths: could humankind destroy the planet? Yet the counter-factual question on this issue, the question that should have mattered but which was never asked or answered, is: would the United States have atom-bombed a white Western country? At the centre of IR was – and remains – the ideology of white supremacy. This is undergirded by the understanding that only Europeans – and whites, to sharpen the point – live 'within' history: all others, as Ashis Nandy (2003, 83–109) has argued, 'live outside' of it.

If these three moments of reconstruction – the South African War, the Paris Peace Conference of 1919 which concluded the First World War, and the ending of the Second World War in 1945 – represented the remaking of the world, what about the ending of the Cold War? It is difficult not to believe that the ending of the Cold War has been one of continuity rather than the much-anticipated fundamental rethink of the nature and idea of the international. The moment was certainly marked by a new vocabulary, of which the word globalisation promised new horizons. However, it quickly became an encryption for the celebration of neoliberal economics and a 'thin' form of democracy that was characterised by Francis Fukuyama as 'the end of history' (Fukuyama 1989). In essence, Fukuyama argued that liberal democracy and capitalism had proved itself superior to any other social system. This theory was seized upon by IR scholars who had, embarrassingly, failed to predict the ending of the Cold War. For IR theorists, the bipolarity that had characterised the Cold War was a stable system for both superpowers. They therefore saw no reason for either power to seek to end it. What they did not envision was that an internal collapse of the Soviet economy matched with the rising opposition of subjugated peoples in Eastern Europe would break the Soviet system from within. This was just one of the reasons that the critical turn in IR theory began around the end of the Cold War and IR began to look beyond the state towards the individual.

However, not long after this embarrassment there was a return to triumphalism. A US president, George H. W. Bush, declared that the 'West had won' the Cold War – but even this was not enough. What lay ahead was a new challenge that one disciple of realist thought called a 'clash of civilizations' (Huntington 1993). Let me insert a personal story here. Just after the Berlin Wall came down in 1989 – the event that symbolised the beginning of the end of the Cold War – I was invited to participate in a high-level panel organised by one of the big think tanks in the world, the New York-based Council on Foreign Relations. My co-panellists included former members of successive American cabinets, a former director of the CIA, and many academic luminaries from the IR community. During the course of several meetings, it became clear to me that Islam was being constructed as a threat to America's 'global interests' and that it would be targeted. This kind of thinking created a kind of intellectual swamp that gave rise to successive wars in Iraq and Afghanistan and, dangerously, for IR a tendency to focus disproportionately on such 'threats'. What this does to how the world is made remains to be seen.

Industrial IR

No academic development has had a greater impact on IR's recent history than the rise of think tanks. This is a big claim, to be sure, so let me illustrate it with a story from my own country. In the post-apartheid years, the emergence of a think tank called the Institute for Security Studies (ISS) shifted the hopes of the immediate post-apartheid years from the high idealism of the Nelson Mandela presidency towards a security-centred society. This, in a country where some ten million children – over 54 per cent – live in poverty. Elsewhere, as others have shown (see Ahmad 2014), think tanks have and continue to play a critical role in making the case for war against Islam in the United States, and in pushing the UK's Blair government to enthusiastically support the invasion of Iraq in 2003 (on this, see Abelson 2014).

Rather than viewing think tankers as neutral and disinterested parties in the making of IR, we must take them seriously. As the German-born critical thinker, Hannah Arendt (1970, 6), put it in her book, *On Violence:*

> There are ... few things that are more frightening than the steadily increasing prestige of scientifically minded brain trusters in the councils of government during the last decades. The trouble is not that they are cold-blooded enough to 'think the unthinkable,' but that they do not think.

In the economic-speak of our times, think-tankers are 'norm-entrepreneurs'; protagonists for one or another position on policy and its outcomes who, while claiming to provide objective analysis, are in fact complicit in pursuing particular agendas: political, economic and social.

Invariably, think-tankers are well schooled in the repertoire of IR; they have mastered its vocabulary and are familiar with its disciplinary traditions. Using this, think-tankers are encouraged to promote the current policy fashion by drawing uncritically on the prevailing meta-narrative. During the Cold War, for instance, think tanks in the West promoted the 'threat' posed by the Soviet Union (and its allies) in much of their work, which was also embedded within different shades of realist thinking.

Early in my own pilgrimage I worked for one such think tank: the South African Institute of International Affairs (SAIIA) which, nowadays, calls itself the country's 'premier research institute on international issues'. It was never branded as such when I worked there – perhaps that was because I was one of only two academic professionals on the staff. The other professional was John Barratt, my boss, who was a former South African diplomat. He had not studied IR, but read modern history at Oxford after taking a first degree – also in history – in South Africa. The watchwords for our work were 'facts' and 'objectivity' – to seek 'truth' in the way that practitioners in the natural sciences do. In this view of scholarship, knowledge was neutral and the role of SAIIA was to present as many opinions as possible in international affairs so that the public could make up their own minds. This was in the 'non-political' spirit of London's Chatham House on which the SAIIA was modelled.

Sustaining this position in the South Africa of the 1970s was bizarre. The apartheid government had cracked down on internal dissent with the result that censorship was pervasive, even in universities. There was, for example, no access to the vigorous debates on the liberation of South Africa that were taking place amongst exiled groups. More seriously, the country's black community had absolutely no voice in the management and the affairs of the SAIIA: they did serve the tea, however. In the 1970s I often thought that the good and the great who gathered in the SAIIA classical-styled headquarters were of the view that those on the other side of apartheid's cruel divide had no imaginary, or, indeed, experience, of the international.

John Barratt was often as frustrated by this state of affairs as was I, and we made several efforts – mostly unsuccessful – to cross the divide. What the corporate sponsors of the SAIIA would have made of these efforts is unknown. What I do know is that on many occasions I faced the raised eyebrows of the white liberals – and the not so liberal – who gathered, say, to deliberate on whether South Africa's outreach to independent black states was compatible with the policy of apartheid, or the unquestioning fealty of the white state towards the West in the face of sanctions (Vale 1989).

We need to pause here and return to Hannah Arendt's concerns: who stands to benefit from the work of think tanks? In the main, the funding is linked to the business sector. The assumption is that the work of think tanks – publications, public commentary, conferencing – reflects the interests of their sponsors and the status quo. Certainly, the conservative inclination of the SAIIA, when I worked there, was a reflection of the interests of South African business in the 1970s, as successive waves of critical scholars, including myself, have been keen to point out. This personal experience confirms four things. First, access to the discipline – certainly in South Africa, but elsewhere too – was a closed shop. IR was an elitist pursuit. Second, the conversations were limited by particular vocabularies. Certainly, they were not critical in the sense of asking deep questions and, in the press of the everyday, reflecting on what we were doing. Third, a particular meta-narrative – the Cold War – framed all the analysis. But mostly, and fourth, think tanks are what sociologists have called 'total institutions' – institutions with tight regimens, tight supervision and rules that 'routine' professional behaviour. These observations were confirmed when, a few years later, I spent some time as a research associate in a more cosmopolitan think tank community at the International Institute for Strategic Studies (IISS) in London.

As the Cold War ended, the meta-narrative of IR shifted. Today, the almost pre-packaged understanding of the 'advantages' of liberal reform – often simply a code for economic austerity – is stock-in-trade for contemporary think tanks. While neoliberal economics as an instrument of social engineering, both domestically and internationally, has increasingly hovered over the discipline, security and geopolitics remain the staple diet of the policy end of IR. In fact, threading these together is not new. The most famous example (yet notoriously overlooked in IR circles) is the Nixon administration's intervention in Chile in September 1973. This coup against the democratically elected government occurred almost at the mid-point of the United States' two-decades-long direct involvement in this country. Driven by Cold War anti-communism, the United States was determined to keep the Marxist-inclined government of Salvador Allende in check. The successful right-wing military coup was a precursor to a policy of social control, which gathered force from 1975 onwards, and was based on neoliberal economic policies. But in its more recent incarnation, under the utopian guise of globalisation, there is a sense that a 'neo-liberal corporate takeover ... has asserted America's centrality in the world' (Buell 2000, 310).

Three further points on think tanks need to be aired. First, as the discipline has become a popular academic subject, more and more IR graduates have entered the work place, and think tanks are significant places of employment. Indeed, it is possible to talk about IR as an academic 'industry' grounded in think tanks. This is linked to the second of my points, that there exists a triangular relationship between think tank, sponsors and the press or social media. Finally, the interaction of people trained in the same grammar and vocabulary often produces groupthink and a closed insider terminology. It becomes impossible to see beyond closed and often self-selecting groups – called 'experts' – who are pre-destined, almost, to repeat the same ideas to each other. Can any of these practices be conducive to sound policy outcomes? This is where the 'critical turn' in IR, which began in the early 1980s and spread in the course of the decade to several of its sub-fields, is especially important for understanding the future of IR and the world it makes. The arrival of critical theories opened up a space to question legitimately the theory and practice of an inner sanctum in the discipline. It certainly enabled me to be self-reflexive of my own thinking and to ask searching questions about the theory and practice of security in southern Africa (Vale 2003).

As in every discipline, and in every facet of life and knowing, sources of certainty have to be questioned continuously and critical perspectives have freed the space for doing so in IR. The constant challenge in our professional lives – especially in IR – is to negotiate the space between understanding what questions are intellectually interesting and which will truly make the world a better place.

Talk, text, technology

Technology matters in the world that IR makes – it always has and it always will. This is because it helps us understand and explain the world and also helps to shape it. So, the same kinds of technology that have helped to develop drones that are killing people in the Middle East and elsewhere have also enabled the delivery of more effective health care in remote parts of the world. Today, technology seems – irrevocably, perhaps – to have changed how scholars and students access information and how it is processed and published in an acceptable and professional way. This is because technology is changing faster than are understandings of the world that IR is making.

Technology also constantly changes the very 'stuff' of IR. For example, the complex and still unresolved relationship between IR and the idea of globalisation may well be the result of IR's failure to understand the fact that new technologies have eroded the discipline's central tenets – those of sovereignty, order, power and the very idea of 'the international'.

Technology may well have finally shattered any hope of a detached, or objective, search for truth that the academic discipline of IR once hoped to tap from the practices of the natural sciences. Can IR scholars pretend to be objective on an issue when technology (media, internet) regularly reminds us that in some distant place, bodies are piling up?

Notwithstanding IR's undertaking to provide understanding and rationality, technology seems to have widened conceptual cracks at the social, political and economic levels. As I write these words, there seems no end to the erosion of this order and the headaches that will follow. Consider three technology-generated issues that immediately knock against IR's busy windows. First, as viruses like Zika, Ebola and HIV/AIDS spread, the invariable question is whether technology can halt this. Second, packaging its ideological message in bundles fashioned by technology, the Islamic State group continues to wreak havoc and draw in supporters globally. Finally, the global monetary system is flummoxed by bitcoin – technology's reimagining of what money is, and can be, at the global level.

Is one tradition of storytelling in IR – that of the state, sovereignty and an international system – at an end? In earlier times, the making of the international was slow and ponderous as letters and directives travelled slowly between the metropole and periphery. Today, this is an instantaneous process – the international is being made and remade by bits, bytes and blogs. The discipline is challenged to respond to this new way of knowing – which makes the book in which this chapter appears – with its presentation in various formats and its open access – an investment in IR's future.

Conclusion

I draw to a close my reflections on the 'doing' of IR by returning to the epigram at the head of this chapter from W. L Watkinson, an English Methodist minister. It is also the motto of Amnesty International. If the idea of 'crossings' in the title comes from my confession, made at the beginning, that the personal, the professional and the political have been interwoven in my approach to IR over four decades, the other image in the title encapsulates a belief that IR – especially in its critical mode – is a kind of candle that casts light in often very dark places.

There is a paradox which stalks the discipline of IR: as it speaks of peace, the principle of sovereignty, which is at the centre of its world view, looks out upon messy – and often very violent – social relationships. These pages have suggested that there are no uncontaminated places in the making and remaking of these social relationships; there is thus no space where IR can escape the hot breath of compromise, concession or conciliation. However, the task, which lies beyond the pages of this book, is to recognise that despite all that we are taught, this is still a largely unexplored world. It remains a place of infinite possibilities and a site of great hope.

References

Abelson, D. E. (2014). 'Old world, new world: the evolution and influence of foreign affairs think-tanks'. *International Affairs* 90(1): 125–42.

Acharya, U. D. (2008). 'War On Terror or Terror Wars: The Problem in Defining Terrorism'. *Development Journal of International Law and Policy* 37(4): 653–79.

Acheson, D. (1962). 'Our Atlantic Alliance: The Political and Economic Strands', speech at the United States Military Academy, West Point, New York, USA, 5 December.

Ahmad, M. I. (2014). *The Road to Iraq: The Making of a Neoconservative War*. Edinburgh: Edinburgh University Press, 1–256.

Appleby, R. S. (2000). *The Ambivalence of the Sacred: Religion, Violence and Reconciliation*. Lanham, MD: Rowman & Littlefield.

Americans for Tax Fairness (2014). *Walmart on Tax Day: How Taxpayers Subsidize America's Biggest Employer and Richest Family.* Washington, DC: Americans for Tax Fairness. Available at: www.americansfortaxfairness. org/files/Walmart-on-Tax-Day-Americans-for-Tax-Fairness-1.pdf

Anderson, C. (2004). 'The Long Tail', *Wired*. Available at: http://www.wired. com/2004/10/tail/

Arendt, H. (1970). *On Violence*. London: Allen Lane.

Asad, Talal (2003). *Formations of the Secular: Christianity, Islam, Modernity*. Stanford, CA: Stanford University Press.

Bacevich, Andrew J. (2016). *America's War for the Greater Middle East*. New York: Random House.

Beck, Guy L. (2012). *Sonic Liturgy: Ritual and Music in Hindu Tradition*. Columbia, SC: University of South Carolina Press.

Berger, Peter L. (1999). 'The Desecularisation of the World: A Global Overview'. In Peter L. Berger (ed.) *The Desecularisation of the World: Resurgent Religion and World Politics,* 1–18. Grand Rapids, MI: Eerdmans.

Blackwood, L., N. Hopkins and S. Reicher (2013). Muslim Encounters at Airports: the production of disengagement. Available at: www.sipr.ac.uk/downloads/AnnRep2011/Muslim_encounters.pdf

Blakeley, R. and M. Raphael (2016). 'Understanding Western State Terrorism. In R. Jackson (ed.) *Routledge Handbook of Critical Terrorism Studies,* ch. 15. Abingdon, UK: Routledge.

Booth, K. (1991). 'Security in anarchy: utopian realism in theory and practice'. *International Affairs* 67(3): 527–45.

Branch, J. (2014). *The Cartographic State: Maps, Territory and the Origins of Sovereignty.* Cambridge: Cambridge University Press.

Broad, W. J. and S. Peçanha (2015). 'The Iran Nuclear Deal: A Simple Guide'. *International New York Times,* 30 March. Available at: www.nytimes.com/interactive/2015/03/30/world/middleeast/100000003603418.mobile.html

Bronner, Simon J. (ed.) (2011). *Revisioning Ritual: Jewish Traditions in Transition.* Oxford: Littman Library of Jewish Civilisation.

Bruce, Steve (2002). *God is Dead: Secularisation in the West.* Malden, MA: Blackwell.

Buchheit, Paul (2013). 'Apple, Walmart, McDonald's: Who's the Biggest Wage Stiffer?'. *AlterNet,* 28 July. Available at: www.alternet.org/labor/apple-walmart-mcdonalds-whos-biggest-wage-stiffer

Buell, F. (2000). 'Ashis Nandy and Globalist Discourse'. In Vinay Lal (ed.) *Dissenting Knowledges, Open Futures: The Multiple Selves and Strange Destinations of Ashis Nandy.* New Delhi: Oxford India Paperbacks, 309–34.

Bush, Ray (2010). 'Food Riots: Poverty, Power and Protest'. *Journal of Agrarian Change* 10(1): 119–29.

Bush, V. (1945). *Science, the Endless Frontier. A Report to the President on a Program for Postwar Scientific Research.* Washington: Office of Scientific Research and Development, 1–256.

AlterNet: *Labor Section*, 28 July 2013. Available at: www.alternet.org/labor/apple-walmart-mcdonalds-whos-biggest-wage-stiffer

Bull, Hedley (1977). *The Anarchical Society*. New York: Columbia University Press.

Chapman, Roger and James Ciment (eds). 2013. *Culture Wars in America: An Encyclopaedia of Issues, Viewpoints, and Voices*, London: Routledge.

Clifford, James (1986). 'Introduction: Partial Truths'. In J. Clifford and G. E. Marcus (eds) *Writing Culture: The Poetics and Politics of Ethnography*, 1–26. Berkeley: University of California Press.

Coggins, B. (2015). 'Does State Failure Cause Terrorism? An Empirical Analysis (1999–2008)'. *Journal of Conflict Resolution* 59(3), 455–83.

Coll, Steve (2014). 'The Unblinking Stare: The Drone War in Pakistan'. *New Yorker*, 24 November. Available at: www.newyorker.com/magazine/2014/11/24/unblinking-stare

Collier, Paul (2008). 'The Politics of Hunger'. *Foreign Affairs* 87(6): 67–79.

Cooper, Andrew F. (2010). 'Beyond the Boardroom: "Multilocation" and the Business Face of Celebrity Diplomacy'. In Morten Ougaard and Anna Leander (eds) *Business and Global Governance*, 218–34. London and New York: Routledge.

Curtis, L. (1918). 'Windows of Freedom'. *The Round Table* 8(3): 1–47.

Curtis, L. (1938). *Civitas Dei: The Commonwealth of God*. London: Macmillan, 1–994.

Da Silva, José Graziano, Mauro Eduardo Del Grossi and Caio Galvão De França (2011). *The Fome Zero (Zero Hunger) Program: The Brazilian Experience*. Brasilia: Ministry of Agrarian Development.

Davies, Thomas (2014). *NGOS: A New History of Transnational Civil Society*. London: C. Hurst & Co.

Dershowitz, Alan M. (2003). *Why Terrorism Works*. New Haven, CT: Yale University Press.

Drezner, D. W. (2014). *The System Worked: How the World Stopped Another Great Depression*. Oxford: Oxford University Press.

Duhigg, Charles and Keith Bradsher (2012). 'How the U.S. Lost Out on iPhone Work'. *New York Times*, 21 January. Available at: www.nytimes.com/2012/01/22/business/apple-america-and-a-squeezed-middle-class.html?

Dunant, Henry (1939). *A Memory of Solferino*. Reprint ed. Geneva: International Committee of the Red Cross.

Engelen, E., Ismail Ertürk, Julie Froud, Sukhdev Johal, Adam Leaver, Michael Moran and Karel Williams (2012). 'Misrule of experts? The Financial Crisis as Elite Debacle'. *Economy and Society* 41(3): 360–82.

Engelhardt, Tom (2010). *The American Way of War: How Bush's Wars Became Obama's*. Chicago: Haymarket Books.

Evans, G and Newnham, R. (1998). *The Penguin Dictionary of International Relations*. London: Penguin.

Finnemore, Martha and Kathryn Sikkink (1998). 'International Norm Dynamics and Political Change'. *International Organization* 52: 887–917.

Firth, S. (2005). *Australia in International Politics: An Introduction to Australian Foreign Policy*. Sydney: Allen & Unwin.

Fox, Jonathan and Shmuel Sandler (2004). *Culture and Religion in International Relations: Bringing Religion into International Relations*. New York: Palgrave Macmillan.

Fox, Jonathan (2008). *A World Survey of Religion and the State*. Cambridge, MA: Cambridge University Press.

Fukuyama, F. (1989). 'The End of History?' *The National Interest* 18(Summer): 3–18.

Gaddis, J. L. (1989). *The Long Peace: Inquiries into the History of the Cold War*. Oxford: Oxford University Press.

Gellers, J.C. (2015). 'Explaining the emergence of constitutional environmental rights: a global quantitative analysis'. *Journal of Human Rights and the Environment* 6(1): 75–97.

Gholz, Eugene, Daryl G. Press and Harvey M. Sapolsky (1997). 'Come Home, America: The Strategy of Restraint in the Face of Temptation'. *International Security* 21(4): 5–48.

Guilhot, N. (2014). 'Imperial Realism: Post-War IR theory and Decolonisation'. *International History Review* 36(4): 698–720.

Haider, Najam. (2011). *The Origins of the Shi'a: Identity, Ritual, and Sacred Space in Eighth-Century Kūfa.* New York: Cambridge University Press.

Hale, Thomas, David Held and Kevin Young (2013). *Gridlock.* Cambridge: Polity Press.

Hardin, G. (1968). 'The Tragedy of the Commons'. *Science* 162(3859): 1243–8.

Haynes, J. (2012). 'Religion, Politics and International Relations: Change and Continuity'. *Global Policy* 3(2): 251–2.

Healey, D. (1989). *The Time of My Life.* London: Penguin.

Hedges, C. (1999). 'Leaders in Bosnia Are Said to Steal up to $1 Billion'. *New York Times*, 17 August. Available at: www.nytimes.com/1999/08/17/world/leaders-in-bosnia-are-said-to-steal-up-to-1-billion.html?pagewanted=all

Heisenberg, W. K. (1962). *Physics and Philosophy: The Revolution in Modern Science.* New York: Harper & Row.

Herre, Roman and Timothé Feodoroff (2014). *Case Dossier: Cambodia – Sugar Cane Plantations, Human Rights Violations and EU's 'Everything but Arms' Initiative.* Heidelberg: FIAN Germany.

Herrington L., A. McKay and J. Haynes (eds) (2015). *Nations Under God: The Geopolitics of Faith in the 21st Century.* Bristol: E-International Relations.

Hoffman, B. (1945). Quoted in B. Cosgrove, 'Hiroshima and Nagasaki: Photos from the Ruins', *Time*. Available at: http://time.com/3494421/hiroshima-and-nagasaki-photos-from-the-ruins/

Hoffman, S. (1977). 'An American Social Science'. *Daedalus* 106(3): 41–60.

Hoffman, B. (2006). *Inside Terrorism*. New York: Columbia University Press.

Hoover, Dennis and Douglas Johnston (eds) (2012). *Religion and Foreign Affairs: Essential Readings*. Waco, TX: Baylor University Press.

Human Rights Watch (2015). *World Report: Egypt*. Available at: www.hrw.org/world-report/2015/country-chapters/egypt

Huntington, Samuel P. (1993). 'The Clash of Civilisations?'. *Foreign Affairs* 72(3): 22–49.

Jackson, R. (2011). *Contemporary State Terrorism*. Abingdon, UK: Routledge.

Jackson, R. (2014). 'As Walmart Grows Globally, So Does Its Workforce'. *Seattle Globalist*, 29 May. Available at: www.seattleglobalist.com/2014/05/29/walmart-grows-globally-so-does-worker-resistance/25891

Kaldor, Mary (1999). *New and Old Wars*. Cambridge: Polity.

Kang, J. C. (2014). 'ISIS's Call of Duty'. *New Yorker*, 18 September. Available at: www.newyorker.com/tech/elements/isis-video-game

Keck, Margaret and Kathryn Sikkink (1998). *Activists Beyond Borders*. New York: Cornell University Press.

Keohane, Robert O. (2002). 'The Globalisation of Informal Violence: Theories of World Politics, and the "Liberalism of Fear"'. *Dialogue-IO* 1: 29–43.

Keohane, R. O. (2016) Interview with E-International Relations. Available at: www.e-ir.info/2016/02/26/interview-robert-o-keohane/

Khrushchev, N. (1962). Quoted in 'Nuclear Test Ban Treaty', *John F. Kennedy Presidential Library online*, www.jfklibrary.org/JFK/JFK-in-History/Nuclear-Test-Ban-Treaty.aspx?p=2 (accessed 12 January 2016).

King, Stephen D. (2013). *When the Money Runs Out: The End of Western Affluence*. New Haven, CT: Yale University Press,

Kissinger, H. A. (1957). *World Restored: Metternich, Castlereagh, and the Problem of Peace, 1812–1822*. New York: Weidenfeld & Nicolson, 1–376.

Koh, Harold Hongju (1997). 'Why Do Nations Obey International Law?' *Yale Law Journal* 106: 2599–659.

Kuhn, Thomas (1962). *The Structure of Scientific Revolutions*. Chicago: University of Chicago Press.

Lamont, M. (2014) 'Malinowski and the "Native Question"'. In Regna Darnell and Frederic W. Gleach (eds) *Anthropologists and Their Traditions across National Borders*, 69–110. Lincoln, NE: University of Nebraska Press.

Linklater, Andrew (1998) 'Cosmopolitan citizenship'. *Citizenship studies* 2(1): 23–41.

Lebow, Richard Ned (2003). *The Tragic Vision of Politics: Ethics, Interests and Orders*. Cambridge: Cambridge University Press.

Leftwich, A. (2004). 'Thinking Politically: On the Politics of Politics'. In A. Leftwich (ed.) *What Is Politics: The Activity and Its Study*. Cambridge: Polity Press, 1–22.

Lowder, Sarah, Jakob Skoet and Saumya Singh (2014). 'What Do We Really Know About the Number and Distribution of Farms and Family Farms in the World?'. *ESA Working Paper*, 14-02, April. Available at: www.fao.org/docrep/019/i3729e/i3729e.pdf

Nandy, A. (2003). *The Romance of the State and the Fate of Dissent in the Tropics*. New Delhi: Oxford India Paperbacks.

Marty, M. E. (2003). "Our Religio-Secular World." *Daedalus* 132(3): 42–8.

Mandaville, P. (2007). *Global Political Islam*. Abingdon, UK: Routledge.

McGlinchey, S., R. Walters and S. Scheinpflug (2017). *International Relations Theory*. Bristol: E-International Relations.

Merton, Thomas (1948). *The Seven-Story Mountain*. San Diego, CA: Harcourt Brace.

Monbiot, George (2003). 'America is a Religion'. *The Guardian*, 29 July. Available at: www.guardian.co.uk/comment/story/0,3604,1007741,00.html

Morgenthau, Hans Joachim (1948). *Politics Among Nations: The Struggle for Power and Peace*. New York: A. A. Knopf.

Mustafa, D. and K. E. Brown (2010). 'The Taliban, Public Space, and Terror in Pakistan' *Eurasian Geography and Economics* 51(4): 496–512

National Strategy for Combating Terrorism, United States, September (2006). Available at: https://georgewbush-whitehouse.archives.gov/nsc/nsct/2006/

Neumann, P. (2013). 'The Trouble with Radicalisation' *International Affairs* 89(4) 873-893.

Nye, J. S. (1990). 'Soft Power'. *Foreign Policy* 80: 153–71.

O'Brien, Robert and Williams, Marc (2010). *Global Political Economy*, 3rd edition. Basingstoke, UK: Palgrave Macmillan.

Ostrom, E. (1990). *Governing the Commons: The Evolution of Institutions for Collective Action*. Cambridge: Cambridge University Press.

Oxfam (2009) 'World Food Day: There Is Enough Food Grown in the World for Everyone', *Oxfam International Press Release*, 16 October. Available at: https://www.oxfam.org/en/pressroom/pressreleases/2009-10-16/world-food-day-there-enough-food-grown-world-everyone-op-ed

Patrikarakos, P. (2012) *Nuclear Iran: The Birth of an Atomic State*. London: I. B. Tauris.

PBS (2009). 'Who Speaks for Islam: What a Billion Muslims Really Think'. *Public Broadcasting Service.* LinkTV, https://youtu.be/Bn12s19X8xU (accessed 20 June 2016).

Pew Research Center (2012). *The Global Religious Landscape: A Report on the Size and Distribution of the World's Major Religious Groups as of 2010*. Washington, DC: Pew Research Center.

Picketty, Thomas (2014) *Capital in the 21st Century*. Boston: Harvard University Press.

Peterson, V. Spike (ed.) (1992). *Gendered States: Feminist (Re)Visions of International Relations Theory*. Boulder, CO: Lynne Reinner Publishers.

Plumer, Brad (2013). 'Senators Release Bipartisan Plan for Immigration Reform'. *Washington Post*, 28 January. Available at: www.washingtonpost. com/news/wonk/wp/2013/01/28/read-senators-release-their-plan-for-immigration-reform/

Pogge, T. (2008). *World Poverty and Human Rights*, 2nd edition. Cambridge: Polity Press.

Pogge, T. (2010). 'Responses to the Critics'. In A. Jaggar (ed.) *Thomas Pogge and His Critics*, 175–250. Cambridge: Polity Press.

Polanyi, Karl (1957). *The Great Transformation*, Boston: Beacon Press.

Posen, Barry (2014). *Restraint: A New Foundation For US Grand Strategy*. Ithaca, NY: Cornell University Press,

Rapoport, D. (2004). 'The Four Waves of Terrorism'. In A. K. Cronin (ed.) *Attacking Terrorism*. Washington, DC: Georgetown University Press, 45–73.

Rees, John A. (2016). 'The Nation and the State'. In J. Arvanitakis (ed.) *Sociologic: Analysing Everyday Life and Culture*, 179–96. South Melbourne: Oxford University Press,

Ricardo, David (1817). *On the Principles of Political Economy and Taxation*, ch. 7. Available at: www.econlib.org/library/Ricardo/ricP.html

Rucker, R. (1983). *The Sex Sphere*. New York: Ace.

Ruggie, G. J. (1982). 'International Regimes, Transactions, and Change: Embedded Liberalism in the Postwar Economic System'. *International Organization* 36(2): 379–415.

Sacks, Jonathan (1997). *The Politics of Hope*. London: Random House.

Sageman, M. (2008). *The Leaderless Jihad: Terror Networks in the Twenty-first Century*. Philadelphia: University of Pennsylvania Press.

Said, Edward W. (1978). *Orientalism*. New York: Random House.

Scholte, Jan Aart (2011). *Building Global Democracy? Civil Society and Accountable Global Governance*. Cambridge: Cambridge University Press.

Scholte, Jan Aart (2014). 'Civil Society and NGOs'. In Thomas G. Weiss and Rorden Wilkinson (eds) *International Organization and Global Governance*, 322–34. London and New York: Routledge.

Sen, Amartya (2009). 'Capitalism Beyond the Crisis'. *New York Review of Books*, 26 March. Available at http://www.nybooks.com/articles/archives/2009/mar/26/capitalism-beyond-the-crisis/

Silber, M. and A. Bhatt (2007). 'Radicalisation in the West: The Home-grown Threat'. New York Police Department. Available at: http://sethgodin.typepad.com/seths_blog/files/NYPD_Report-Radicalization_in_the_West.pdf

Silke, A. (2008). 'Holy Warriors: Exploring the Psychological Processes of Jihadi Radicalization'. *European Journal of Criminology,* 5(1): 99–123.

Singer, J. D. (1961). 'The Level-of-Analysis Problem in International Relations'. *World Politics* 14(1): 77–92.

Sinha, S. and S. C. Beachy (2015). 'Timeline on Iran's Nuclear Program'. *New York Times*, 2 April. Available at: www.nytimes.com/interactive/2014/11/20/world/middleeast/Iran-nuclear-timeline.html#/#time243_10809

Simons, A. and D. Tucker (2007). 'The Misleading Problem of Failed States: A "Socio-geography" of Terrorism in the Post-9/11 Era'. *Third World Quarterly* 28(2): 387–401.

Sherman, W. (2016). Interviewed on 'Our World: Iran's Nuclear Deal'. *BBC News*, 14 July.

Singer, P. (1972). 'Famine, Affluence and Morality'. *Philosophy and Public Affairs*, 1: 229–43.

Smith, A. (1776). *The Wealth of Nations*. London: W. Strahan & T. Cadell.

Steinbeck, John (1939). *The Grapes of Wrath*. London: Penguin Classics.

Stewart, F. (1991). 'The Many Faces of Adjustment'. *World Development* 19(12): 1847–64.

Stiglitz, Joseph E. (2002). *Globalization and its Discontents*. London: Penguin.

The National Security Strategy of the United States of America (March 2006). Available at: http://georgewbush-whitehouse.archives.gov/nsc/nss/2006/

Thomas, Scott M. (2005). *The Global Resurgence of Religion and the Transformation of International Relations: The Struggle for the Soul of the Twenty-First Century*. New York: Palgrave Macmillan.

Toft, M.D., D. Philpott and T. Shah (2011). *God's Century: Resurgent Religion and Global Politics*. New York: W. W. Norton.

Toki, Valmaine (2010). 'The Treaty of Waitangi in New Zealand's Law and Constitution'. *Commonwealth Law Bulletin* 36(2): 398–400.

Tyndale, Wendy (ed.) (2006). *Visions of Development: Faith-Based Initiatives*. Aldershot, UK: Ashgate.

UNICEF (2015). 'Progress for Children: Beyond Averages, Learning from the MDGs'. Available at: http://data.unicef.org/resources/progress-for-children-report.html

United Nations (2011). 'The Global Social Crisis: Report on the World Social Situation'. Available at: www.un.org/esa/socdev/rwss/docs/2011/rwss2011.pdf

Vale, P. (1989). 'Whose World Is It Anyway? International Relations in South Africa'. In Hugh C. Dyer and Leon Mangasarian (eds) *The Study of International Relations: The State of the Art*. New York: Palgrave Macmillan, 201–20.

Vale, P. (2003). *Security and Politics in South Africa: The Regional Dimension*. London: Lynne Rienner.

Vale, P. (2016a). 'Inclusion and Exclusion'. *International Studies Review* 18(1): 159–62.

Vale, P. (2016b). 'Unlocking Social Puzzles: Colony, Crime and Chronical – An Interview with Charles van Onselen'. *Thesis Eleven* 136(1): 35–48.

Waal, F. de (1982). *Chimpanzee Politics: Power and Sex among Apes.* London: Jonathan Cape.

Walker, Neil (2014). *Intimations of Global Law.* Cambridge: Cambridge University Press

Walter, Maggie (2016). 'Researching the World Around Us'. In J. Arvanitakis (ed.) *Sociologic: Analysing Everyday Life and Culture*, 57–79. South Melbourne, Australia: Oxford University Press.

Waltz, K. (1959). *Man, the State and War: A Theoretical Analysis.* New York: Columbia University Press.

Walzer, Michael (2015). *The Paradox of Liberation: Secular Revolutions and Religious Counterrevolutions.* New Haven, CT: Yale University Press.

Wiktorowicz, Q. (2006). 'Anatomy of the Salafi movement'. *Studies in Conflict and Terrorism* 29(3): 207–39.

Weber, M. (1965). *Politics as a Vocation*, 15th edition. Philadelphia: Fortress Press.

Weis, Tony (2007). *The Global Food Economy: The Battle for the Future of Farming.* Black Point, Canada: Fernwood Publishing.

Wendt, Alexander (1992). 'Anarchy is what States Make of it: The Social Construction of Power Politics'. *International Organization*, 46(2): 391–425.

Woodhead, Linda (2011). 'Five concepts of religion', *International Review of Sociology* 21(1): 121–43.

Zinn, H. (1980). *A People's History of the United State.* London and New York: Longman.

Note on Indexing

E-IR's publications do not feature indexes due to the prohibitive costs of assembling them. If you are reading this book in paperback and want to find a particular word or phrase you can do so by downloading a free PDF version of this book from the E-IR website.

View the e-book in any standard PDF reader such as Adobe Acrobat Reader (pc) or Preview (mac) and enter your search terms in the search box. You can then navigate through the search results and find what you are looking for. In practice, this method can prove much more targeted and effective than consulting an index.

If you are using apps (or devices) such as iBooks or Kindle to read our e-books, you should also find word search functionality in those.

You can find all of our e-books at: http://www.e-ir.info/publications

Lightning Source UK Ltd.
Milton Keynes UK
UKHW021839051020
371060UK00009B/2025

9 781910 814178